Sven Janssen
BRITISH AND GERMAN BANKING STRATEGIES

Alexandros-Andreas Kyrtsis (*editor*)
FINANCIAL MARKETS AND ORGANIZATIONAL TECHNOLOGIES
System Architectures, Practices and Risks in the Era of Deregulation

Caterina Lucarelli and Gianni Brighetti (*editors*)
RISK TOLERANCE IN FINANCIAL DECISION MAKING

Roman Matousek (*editor*)
MONEY, BANKING AND FINANCIAL MARKETS IN CENTRAL AND EASTERN EUROPE
20 Years of Transition

Philip Molyneux (*editor*)

BANK PERFORMANCE, RISK AND FIRM FINANCING

Philip Molyneux (*editor*)
BANK STRATEGY, GOVERNANCE AND RATINGS

Imad A. Moosa
THE MYTH OF TOO BIG TO FAIL

Simon Mouatt and Carl Adams (*editors*)
CORPORATE AND SOCIAL TRANSFORMATION OF MONEY AND BANKING
Breaking the Serfdom

Anders Ögren (*editor*)
THE SWEDISH FINANCIAL REVOLUTION

Özlem Olgu
EUROPEAN BANKING
Enlargement, Structural Changes and Recent Developments

Ramkishen S. Rajan
EMERGING ASIA
Essays on Crises, Capital Flows, FDI and Exchange Rate

Allesandro Roselli
FINANCIAL STRUCTURES AND REGULATION: A COMPARISON OF CRISES IN THE UK,
USA AND ITALY

Yasushi Suzuki
JAPAN'S FINANCIAL SLUMP
Collapse of the Monitoring System under Institutional and Transition Failures

Ruth Wandhöfer
EU PAYMENTS INTEGRATION
The Tale of SEPA, PSD and Other Milestones Along the Road

The full list of titles available is on the website:
www.palgrave.com/finance/sbfi.asp

Palgrave Macmillan Studies in Banking and Financial Institutions
Series Standing Order ISBN 978–1–4039–4872–4

You can receive future titles in this series as they are published by placing a standing order.
Please contact your bookseller or, in case of difficulty, write to us at the address below
with your name and address, the title of the series and the ISBN quoted above. Customer
Services Department, Macmillan Distribution Ltd, Houndmills, Basingstoke, Hampshire
RG21 6XS, England

Bancassurance in Europe

Past, Present and Future

Edited by

Franco Fiordelisi

Ornella Ricci

First published 2012 by
PALGRAVE MACMILLAN

Palgrave Macmillan in the UK is an imprint of Macmillan Publishers Limited, registered in England, company number 785998, of Houndmills, Basingstoke, Hampshire RG21 6XS.

Palgrave Macmillan in the US is a division of St Martin's Press LLC, 175 Fifth Avenue, New York, NY 10010.

Palgrave Macmillan is the global academic imprint of the above companies and has companies and representatives throughout the world.

Palgrave® and Macmillan® are registered trademarks in the United States, the United Kingdom, Europe and other countries.

ISBN 978-1-349-32259-6   ISBN 978-0-230-35828-7 (eBook)
DOI 10.1057/9780230358287

This book is printed on paper suitable for recycling and made from fully managed and sustained forest sources. Logging, pulping and manufacturing processes are expected to conform to the environmental regulations of the country of origin.

A catalogue record for this book is available from the British Library.

Library of Congress Cataloging-in-Publication Data
Bancassurance in Europe : past, present and future / edited by
Franco Fiordelisi, Ornella Ricci.
p. cm.
Includes bibliographical references and index.

1. Banks and banking—Insurance business—Europe.   I. Fiordelisi, Franco, 1972– II. Ricci, Ornella, 1982–
HG1616.I47B338 2012
368.8'540094—dc23   2011040385

10   9   8   7   6   5   4   3   2   1
21   20   19   18   17   16   15   14   13   12

to Patrizia and Anna, the joys of my life
Franco F.

to Daniele, for his constant support and patience with me
Ornella R.

Contents

List of Tables

List of Figures

List of Boxes

Notes on Contributors

Massimo Caratelli is Assistant Professor of Banking and Finance in the Faculty of Economics at the University of Rome III, Italy. His research interests include the distribution of financial services, clients' needs and transparency.

Franco Fiordelisi is Professor of Banking and Finance in the Faculty of Economics at the University of Rome III, Italy. He is also Visiting Research Fellow at Bangor Business School, Bangor University, UK, the Essex Finance Centre of the University of Essex, UK, the ECB and the Olin Business School of the Washington University in St Louis (U.S.). He is author of publications in several journals: *Journal of Banking & Finance, Omega – The International Journal of Management, European Financial Management, European Journal of Finance, Applied Economics, Applied Financial Economics*. His recent books include *Shareholder Value in European Banking* (Palgrave Macmillan, 2006), *New Drivers of Performance in a Changing Financial World* (Palgrave Macmillan, 2008), *Mergers and Acquisitions in European Banking* (Palgrave Macmillan, 2009), *New Issues in Financial and Credit Markets* (Palgrave Macmillan, 2010) and *New Issues in Financial Institutions Management* (Palgrave Macmillan, 2010).

Ornella Ricci is Assistant Professor of Banking and Finance in the Faculty of Economics at the University of Rome III, Italy. Her main research interests focus on financial conglomeration and bancassurance. She is author of several publications on financial institutions, including articles in the *European Journal of Finance* and *Applied Financial Economics*.

Maria Grazia Starita is Assistant Professor of Banking and Finance at the University of Naples Parthenope, Italy. Her research topics are insurance companies, pension funds and Islamic insurance.

Sabrina Pucci is Full Professor of Accounting in the Faculty of Economics at the University of Rome III, Italy. Her main research interests include the management of insurance companies, the analysis of financial statements and the international accounting standards.

Introduction

Bancassurance is one of the most important forms of business collaboration in the European financial services industry. Initially, the development of bancassurance was the result of the disintermediation process and the relaxation of regulatory barriers to financial conglomeration. Over the last decade, the cooperation between banks and insurance companies has increased continuously from the initial cross-selling agreements to strategic alliances and ownership links: this process was driven by the increasing investor demand for long-term savings products, growth in life expectancy and the crisis of social security systems.

The growth of bancassurance has been particularly impressive in countries where the financial services industry is characterized by a strong orientation towards the relationship banking model and a lower penetration of insurance products. In many European countries (for example, France, Italy, Spain and Portugal), bank branches have become the main distribution channel for life policies, while in others, for example, the UK and Germany, agents and brokers have retained the majority of the market.

The cooperation between banks and insurance companies is well developed for life policies, but still at an initial stage for property and casualty (P&C) products. This is probably due to the fact that P&C products show few similarities with the banking business and require more efforts to provide branch staff with the right specific competences. Banks have only recently extended their offering from P&C policies bundled with banking products, that is, payment protection and home insurance, to non-bank-related products, such as car, travel, pet and health insurance. These products may involve high underwriting risk and imply some inefficiencies and difficulties in the claim management process – something very far from the traditional banking business.

On the other hand, some P&C products have a very interesting growth potential as in the case of health insurance covering private medical expenditure, which is becoming increasingly relevant as a consequence of the decrease in social welfare benefits.

Our book provides an innovative analysis of the bancassurance phenomenon by combining both theoretical and empirical research methods. Firstly, our book provides a description of bancassurance, examining its historical roots and main drivers of development. During the 1990s, the success of bancassurance was driven mainly by high financial content products (that is, indexed and unit-linked policies) which were easy to sell in a period of positive growth for capital markets, and was also affected by the dramatic expansion of the Internet. At the end of this euphoric phase, linked policies became much less attractive for investors who turned their attention back to traditional savings products. This change in customers' preferences has been reinforced by the advent of the global financial crisis which started in the second half of 2007, generating huge losses for investors all over the world. It is possible to posit that there will be a further development of insurance products providing a 'second pillar' in addition to public social protection and guaranteeing a more stable income over the life cycle. As a consequence, bancassurance companies should be able not only to continuously adapt their offering to changing financial needs, but also to address new targets of customers. It is probable that their traditional focus will move from middle aged, affluent customers – with considerable savings to invest – towards mass-market clients with the need of a supplementary pension to maintain an adequate standard of living after retirement.

Secondly, our book provides an in-depth analysis of the accounting principles and regulatory constraints in bancassurance, outlining their main evolutions in more recent years. The insurance industry is facing an unprecedented phase of regulatory changes, investing accounting rules (IAS/IFRS) and capital requirements. Solvency 2 will force insurance companies to identify the right trade-off between the economic contribution and risk profile of every offered product. Even though it could also be an opportunity to redesign and innovate products, as well as improving their pricing, the most important and immediate consequence will be an increase in the cost of running the insurance business. In addition to this, as a response to the global financial crisis, the Basel Committee for Banking Supervision has recently issued some new rules to strengthen bank capitalization and liquidity reserves. The combined impact of Solvency 2 and Basel III provisions may exert a strong pressure on bancassurance combinations, reducing the capital benefits associated with this model. As a consequence, many banks are rethinking their strategy, sometimes deciding to refocus on their core business. At the same time, the financial crisis has also outlined the important role played by insurance profits, which were able to partially offset the slowdown in credit-based products. The fundamental question is whether it is preferable to act as a simple distributor of insurance products, gaining commissions free of capital and risk implications, or to be directly involved in the underwriting activity in order to access potential greater synergies and returns. Obviously, there is no one correct answer to this question, because many different exogenous and endogenous factors may contribute to the success or failure of bancassurance. A precious help can derive from the academic literature, in order to draw some useful directions from both theoretical and empirical studies devoted to financial conglomeration and bancassurance.

Thirdly, our book reviews the limited number of empirical studies dealing with bancassurance. Furthermore, most of these are based on simulated or effective M&As between banks and insurance companies, assessing risk/return effects and generally adopting a short-term perspective. Surprisingly, even though cost and revenue synergies are commonly recognized as one of the main economic rationales for financial conglomeration, the efficiency issue is still poorly investigated.

Finally, we present some empirical investigations undertaken to measure potential efficiency gains on both the cost and the profit sides. First of all, we run an exploratory study using a European sample to compare cost and profit efficiency between banks diversifying into the life insurance industry and their more specialized competitors. We find that the two subgroups present quite similar levels of performance and that differences are mainly explained by some firm-specific factors, such as size and capitalization, that are beyond management control in the short run, but able to influence the distance from the best practice. Considering that findings appear very sensitive to the applied input and output specification for cost and profit functions, we may conclude that the analysis does not provide any strong evidence in favour of bancassurance. Secondly, we compare bancassurance gains for banks and insurance companies focusing on the Italian market. We show that the use of bank branches provides a cost advantage with respect to other distribution channels, but there is no evidence of profit synergies, from neither the banking nor the insurance standpoint. It could be due to the differing fortunes of products with a high financial content, which generally dominate the offerings of bancassurance companies. This result reinforces the conclusion that the combination of products should be revised continuously in the light of customer needs and the evolution of financial markets. Furthermore, the bancassurance cost advantage (results in) depends on distribution economies, while the presence of a bank in the ownership structure of the insurance company does not prove to be a relevant determinant of performance, neither for captive companies nor for joint ventures. As a consequence, the combination of products should be continuously revised in the light of customer needs and the evolution of the financial market, and the parties involved should also consider more flexible and reversible forms of cooperation, such as cross-selling agreements and non-equity strategic alliances.

We believe that our book provides a useful first, in-depth step in exploring the bancassurance business, an often-discussed but little researched topic. Further research may fruitfully examine cost and revenue synergies and, more broadly, the bancassurance value creation strategies. Last, but not least, we wish to thank Yener Altunbas, Alessandro Carretta, Barbara Casu, Claudia Girardone, John Goddard, Phil Molyneux, Daniele Previati, Thomas Weyman Jones and John Williams. We also thank the Essex Finance Centre of the Essex Business School, the Association of Italian Insurers (Associazione Nazionale fra le Imprese Assicuratrici – ANIA) and the Italian Banking Association (Associazione Bancaria Italiana – ABI) for their assistance in data collection. All errors, of course, rest with the authors. We would also like to acknowledge financial support from the Dipartimento di Scienze Aziendali ed Economico-Giuridiche of the University of Rome III, Italy.

Rome, 1 May 2011
Franco Fiordelisi
Ornella Ricci

1
The Development of Bancassurance in Europe

Ornella Ricci

1.1 Introduction

The first use of the term *bancassurance* was in France, where cooperation between banks and insurance companies started earlier than in other European countries. This word was originally coined to indicate the simple distribution of insurance products by bank branches, while now it is used to describe all kinds of relationships between the banking and the insurance industries. Along with the development of the phenomenon, bancassurance definitions are becoming more and more general, as in the following examples:

> Bancassurance is basically the provision of and selling of banking and insurance products by the same organisation under the same roof. (Elkington, 1993, p. 2)

> Bancassurance can be described as a strategy adopted by banks or insurance companies aiming to operate the financial market in a more or less integrated manner. (Swiss RE, 1992, p.4)

The bancassurance strategy is aimed at cross-selling insurance products to bank customers and can be realized in a number of different ways: the bank can play a simple brokerage role, participate in a strategic alliance or a joint venture with an insurance partner or bear the underwriting risk of the policy through its own captive company. In any case, as outlined in Van den Berghe and Verweire (1998), it is important to distinguish bancassurance from different concepts, such as *assur finance* and *all finance*. Assurfinance is the provision of financial/banking products by insurers. Even though there is no conclusive evidence, it seems to be a less successful trend with respect to bancassurance, probably because the banks are in a better position to be considered by customers as a unique intermediary able to satisfy all their financial needs.

The term 'all finance' is quite a general one, indicating the bundling of different products to offer integrated and personalized financial solutions to customers. Institutions involved in all finance are generally referred to as financial conglomerates. It is difficult to find a single generally accepted definition of financial conglomerates in the economic literature: for example, in Vander Vennet (2002, p.254) they are defined as 'financial institutions that offer the entire range of financial services'. In general, from an economic perspective, a financial conglomerate is an institution operating in more than one of the following businesses: banking, securities and insurance. Recently, the concept has been fairly delimited by EU regulation: the Directive 87/2002/CE classifies a group as a financial conglomerate if engaged in both the banking and the insurance activities in a significant way (with reference to total assets or capital requirements), while the mix of commercial banking and underwriting securities is not identified as a conglomerate.[1] As a result, it is possible to affirm that regulators are more concerned about financial conglomeration when assuming the form of bancassurance.

The aim of this chapter is to analyze the main aspects of the bancassurance phenomenon, with a specific focus on European countries and some comparisons with the US experience. The remainder is organized as follows:

- section 1.2 provides a general view of the context in which the bancassurance phenomenon developed, identifying both the main exogenous determinants and economic rationales for the firms involved;
- section 1.3 summarizes the main steps in the evolution of bancassurance as a new business model for financial firms. In addition to this, it describes the features of several organizational models showing how the cooperation between banks and insurers works;
- section 1.4 reports the main conclusions, serving as a general framework for the remainder of the book.

1.2 The main determinants of bancassurance

Bancassurance can be considered one of the most important trends in the evolution of modern European banking, resulting from several interconnected drivers of change that have been of interest to the financial services industry in the last 30 years. First of all, it is important to outline that, with some differences between countries, banking markets were mainly domestically oriented, characterized by severe regulation and low competitiveness up to the 1990s. The traditional deposit and lending business was absolutely dominant in the portfolio of banking activities with net interest margin representing the main revenue stream. Competitive pressures from non-banking financial institutions and from foreign competitors were inhibited by the high level of regulatory restrictions and by material obstacles to long-distance relationships. As a consequence, shareholders' value creation and customers' satisfaction had still not emerged as absolute priorities in banking management. In this framework, the connections between different sectors of the financial services industry – banking, securities and insurance – were quite limited. From the end of the 1980s the scenery has evolved substantially, thanks to deregulation, globalization and progress in information and communication technologies (ICT). As outlined in Casu et al. (2006), limitations to the free flow of capital across national boundaries have been progressively removed, together with portfolio restrictions used to limit the freedom of banks in the allocation of their resources. The role of state-owned institutions, still relevant in some countries (for example, Italy), was also reduced as a result of privatization. The development of ICT technologies, especially internet-based ones, has led to a decline in the cost of managing information, communicating with customers and realizing transactions with distant counterparts, contributing to the internationalization of the competitive arena.

In Europe, the convergence between different sectors of the financial industry has been encouraged by the liberalization process which had the intention of creating a single market for financial services. The 1989 Second Banking Directive introduced the universal banking model[2] which allowed banks to operate directly in a large set of financial activities, such as the trading and underwriting of securities or asset management. Even though the undertaking of insurance activity remained reserved to specialized companies, banks were allowed to hold unlimited reciprocal participation in insurance firms. Together with the universal banking model, the Directive also established the mutual recognition of licences issued in any Member State (single passport) and the home country control principle for supervision, realizing a fundamental step in EU financial integration and giving further impulse to competition. In the US, regulatory hedges between different financial institutions were removed by the 1999 Gramm–Leach–Bliley Act, allowing banks to become financial holding companies engaged in the securities and/or the insurance business.

Box 1.1 The US regulatory framework

The passage of the 1999 Gramm–Leach–Bliley Act (GLBA), also known as the Financial Services Modernization Act (FSMA), eliminated most of the remaining barriers to consolidation and conglomeration in the US financial services industry. The first strong limitation to bank diversification was set by the National Banking Act of 1864, which allowed only activities incidental to banking and necessary to carry on the traditional deposit and lending business. Insurance was not considered to match these characteristics and, consequently, banks were not granted the right to underwrite and distribute policies. Commercial and investment banking were separated in 1933 by the Glass–Steagall Act in order to avoid excessive risk taking and restore public confidence in the banking system following the Great Depression at the end of the 1920s. Section 20 of this act prohibited banks from affiliation with entities mainly engaged in the underwriting and sale of securities. Banks have tried to circumvent limitations to their scope expansion using non-bank subsidiaries, but the 1956 Bank Holding Company Act restricted corporate affiliates to activities closely related or incidental to banking.

Many years later, some limitations to bank diversification were relaxed by regulatory rulings and market practice for both securities and insurance activities. In 1987 commercial banks were allowed to establish 'Section 20 subsidiaries' operating in the securities business on the condition that their revenues should not exceed 5 per cent of total gross income. Then, this maximum weight was progressively augmented, up to 25 per cent in 1997. So it is possible to affirm that, even before the passage of the GLBA in 1999, commercial banks could engage in the security business; on the other hand, the expansion of investment banks or security firms into commercial banking, was still not permitted. Regarding the insurance case, in the 1980s the Office of the Comptroller of Currency (OCC) declared annuities to be a general investment product that could be provided by banks. In addition to this, banks operating in small towns with less than 5,000 inhabitants were allowed to sell all types of insurance products to customers located everywhere. In the mid-1990s the OCC rulings were upheld by Supreme Court cases: 'the door for national banks to engage in insurance agency activity has been open; however, with limited exceptions, insurance underwriting was effectively separated from banking' (Hendershott et al., 2002, p. 57).

The 1999 GLBA removed the remaining barriers, allowing mergers between banks, security firms and insurance companies. Furthermore, newly established Financial Holding Companies (FHCs) may engage in banking, securities, insurance agency and underwriting without any limitations on revenue. The safety and soundness of these entities should have been guaranteed by a set of management rules and capitalization requisites. The global financial crisis triggered by subprime mortgages in summer 2007 has renewed concerns about excessive risk-taking positing the question of a possible revision of the GLBA.

As outlined by the National Bank of Belgium (2002), the rise of financial conglomerates is also the result of strong competitive pressures faced by banks on both the asset and the liabilities sides of their balance sheet. This trend is observable in all European countries, especially with reference to the period from the mid-1990s to the year 2000, starting after the main deregulating interventions and experiencing a phase of exceptional growth of capital markets.

On the asset side, the development of more efficient capital markets has provided many firms with convenient access to direct finance, allowing them to substitute bank loans with alternative and cheaper sources of funding. Figure 1.1 shows time series data for the composition of financial liabilities in the balance sheet of European non-financial corporations, with a specific focus on five large countries: France, Germany, Italy, Spain and the UK. Focusing on the period from 1996 to 2000, all countries – with the exception of Spain – experienced a significant decrease in the weight of loans with respect to bonds, shares, quotes and other financial liabilities. At the Euro area level, the registered decline was about 6 per cent.

At the same time, there has been a dramatic growth in the disposable set of investment opportunities. Household savings have moved from short-term, low-yield bank deposits to more attractive long-term, high-yield financial assets. This tendency has been fostered by various factors, such as higher levels of prosperity, longer life expectancies and lower inflation rates (Genetay and Molyneux, 1998). The emergence of mutual funds and insurance policies has led to a further decrease in deposits with a consequent increase in the banks' cost of funding. As shown in Figure 1.2, the weight of cash and deposits in the composition of

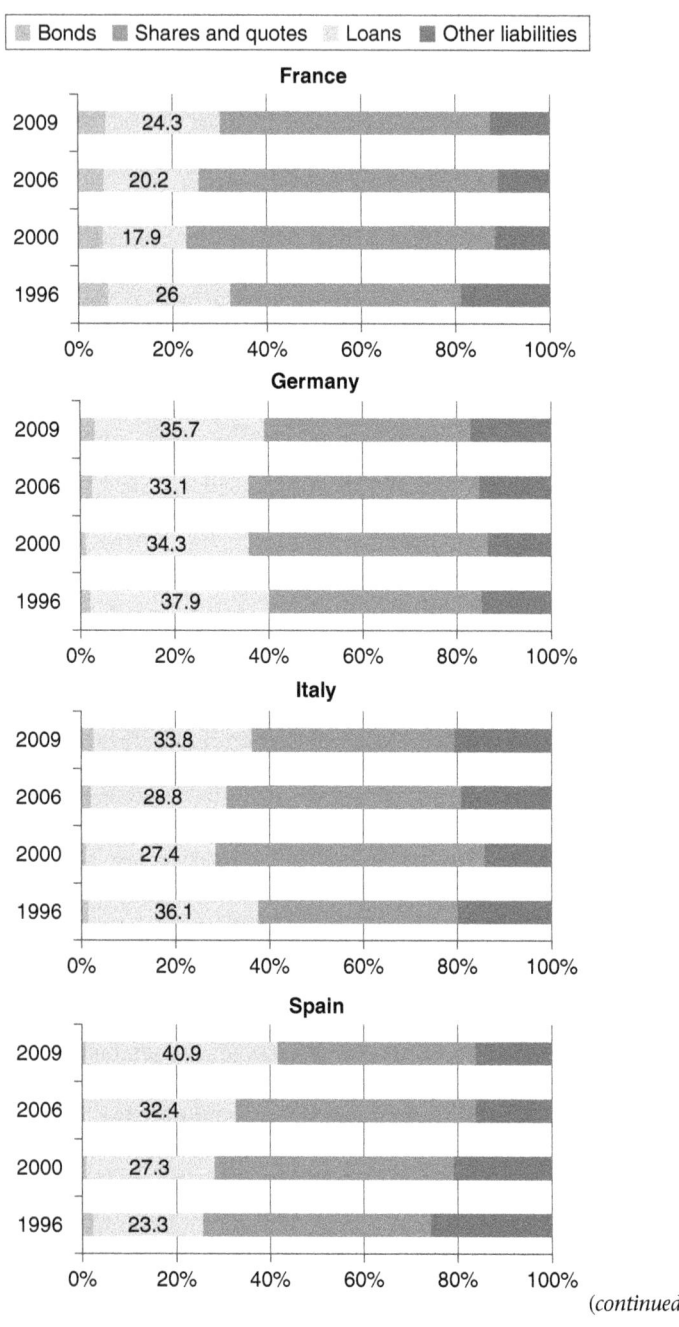

(*continued*)

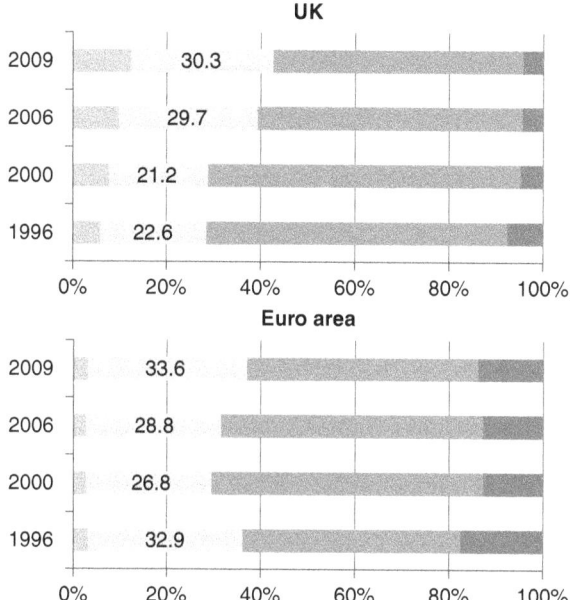

Figure 1.1 The composition of financial liabilities in European non-financial firms over 1996–2009
Source: Author's elaboration on data provided by the Bank of Italy in its Annual Reports. The Euro area has a time-changing composition.

household financial assets has declined significantly between 1996 and 2000 in all European countries with respect to bonds, shares, mutual funds and other investments (that is, insurance policies and pension funds). At the Euro area level, the registered decline was about 8.6 per cent.

The disintermediation process has exerted strong pressure on bank profits. One of the main responses has been the engagement in activities different from the traditional deposit and lending business, with a consequent drop in the weight of net interest income in total operating revenues. With reference to France, where the bancassurance phenomenon started, the ratio of net interest income to total revenues declined from 77.4 per cent in 1990 to 39.1 per cent in 2000 (OECD statistics).

Banks have reacted to this adverse evolution of the financial services industry by trying to internalize the trend, expanding into the insurance

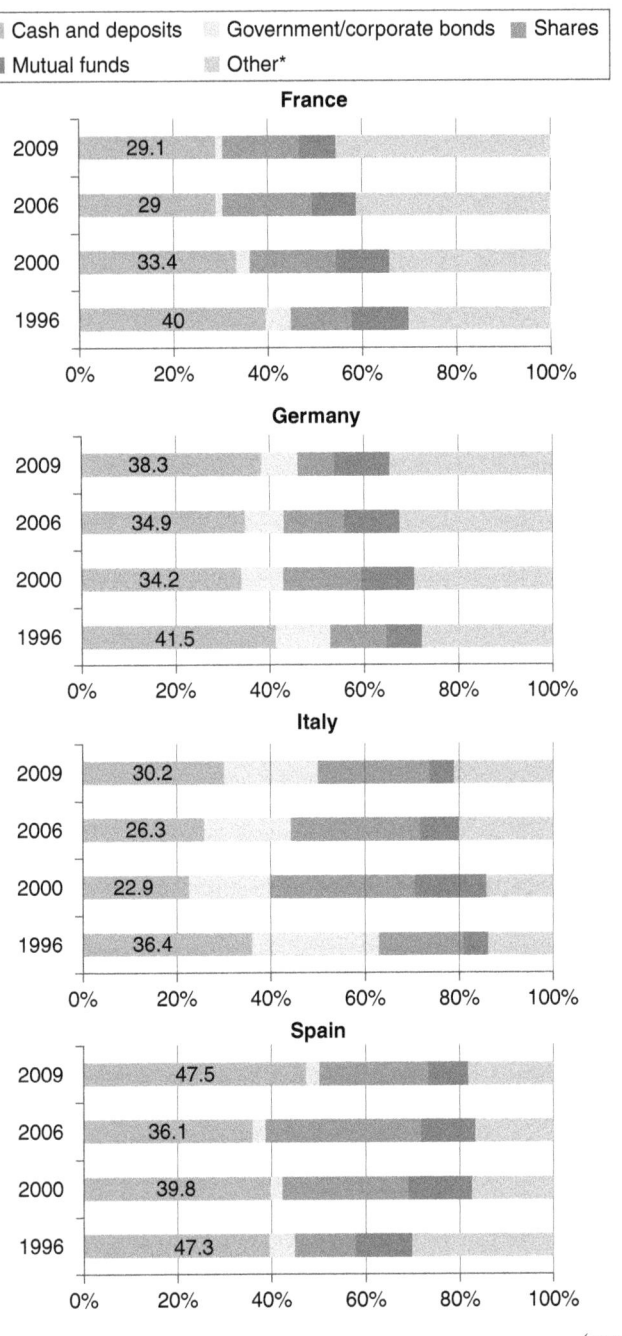

(*continued*)

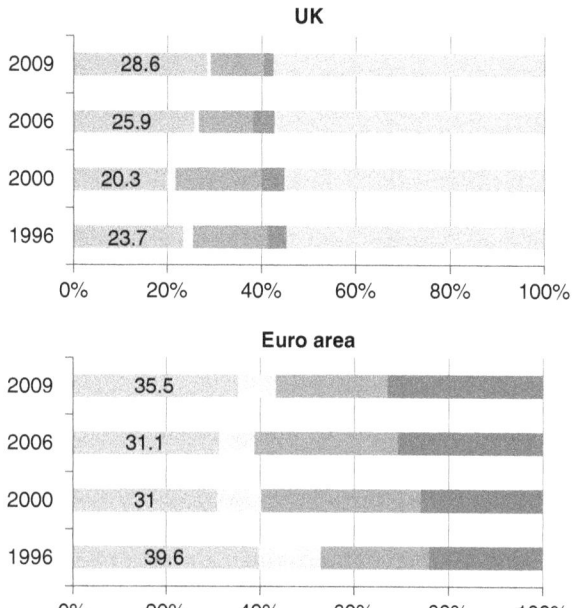

Figure 1.2 The composition of financial assets owned by European households over 1996–2009

Note: *'Other' comprises pension funds, insurance policies and other minor items.
Source: Author's elaboration on data provided by the Bank of Italy in its Annual Reports. The Euro area has a time-changing composition. For the Euro area, the distinction between the investment in shares and in mutual funds was not available for the entire observed period.

and asset management industries. Life insurance has appeared as a particularly interesting opportunity for many reasons, including:

1. the progressive ageing of the population and the contemporaneous decrease in welfare state protection offered by governments;
2. the positive perspectives for the insurance market;
3. the existence of some similarities and complementaries between the banking and the insurance industries.

Starting from the 1950s all developed countries have experienced relevant demographic changes, that is, a decline in the fertility rate and an increase in life expectancy, resulting in the progressive ageing of the population. Several decades later, this trend has contributed, in combination with a slowdown in economic growth and an increase in public debt, to the crisis of social security systems based on 'pay-as-you-go' financing, forcing governments to gradually reduce the level of payable benefits. As a consequence, the need for a private supplementary pension has become more evident and urgent, contributing to the development of pension funds and insurance products, such as individual deferred annuities, able to guarantee more stable income over the life cycle. In several European countries, for example, France, Italy and Spain, long-term savings products have also benefited from consistent tax advantages (Swiss Re, 2007).

In Europe, the increasing demand for long-term savings products has often been accompanied by low penetration rates of life insurance. In fact, only a few countries, such as the UK and the Netherlands, had already established a tradition of household investment in life policies and pension funds. This made the expansion into the insurance industry even more attractive for banks. As noted by the National Bank of Belgium (2001), countries that have registered higher growth rates for life insurance are the same countries where the bancassurance phenomenon has experienced greater success. Even though it may be difficult to infer the direction of causality, it is possible to affirm that banks have been attracted by a market in expansion and have themselves contributed to its growth.

Finally, the convergence between the banking and the insurance industries has also been fostered by the existence of some similarities and complementary aspects from both an activity and a product perspective. Even though the core business of a bank and an insurance company are quite different, they are both financial intermediaries collecting individual savings and channelling them into the capital market. Furthermore, they are both engaged in information-intensive activities in which laws of large numbers, liquidity and risk management are essential (Fields et al., 2007). In addition to this, banking and insurance products can serve as savings vehicles in a similar way or can be complementary in the same purchase (Genetay and Molyneux, 1998): in mortgage contracts, for example, banks often ask their borrowers to insure against death, unemployment and property damage. It is worth noticing that similarities and complementaries are more evident for banking and life insurance with respect to property and casualty (P&C) insurance, explaining why bancassurance expanded almost everywhere for the former and is generally still at an initial stage for the latter.[3]

The rise of bancassurance involves more than just the evolution of the financial services industry and the attractiveness of life business.

It is also possible to identify other strategic economic rationales for conglomeration, on both the supply and demand sides.

On the supply side, the convergence between the banking and the insurance industry can be explained by the potential exploitation of economies of both scale and scope. Banks sustain huge fixed costs for the compensation of their employees and the maintenance of a capillary net of branches. This cost may be split over a larger variety of products, if the bank is engaged in a bancassurance strategy, giving the opportunity to increase staff productivity. From their standpoint, insurance companies can use bank branches to access new customers, through a channel that has often proven to be less expensive than agents and brokers (Swiss RE, 2007). In fact, from a theoretical point of view, branch employees could be rewarded with lower commissions than the traditional insurance sales force. This may also allow the provision of products that would otherwise be unfeasible, because of the excessive weight of sales costs on premiums, making the final price uncompetitive (Munich RE, 2001). However, it is quite difficult to quantify the actual bancassurance cost advantage and assess whether it is reflected in lower pricing to customers or absorbed by bank profits (Davis, 2007).

Relevant cost economies may also arise in relation to the cost of managing customer databases and IT systems more generally. Furthermore, frequent interaction with clients produces a deep knowledge of their financial needs and attitude to risk, representing a relevant advantage with respect to competitors. This also helps to explain why bancassurance is more developed in continental Europe, which is generally more oriented to relationship banking, than in the Anglo-Saxon countries, which are more oriented to transaction banking.

On the demand side, it is worth noticing that scope economies may also arise from revenues, if customers are willing to pay higher prices for one-stop banking, because of reductions in user transaction fees and search costs associated with consuming different financial services offered by the same provider, often at the same location. Traditionally, banks have been in an ideal position to serve as a financial one-stop shop, because of their strong relationship with customers and their good reputation. Insurance companies, by contrast, may experience conflicts with customers, frequently arising in the management of claims. More generally, in the light of the increasing complexity of financial needs, the provision of a complete and diversified range of products may be necessary in order to keep customer loyalty and avoid customer mobility. This is particularly important because the increase of activity volume through customer retention, cross- and up-selling is less expensive than the search for new clients.

In addition to supply- and demand-side economic rationales, financial conglomeration can also be explained for agency reasons, such as the managers' desire for empire building, given that status and compensation generally depend on company size. In his work, Dierick (2004) points out that efficiencies can turn into inefficiencies if the financial entity becomes too complex, affected by coordination problems and conflicts of interest. Furthermore, there are other conglomeration risks, particularly relevant from the supervisor perspective:[4]

- regulatory arbitrage: conglomerates can meet regulatory requirements on a formal basis, but not from a substantial point of view. The main regulatory concerns regard intra-group transactions and the problem of multiple gearing (that is, the use of the same capital to cover different risks in several entities of the conglomerate);
- contagion: difficulties experienced by one component can affect the entire conglomerate, due to internal links and the use of common brands. For example, a fraud occurring in a single business area can impact the whole group reputation;
- moral hazard: if the conglomerate is perceived as 'too-big-to-fail' or too systematically important to fail it may engage in very risky activities having the implicit guarantee of public intervention in case of an illiquidity or insolvency crisis;
- lack of transparency: a large and complex structure may be difficult to analyze for both investors and supervisors;
- abuse of economic power: the rise of financial conglomerates may lead to an increase in market concentration to the detriment of competition. However, as observed by Van den Berghe and Verweire (2001) the effect of conglomeration on competition can be hard to predict, because of the passage from an industry-based to product-based competition. So, even though there is a trend towards greater consolidation at the industry level the opening of some product markets to new firms may result in an increase in competition.

1.3 The development of bancassurance in Europe

As observed by DBRS (2006, p. 3), 'the combination of banking and insurance activities has undergone a Darwinian process, evolving from relatively crude forms of distribution, through business combinations and acquisitions, toward more complex forms of business integration'. This evolution process has been influenced by various factors, such as regulatory constraints and the characteristics of the banking and the insurance industries, resulting in some differences between countries.[5] With reference to the case of France, Daniel[6] (1995) distinguishes three different stages of bancassurance development:

- in the first stage, up to 1980, banks provide only insurance products strictly linked to their traditional activity, for example related to consumer credit or mortgages;
- the second stage starts in the early 1980s, when banks begin to offer life insurance products with a saving function (for example, annuity policies);
- the third stage begins at the end of the 1980s with a real boom in the 1990s: banks can offer a wider range of insurance products, also with a high financial content, such as index- or unit-linked policies.

Changes in the range of products offered have led to an increase in the level of integration between the bank and the partner insurance company: despite the existence of some exceptions (for example, the UK), it is possible to sustain that simple distribution agreements during the 1970s and the 1980s became a mix of partnerships and share exchanges in the early 1990s (Molyneux, 2002). This evolution is also confirmed when considering data on M&As involving European banks and insurance companies. Focusing on the last decade, it is possible to discern a different trend. Figures on the number of transactions, reported in Figure 1.3, show that the convergence process has been more frequently guided by banks and was particularly intensive between 1999 and 2000. It then decelerated from 2001 to 2003 to intensify again from 2004 to 2007. Finally, the global financial crisis triggered by US subprime mortgages has caused a significant slowdown.

The appearance of more complex and integrated models has not led to the disappearance of the previous ones: currently, it is possible to observe several forms of bancassurance, which are more or less successful depending on the institutional and economic framework, types of business mix and the objectives of the firms involved. First of all, it is important to notice that insurance companies are subject to the specialization principle: as a consequence, the combination with banking, or any other business, in the same legal entity is not permitted by law and other organizational models have to be used (Dierick, 2004). The main two variables that distinguish the form of cooperation are

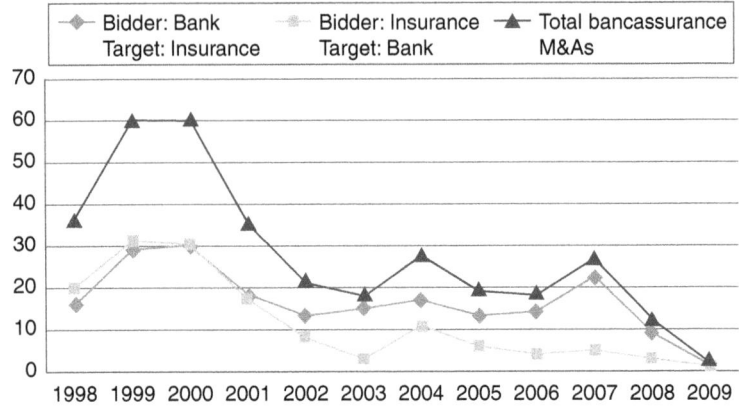

Figure 1.3   Bancassurance M&As, 1998–2009
Source: Author's elaboration on Thompson Banker One data.

the percentage of financial ownership and the level of integration from a strategic and management perspective (Davis, 2007). From the existing literature (Hoschka, 1994; Van den Berghe and Verweire, 2001; Voutilainen, 2005; Staikouras, 2006; Fitch Ratings, 2006), it is possible to distinguish between several models:

1 *cross-selling agreements*;
2 *cooperation between independent partners*;
3 *control by ownersip*.

   1. Cross-selling agreements. Thanks to a simple partnership, banks sell insurance products through their branches, on behalf of a single company or several companies. In this case the two partners do not constitute a special entity to conduct the insurance business, whose profitability and risks remain entirely accounted for in the insurer balance sheet. The bank does not own any stake in the insurance company and typically receives commissions for its distribution service (that are compensated by fees charged to customers). This kind of agreement has many advantages: it is simple and reversible, not implying any change in the ownership structure or in the organizational model of the firms involved, that remain absolutely independent. Start-up is quick and relatively cheap, given that fixed costs are already sustained by existing entities. Furthermore, there are no consequences in

the allocation of economic and regulatory capital. On the other hand, there are also some drawbacks: for example, conflicts of interest between banking and insurance products sharing the same distribution channel are more likely in the absence of coordination between two different managements. There may be low levels of brand recognition by customers. It is also important to notice that banks can only offer simple and standardised insurance products that do not require highly specialised consulting services. These days simple cross-selling agreements are generally signed by banks that approach the insurance business for the first time or by small institutions without the necessary resources and know-how to develop stand-alone bancassurance.

2. Cooperation between independent partners, realised through strategic alliances (often reinforced by cross-ownerships in the form of minority stakes) or joint ventures. Surely, a joint venture is a stronger form of cooperation, with the constitution of a new entity devoted to the bancassurance business. In this way, it is possible to realise a strategic partnership maintaining the independence of partners and to exploit in the best way the skills of every participant, enforcing their specializations: insurance companies take care of product design, while banks realize distribution, generally on an exclusive basis. The joint venture company pays distribution commissions to the bank that also benefits from dividends. These alliances can reach significant synergies concerning know-how, human capital, cross-selling and scope economies, but it is necessary that the two partners share the same strategy and the same engagement in resources. In addition to this, some problems may arise because of the cannibalization of the traditional insurer distribution channels and because of the tendency of the bank to capture the majority of the value. At the beginning joint ventures are often founded with an equal sharing between the partners; it is also frequent that this is a temporary partnership that ends with the exit of one of the two participants or the sale of the company on the market.

3. Control by ownership. The banking and the insurance activities are under the direction of the same ultimate owner. It is possible to distinguish two cases:

   o the bank establishes a subsidiary completely dedicated to the insurance business, or acquires the majority of an insurance company already operating on the market. The share is generally very high, near to 100 per cent, because the bank wants to have full control of the business. Legal separation with the company is due to regulatory constraints, but there is a strong integration in strategy and management. This 'captive' model allows the bank to use information at its disposal, designing products suitable for well-known customers' needs and avoiding the danger of 'cannibalization' (Berghendal, 1995). Frequently several small banks, usually cooperatives, share a common insurance captive company or the stake in a bancassurance company with the involvement of an external insurer;

o the same holding company controls the banks and the insurance companies. In this case there can be different levels of integration: there can be a unique strategic design or little effort to coordinate the two activities. In the latter case, the conglomerate structure allows earnings diversification and a large capital base, but poor realization of cost and revenue synergies.

It is worth noticing that stronger forms of cooperation (for example, joint ventures or captive companies) require a greater effort in coordination than simple distribution agreements or strategic alliances, a more stable relationship and changes in the ownership structure or in the organizational model of the firms involved. On the other hand, they permit to better exploit the skills of each subject enforcing their specialization, raising up the opportunity to realize cost and revenue synergies. The main advantages and drawbacks of several bancassurance models are summarised in Table 1.1.

As outlined in Staikouras (2006), it is difficult to identify the best corporate structure, because bancassurance success depends on a large variety of factors that the author classifies into three categories: market factors, strategic factors and operational factors. Market factors are exogenous in nature so that bancassurance companies can have a limited control of them: apart from the aforementioned regulatory constraints, the evolution of the financial services industry and tax environment, a relevant role is also played by economic growth and demographic features. For example, one ideal target for bancassurance are emerging countries with progressively improving fundamentals or developed economies in which new needs are emerging, for example, those connected to retirement. From a strategic and operational perspective, it is crucial to have flexibility in terms of a number of factors: accepting and adopting each other's culture; having a proper corporate governance model; management initiative; strong corporate

Table 1.1 Advantages and disadvantages of alternative bancassurance models

Model	Advantages	Disadvantages
Cross-selling agreement	✓ quick and simple ✓ reversible ✓ partners remain independent	➢ provision of basic products ➢ limited exploitation of synergies ➢ possible conflicts of interest
Cooperation between independent partners	✓ enhancement of specific competences ✓ partners remain independent	➢ possibly clashing cultures ➢ problems of coordination and value sharing
Control by ownership	✓ unique strategic design ✓ maximum potential for synergies	➢ long term capital commitment ➢ complexity and agency problems

Source: Author's elaboration.

brand value, reputation, customer relationship management and technology. The issue of potentially clashing cultures has to be considered carefully. Banking and insurance companies have different standpoints regarding employees' compensation, marketing and customer advice:

> the insurer is a salesman, constantly on the move, whereas the banker works in a branch. The insurer seeks out the prospective customer, talks to him personally, is trained to talk and explain risk and assumes risk on behalf of the company. The banker waits for the customer at a sale's point, addresses issues to a group of customers, while he is trained to secure risk on behalf of the bank. (Staikouras, 2006; p. 134)

After the global financial crisis, which began in the summer of 2007, the search for the optimal supply model has become increasingly important for practitioners, leading some institutions to rethink their bancassurance strategy. A survey conducted by Ernst & Young (2010) reveals that managers' preferences are moving from proprietary models to joint ventures and reinsurance agreements, because of a 'combination of capital constraints, loss-making portfolios in some areas, a greater emphasis on risk management and a more risk-averse mentality' (Ernst & Young, 2010, p. 16).

1.4 Conclusions

This chapter has shown that the trend towards conglomeration has been motivated by relevant changes in the financial services industry, including deregulation, globalization and the development of ICT. Banks have entered securities and insurance activities in order to offset the slowdown in their traditional deposits and lending business resulting from the development of more efficient capital markets and the increasing household demand for long-term, high-yield investments. In this framework, bancassurance has had a particular success, fostered by demographic changes, decreasing guarantees offered by public pension schemes and fiscal incentives.

The period from the 1970s to the 1990s saw a transformation from the provision of basic policies strictly linked to bank loans to a fully integrated range of products able to satisfy all customers' financial needs. This evolution has been accompanied by the development of different organizational models, ranging from simple distribution agreements to full control by ownership.

The viability of bancassurance as a business model for financial firms has always been widely discussed by both academics and practitioners. With the advent of the global financial crisis and the decision of some financial institutions to refocus on their core business, the debate between advocates and sceptics of bancassurance is becoming even more heated. A relevant case is the Belgian financial conglomerate ING announcing its decision to separate its banking from its insurance business in October 2009. Actually, some important bancassurance divestitures also took place before the crisis period – for example, Credit Suisse selling Winterthur to AXA in June 2006. However, it is also possible to find examples in the opposite direction: Intesa Sanpaolo has recently received permission from the anti-trust authority to proceed with the total acquisition of Intesa Vita, born as a joint venture with the insurer Alleanza Assicurazioni (now part of the Generali Group). Furthermore, looking at the three principal banking groups from five large European countries – France, Germany, Italy, Spain and the UK – it is possible to observe that most of them have a bancassurance company, fully or partially owned (see Table 1.2).

This reinforces the conclusion that, at present, it is not possible to identify an ideal form of bancassurance, because the success of cooperation between banks and insurance companies depends upon many factors, both market-based and strategic or operational. To sum up, bancassurance can experience alternate fortunes across time and countries, but remains a central current phenomenon of the modern financial services industry.

Table 1.2 Top 3 banking groups and their main related insurer in Europe

Country	Country rank	Banking group name	Main related insurer	% Ownership
FRANCE	1	BNP PARIBAS	BNP PARIBAS ASSURANCE	100
FRANCE	2	CREDIT AGRICOLE	PREDICA	MO*
FRANCE	3	SOCIETE GENERALE	SOGECAP	100
GERMANY	1	DEUTSCHE BANK	X	X
GERMANY	2	COMMERZ BANK	X	X
GERMANY	3	DZ BANK	R + VVERSICHERUNG AKTIENGESELLSCHAFT	>73
ITALY	1	UNICREDIT	CREDITRAS VITA SPA	50
ITALY	2	INTESA SANPAOLO	EURIZON VITA SPA	>50
ITALY	3	MONTE DEI PASCHI DI SIENA	AXA MPS ASSICURAZIONI VITA	50
SPAIN	1	BANCO SANTANDER	SANTANDER SEGUROS Y REASEGUROS C. ASEGURADORA	100
SPAIN	2	BBVA	BBVA SEGUROS SA DE SEGUROS Y REASEGUROS	100
SPAIN	3	LA CAIXA	VIDA-CAIXA SA DE SEGUROS Y REASEGUROS	100
UK	1	BARCLAYS BANK PLC	X	X
UK	2	ROYAL BANK OF SCOTLAND	RBS INSURANCE GROUP LIMITED	100
UK	3	HSBC	HSBC LIFE (UK)	100

* MO: *Mostly Owned.*
Source: Author's elaboration on Bankscope data. The three largest banking groups in each country are identified on the base of total equity at the end of the year 2009.

Notes

1. For more details on regulatory issues, see Chapter 4.
2. See Chapter 4 for more details.
3. For more details, see Chapters 2 and 3.
4. For more details, see Chapter 4.
5. For more details, see Chapter 2.
6. For a detailed analysis of the historical development of bancassurance see Elkington, 1993; Hoschka, 1994; Genetay and Molyneux, 1998; Locatelli et al., 2003.

References

Berghendal, G. (1995) 'The Profitability of Bancassurance for European Banks', *International Journal of Bank Marketing*, XIII, 1, 17–28.

Casu, B., C. Girardone and P. Molyneux (2006) *Introduction to Banking* (London: FT Prentice Hall).

Davis, S.I. (2007) 'Bancassurance: The Lessons of Global Experience in Banking and Insurance Collaboration', VRL KnowledgeBank Ltd. Available online at www.patersons.com.

Dierick, F. (2004) 'The Supervision of Mixed Financial Services Groups in Europe', European Central Bank, Occasional Paper Series no. 20/2004.

Daniel, J.P. (1995) *Les Enjeux de la Bancassurance* (Paris: Edition de Verneuil).

DBRS-Dominion Bond Rating Service (2006), 'European Bancassurance Overview and Rating Methodology', June.

Elkington, W. (1993) 'Bancassurance', *Chartered Building Societies Institutions Journal*, March, 2–3.

Ernst & Young (2010) 'Bancassurance: A Winning Formula', July.

Fields, L., D. Fraser and J. Kolari (2007) 'Bidder Returns in Bancassurance Mergers: Is There Evidence of Synergy?' *Journal of Banking & Finance*, XXXI, 12, 3646–62.

Fitch Ratings (2006) 'Bancassurance or not Bancassurance?', February.

Genetay, N. and P. Molyneux (1998) *Bancassurance* (London: Palgrave Macmillan).

Hendershott, R.J., D.E. Lee and J.G. Tompkins (2002) 'Winners and Losers as Financial Service Providers Converge: Evidence from the Financial Modernization Act of 1999', *The Financial Review*, XXXVII, 1, 53–72.

Hoschka, T.C. (1994) *Bancassurance in Europe* (London: Macmillan).

Locatelli, R., C. Morpugno and A. Zanette (2003) 'L'integrazione tra banche e compagnie di assicurazione e il modello dei conglomerati finanziari in Europa', in F. Cesarini (ed.) *Le strategie delle grandi banche in Europa* (Rome: Bancaria Editrice).

Molyneux, P. (2002) 'Evoluzione dei rapporti tra banca e assicurazione: lo scenario internazionale', *Evoluzione Bancassurance*.

Munich Re (2001) 'Bancassurance in Practice'. Available online at www.munichre.com.

National Bank of Belgium (2001) 'La Bancassurance', *Revue Economique*, May, 9–33.

National Bank of Belgium (2002) 'Financial Conglomerates', *Financial Stability Revue*, Issue 1, 61–78.

Staikouras, S.K. (2006) 'Business Opportunities and Market Realities in Financial Conglomerates', *The Geneva Papers*, XXXI, 1, 124–48.

Swiss RE (1992) 'Bancassurance', *Sigma*, no. 2/1992. Zurich: Swiss Reinsurance Company, Economic Research & Consulting.

Swiss RE (2007) 'Bancassurance: Emerging Trends, Opportunities and Challenges', *Sigma*, no. 5/2007. Zurich: Swiss Reinsurance Company, Economic Research & Consulting.

Van den Berghe, L. and K. Verweire (1998) *Creating the Future with All Finance and Financial Conglomerates* (Dordrecht: Kluwer Academic Publishers).

Van den Berghe, L. and K. Verweire (2001) 'Convergence in the Financial Services Industry', *The Geneva Papers*, XXVI, 2, 173–83.

Vander Vennet, R. (2002) 'Cost and Profit Efficiency of Financial Conglomerates and Universal Banks in Europe', *Journal of Money, Credit and Banking*, XXXIV, 1, 254–82.

Voutilainen, R. (2005) 'Comparing Alternative Structures of Financial Alliances', *The Geneva Papers*, XXX, 327–42.

2
Bancassurance Products
Maria Grazia Starita

2.1 Introduction

The aim of this chapter is to analyze the main features of bancassurance products and their evolution over time. Generally, bancassurer products have a low insurance content if they belong to the life business, or a high degree of standardization, if they belong to the non-life business. These characteristics derive from the skills and knowledge of the banks which approach the insurance business. In fact, the bancassurance products were initially born as banking-related products and bank branches have gradually become one of the most important distribution channels of insurance policies. Bancassurers are able to combine the information about the financial behaviour of their clients with their insurance needs. In the first step of the bancassurance development process, bancassurers focused on life products because of their high saving content and because of the many similarities and complementaries these had with the asset management activity. The share of the written premium addressed to cover the mortality/longevity risk was equal to zero or limited to a small amount and the claim management process was quite simple. In the second step of the development process, bancassurers have also approached the non-life business with some standardized products or with the help of reinsurers. The variables of customization of non-life products are few (above all, the age of the policyholder) and the claim management process is in outsourcing. It is likely that bancassurers will expand their product range in the near future, strengthening the offer of insurance policies with a less direct link with the traditional banking activity.

The remainder of the chapter is organized as follows: section 2.2 reviews the financial needs in order to outline the main business opportunities for bancassurance. Some financial needs can be easily satisfied by bancassurance products while those requiring high customization can be effectively satisfied only by insurance undertakings (for example, annuities or critical illness insurance). Section 2.3 analyzes the traditional bancassurance products: unit-linked policies, index-linked policies and with-profit policies. These policies have a high-saving and a low-insurance content. Section 2.4 defines the characteristics of the recent development of bancassurance through products different from those analyzed in the previous section. Thanks to their relevant placement power, bancassurers can now offer some policies covering specific insurance needs, such as home insurance and payment protection insurance. These policies are classified according to the link with banking products (mortgages, personal loans, banking accounts, asset management, and so on) and to the degree of the implied underwriting risk. Finally, section 2.5 analyzes the challenges and the threats linked to the traditional and new bancassurance products, while section 2.6 presents some conclusions.

2.2   Financial needs and bancassurance products

According to the insurance penetration rates (CEA, 2010), the most important European markets are France, Germany, Italy, Spain and the United Kingdom. We do not take into account the organizational models for the cooperation between banks and insurance companies (see Chapter 1 and Chapter 3), but we focus on bancassurers' products, also providing some examples of existing policies, referring to the markets above mentioned. In order to identify the main bancassurance products we need to analyze the customers' needs first.

The financial literature traditionally identifies five different types of financial needs linked to: borrowing, investment, insurance, life protection and pensions. All of these can be directly satisfied with insurance products except for the borrowing needs, but we take into account only bancassurance products. Borrowing needs are normally satisfied by products provided by banks. Investment needs can be satisfied by unit-linked, index-linked and traditional policies. These policies are normally provided by insurance companies and also by bancassurers, thanks to the similarities with asset management services and to the complementarities with banking products. Insurance needs, instead, are connected to the necessity to protect one's house, car, journeys, ... and they are normally satisfied by home insurance, car insurance and travel insurance, respectively. Some of these are offered by bancassurers. Life protection needs normally cover the following events: death, sickness and illness, dread disease, critical illness, long-term care and so on. The financial consequences of these events are respectively covered by: life assurance, payment protection insurance, permanent health insurance, critical illness policies, long-term care policies. Some of these policies (especially the last three types) are only sold by insurance undertakings because of the high cost of acquisition (for example, the health questionnaire) and maintenance of the policy (for example, the cost of claim assessment). In addition to this, customers often require advice from specialized professionals to make sure that they are buying the policy most appropriate to their needs. The dramatic decrease of the protection degree of welfare state implies researching standardized covers for everyone. In the near future the standardized versions of these policies could also be sold by bancassurers. Finally, pension needs are linked to the maintenance of a stable standard of living after retirement. These needs are generally satisfied by annuities and personal pensions. These products are normally sold by insurance undertakings and now also by bancassurers.

The range of products actually provided by intermediaries in order to satisfy each type of financial need varies according to national legislation, local specificities and consumer preferences. Figure 2.1 shows the range of products generally sold by bancassurers in Europe.

For example, the success of bancassurance in France can be explained by the ability of firms to combine life business products (for example, unit-linked policies) with the classic savings products (such as saving accounts), increasing the share of customers' long-term savings managed by banks.

The ability of these products to satisfy financial needs depends strictly on the customers' degree of financial capability. Most people today own and understand bonds, mutual funds, savings accounts and workplace retirement plans, but there is a lack of understanding in relation to pension funds, individual retirement accounts, annuities, long-term care insurance and health insurance: this may affect the ability to achieve the household financial goals (retirement, family's future well-being, protection of assets, generation of future income, and so on). The challenge is to ensure that contribution levels and the consequent retirement plan coverage are sufficient to meet customers' financial needs in the post-retirement age, compensating the decreasing level of protection offered by social security. At the same time the challenge is to protect the family's future well-being and to provide financial security through the insurance goals. The high costs of assisted living and nursing home care can have a devastating effect on retirement savings and estate planning.

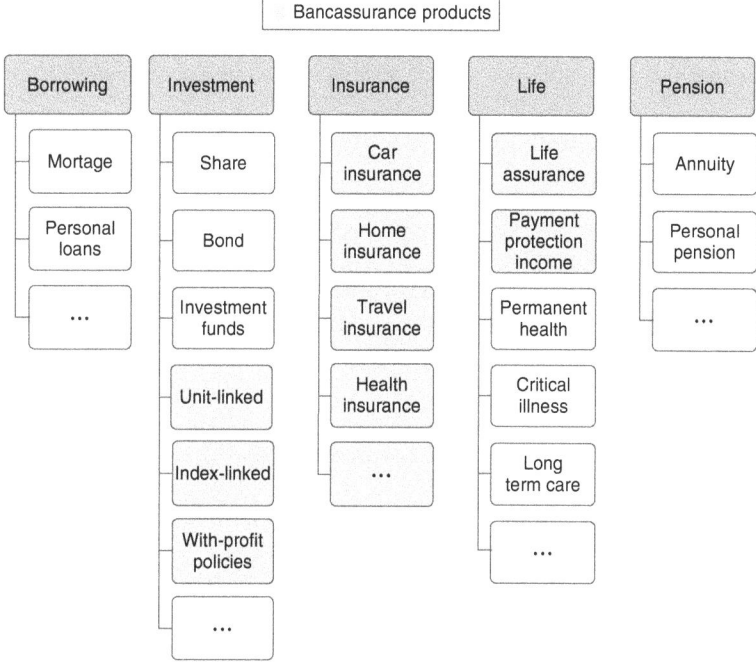

Figure 2.1 Financial needs and bancassurance products
Source: Author's own elaboration.

The literature (Lusardi and Mitchell, 2007; Mitchell and Moore, 1998) analyzes the barriers to private saving, such as: the poor quality of information guiding people in the difficult decision of how much and how best to save and to protect; the poor coverage of voluntary pension schemes; and, above all, an insufficient available income. On the other hand, the reforms of the 'pay-as-you-go' state pension systems imply significant reductions in the generosity of State pensions.

The development of long-term regular savings products which are easily accessible and have a high degree of flexibility and liquidity is necessary to meet individual preferences. This would be particularly significant in a rapidly evolving economic context, as such products would provide customers with the flexibility to respond to changing needs and to the uncertain financial futures that come with them. The bancassurers may have an important role in the increase of long term savings and in the upgrade of insurance culture.

Firstly, we analyze the life business products satisfying investment and/or pension needs (section 2.3) and secondly we focus on products normally linked to insurance and life protection needs (section 2.4).

2.3   Bancassurance products satisfying investment and pension needs

According to the aim of the following analysis, we can subdivide the premium of a life policy into two main components: the risk premium and the saving premium. The first component is an amortization to cover the actuarial risk (the mortality risk or the longevity risk), while the second is an investment to cover the guaranteed amount, if any. The cost of acquiring and maintaining the policy, the cost of risk, the cost of compliance with capital requirements (reserves, underlying portfolio and absorbed capital) and the profit margin of the intermediary are not considered.

Firstly, we analyze those policies with a high financial content which are linked to investment funds (that is, Undertakings for Collective Investment in Transferable Securities (UCITSs)), internal funds held by the insurance undertaking or share indexes and which are quite similar to the asset management range of products. For these policies the saving premium is more than the risk premium. They provide for a return of the reserve in case of death/life (or surrender) or they offer the transformation of the accumulated funds into annuities. The asset management of the pool of premiums is trusted by insurance undertakings (without any smoothing policy of returns as in the traditional policies) or is left to investment companies (as in policies linked to UCITSs) or directly to the market (as in policies linked to a share index). Policies with a high financial content are savings products with easy access and limited degree of flexibility and liquidity (the policyholder can surrender the policy generally after the first or fifth year) to meet individual preferences.

Secondly, we identify the characteristics of traditional policies with a saving content normally linked to a with-profit fund. In relation to these policies, the saving premium is more than the risk premium but the asset management is directly linked to a with-profit fund. The most important characteristic of the asset management of with-profit fund is the smoothing policy and the assignment of a series of regular bonuses. These products normally provide a life or death coverage.

According to the EU Directive 2002/89/EC, life assurance and annuities can be linked to investment funds. We have three types of reference entities: UCITSs, internal funds held by insurance undertakings and share indexes. Commonly, the policies linked to UCITSs and internal funds are called unit-linked policies while the policies linked to share indexes are called index-linked policies. First we will analyze the unit-linked policies.

The premium is transformed into units of one or more UCITSs or into internal funds at the start date and the final amount is also expressed into units at the end date. Customers invest into a wide range of different funds or funds of funds (portfolios of carefully selected funds): it is possible to split the premium less the initial charges among several investment funds. By pooling together the savings of many customers, the fund manager can invest in a much larger spread of assets than the customer could do by himself, providing a relevant diversification benefit. A defined rate of return at the end of the contract or life covers during the investment horizon can be guaranteed. Generally, the life cover can vary according to the age of the customer. The performance of the contract depends on the performance of the investment fund: the value of the policy can go down as well as up,which means that the derived income can vary in a sensitive way. The most important threat is represented by the payment of an amount less than the premium originally invested. Consequently, the amount that the customer will get back depends on several factors: the performance of chosen funds, insurance undertakings/bancassurers' charges, the length of the period of investment and any eventual withdrawals made during the contract period. If the customer needs to access his money in the first year of the contract, the insurance undertaking/bancassurer can charge additional costs. In the case of death, the amount the insurer/bancassurer will pay depends on the value of the units chosen and on a bonus, if any. The customer can move his units among funds through switching.

The customer's choice of investment funds (UCITSs or internal funds) could be based on his objectives and his attitude to or tolerance of investment risk. The level of risk and return attached to unit-linked policies can be understood more easily by a consideration of the fund category (cash, bonds, equities, properties, and so on), the asset classes which fall into each fund (global equities, European equities, emerging market equities), the investment strategy, the degree of activism of the fund manager, the benchmark and the rating (if any). In particular, the benchmark or the pool of benchmarks is a synthetic measure of the approximate risk and return of each fund as the rating.[1] Box 2.1 shows as an example the main features of a unit-linked policy offered by an Italian bancassurer, recommended for customers with a medium risk tolerance.

From the point of view of costs, it is possible to identify three types of charges: initial charges, annual management charges, fund charges and

Box 2.1   Unit-linked policy

name of product: Stereo – Programma Guidattiva

bancassurer: PosteVita

premium: a lump sum. The minimum amount is €1,500

maturity: seven years (from 2008 until 2015)

reference entity: sub-fund of Luxembourg open-ended investment company with variable share capital (UCITS)

name of reference entity: Market II Fast Guaranteed Fund

investment strategy: in the case of life, the value of the policy will depend on the performance of the reference entity. The performance is linked to two indexes through a swap agreement: the first index tracks a dynamic long-short strategy, either long or short at any one time, on EUREX DJ EURO STOXX 50 futures contracts, while the second index tracks a dynamically adjusted long-short strategy, both long and short at the same time, on some of the largest European stocks by market capitalization

financial guarantee: a minimum rate of return of 11 per cent at the end of the contract

guarantor: ABN AMRO Bank N.V. (London Branch) and now the Royal Bank of Scotland (London Branch)

life cover (insurance content): the cost of life cover is 0.50 per cent of the premium. In the case of death, the payment depends on the value of the units at that moment and on the number of units. If this amount is less than the premium paid, the bancassurer adds a bonus equal to the difference between the premium paid and the amount available up to €5,000

fees and charges: the bancassurer management charge is 5.70 per cent of the premium, while the annual management fee is 0.28 per cent of the Net Asset Value of the fund

surrender value: the policyholder can surrender the policy only after one year. The surrender value is equal to the product between the value of the units at that moment and the number of units

options: at the end of the contract the policyholder can decide to transform the amount of the policy into a with-profit annuity

Source: PosteVita, 2008. Stereo – Policy terms and conditions (*Fascicolo informativo*).

---

early exit charges. In particular, annual management charges are taken to cover the expenses of maintaining the product. These charges can be the same throughout the term of the investment (the level can depend on the amount invested) or can be decreasing. The fund charges cover the basic management charge and expenses connected with buying, selling, valuing, owning and maintaining the underlying assets. The early exit charge can be a percentage of the amount the customer wants to withdraw and is taken from the value of the funds at the exit moment.

The insurance undertaking normally has a broad range of internal funds or the ability to choose from the numerous funds of the investment companies within its own group. The bank normally engineers unit-linked policies through the funds managed by the investment companies of its own group. Bancassurers normally provide unit-linked policies with UCITSs managed by investment companies of their own group or unit-linked policies with funds managed by insurance undertakings of the group. The range of funds of bancassurers is the same as that of the bank or entity/entities to which it belongs, and there is no concern of 'cannibalism' for the investment funds provided by the banks (for example, collective investment schemes) thanks to the existence of a life insurance cover (even if small) in unit-linked policies. In both France and Italy, bancassurers distribute their unit-linked policies at a lower cost than insurance undertakings: they balance lower premium-based commissions with asset-based commissions that are the major remuneration for the banks. Insurance undertakings, instead, have high agents' commissions and a high cost of salesmen (CEA, 2010).

We move on to analyze the index-linked policies that are connected to a share index or to a basket of indexes. The mechanism through which the policy is linked to a share index is an option. Insurance undertakings and bancassurers often combine a zero coupon bond with a plain vanilla option or with an exotic option (floor, cap, knock-in, and knock-out are the most common types). The option of the index-linked in Box 2.2 is a plain vanilla option.

Box 2.2 Index-linked policy

name of product: Programma Garantito Terra

bancassurer: PosteVita

premium: a lump sum equal to at least €1,500

maturity: seven years (from 2010 until 2017)

reference entity: Dow Jones EURO STOXX50

investment strategy: the performance of the contract depends on the Dow Jones EURO STOXX50. The value of the index at the end of the contract is equal to the mean of the values reported at these reference dates: 10/07/2017; 11/07/2017; 12/07/2017; 13/07/2017. The 20.16 per cent increase in the index represents the bonus at the end of the contract if the policyholder is in live. If the performance of the index is negative the final amount is equal to the premium paid at the start date. There are three intermediate bonuses if the policyholder is in life at each reference date: at 2011 the bonus is 4 per cent of the premium; at 2013 the bonus is equal to 4.5 per cent of the premium; at 2015 the bonus is 5 per cent of the premium

financial guarantee: the zero coupon bond guarantees the final amount is at least equal to the premium paid at the start date

asset manager: PosteVita

guarantor: PosteVita

life cover (insurance content): the cost of life cover is 0.50 per cent of the premium. In the case of death, the payment is equal to the best of: (1) the premium paid at the start date; (2) the surrender value at the date of the death

fees and charges: bancassurer management charge is 5.70 per cent of the premium

surrender value: the surrender value is equal to the sum of the following elements: (1) the value of premium less the value of the time between the surrender date and the end date of the contract; (2) the intermediate bonus less the value of the time between the surrender date and the end date of the contract; (3) the 15 per cent of the increase of the index from the start date until the surrender date

Source: PosteVita, 2009. Programma Garantito Terra – Policy terms and conditions (*Fascicolo informativo*).

Table 2.1   An example of premium breakdown of an index-linked policy

Premium	100.00%
Life cover	0.50%
Amount invested gross of fees and charges	**99.50%**
Fees and charges	5.70%
Net amount invested by bancassurer	**93.80%**
of which:	
Zero coupon bond	*89.13%*
Price of option	
(share index: Dow Jones EURO STOXX50)	*4.67%*

Source: PosteVita, 2009. Programma Garantito Terra – Policy terms and conditions (Fascicolo informativo).

The premium is subdivided into the following components (see Table 2.1): (1) life cover if any (the risk premium as described above). This is the solo element of life insurance provided: typically, this policy adds 1 per cent or less to the value of investment if it is paid out after the death of the policyholder; (2) the charge of intermediary; (3) the zero coupon bond. On the redemption date the par value covers both the cost of bond and the price of option; (4) the price of the option. Typically these options are negotiated OTC (Over The Counter).

According to the EU disclosure regulation, in the policy documents the insurer/bancassurer must indicate a range of expected scenarios and the values of the underlying option according to the index share. Consequently the performance of these policies depends on: (1) the investment risk: thanks to the option, the final amount depends on the share index at each reference date; (2) the credit risk: the assessment of the bond-originator credit risk is very important.[2]

Bancassurers' index-linked products are long-term investments with low fees on premiums against the higher fee of traditional policies sold by insurers. This advantage depends on the spread between the interest granted to the policyholders and the yield earned on the assets. Bancassurers also take advantage of their knowledge of the stock markets to construct the index-linked policies. These products are very popular with elderly and wealthy clients who pay large premiums to bancassurers (the average premium was more than €20,000 for French, Italian and Spanish markets in 2009 (CEA, 2010)).

In some countries bancassurers combine these policies with mortgages. In the UK the endowment mortgage policy is an investment taken out to pay off the original loan when the mortgage term ends. There is usually no guarantee that the policy will pay out enough to repay the mortgage at the end of the policy.[3] These policies were most commonly used as a way of repaying a mortgage by home buyers in the 1980s and 1990s, but are less popular now due to the fact that many of them have failed to reach the capital sum required to pay off the mortgage at the end of the term.[4]

We proceed by analysing the traditional policies or with-profit policies. From an economic point of view the with-profit investments can take the forms of with-profit policy, endowment, annuity, pension and investment bond (in the UK). A with-profit policy is a long-term investment which grows through adding bonuses. Often it includes some life covers and pays out a guaranteed amount at the end of the policy in accordance with the conditions set out in the contract. Premiums from all policyholders are pooled into a with-profit fund managed by the insurance company/bancassurer. The insurance company/bancassurer invests the with-profit fund in different asset classes, normally gilts, corporate bonds, shares, properties and cash deposits. The pool of premiums is not subdivided into units or basis points as for unit-linked and index-linked policies: the value of participation does not change every day as the investments are reported at the acquisition cost. Box 2.3 shows an example of a with-profit policy offered by an Italian bancassurer, where the rate of return is obtained as the ratio between the sum of dividends, interests, realized gains/losses and the average size of fund.

In France, Italy and Spain the traditional policies were the most important product in the first stage of bancassurance development. In the UK there are two types of with-profit policies: the conventional and the unitized with-profit policies. The premium of the conventional with-profit policy is addressed in the pool while the premium of the unitised with-profit funds is transformed in units at the current price. If the price is fixed, the annual bonuses add extra units to the policy at the same price whereas if the price is variable the unit price increases with regular bonuses.

The performance of a with-profit fund is divided among policyholders by adding bonuses and depends on the smoothing policy (in all countries) and the presence of a market value reduction mechanism (only in the UK). There are two types of bonuses: the annual bonus (or the reversionary bonus) and the final bonus (or the terminal bonus).[5] Insurers/bancassurers do not have to add a bonus each year but, once an annual bonus has been added, it cannot be taken away if the policyholders continue to meet the terms and conditions set out in the policy documents and do not cash in the policy earlier: this is the most important difference between traditional policies and unit-linked policies.

Box 2.3 With-profit policy

name of product: Eurizonvita Valore Garanzia

bancassurer: Eurizonvita

premium: a lump sum. The minimum amount is €5,000. It is possible to add other premiums during the contract

maturity: whole of life

reference entity: with-profit fund

name of reference entity: Fondo Vivadue

investment strategy: the with-profit fund invests in government and corporate bonds. The annual bonus depends on the return of the with-profit fund and on the management fee. The rate of return is obtained as the ratio between the sum of dividends, interests and realized gains/losses and the average size of fund

financial guarantee: a minimum rate of return of 1.5 per cent

asset manager: Eurizonvita SpA

guarantor: Eurizonvita SpA

life cover (insurance content): in the case of death, the payment depends on the value of the contract at that moment

fees and charges: initial charge is 1.50 per cent of the premium, while management fee is 1.20 per cent of the insured amount

options: after five years the policyholder can choose from five options: (1) the surrender of the annual bonus (this option is exercisable only after one year); (2) the surrender according to a predefined programme; (3) the transformation of the with-profit policy into an annuity; (4) the transformation of the with-profit policy into a reversible annuity; (5) the transformation of the with-profit policy into an annuity with a guarantee period of five years

Source: EurizonVita, 2009. Eurizon Valore Garanzia – Policy terms and conditions (*Fascicolo informativo*).

How is the annual bonus to be estimated?

The annual bonus is a function of market conditions, of the rate of return expected from the underlying investments from time to time and, finally, of the current and future financial strength of the issuer. In Italy the annual bonus, as the final bonus, depends on the comparison between the rate of policyholders' participation (at least 80 per cent), the rate of return of investments and a minimum (fixed) rate of return. The final bonus is used to top up the value of fair share of the policy at the maturity date.

How is the final amount to be estimated?

The rate of the final bonus is reviewed annually on the basis of the volumes of transfers and surrenders, the value of remaining policies and the smoothing losses, if any. If the policyholder decides to cash in his policy earlier he may also receive a final bonus, but this is likely to be less than the bonus he would receive if he kept his policy to maturity.

But how is the estimation made of the appropriate amount to pay individual with-profit policyholders?

In the UK the amount to pay as final bonus is calculated through the 'asset share'. The 'asset share' is a measure of the share of the asset attributable to a with-profit policy. It is calculated as the accumulation of premiums, at investment rates of return equal to the rate earned on the assets, minus an allowance for expenses incurred; the weight of taxation; the cost of benefits provided; any charges for the cost of guarantees or the use of capital. The intermediary manages the with-profit fund with the aim of making total aggregate maturity payouts of 100 per cent of the asset share.

The smoothing policy allows the insurer/bancassurer to hold back some of the investment returns in good years and to use it to top up bonuses when markets fall. If investment returns are poor year after year or if there is a financial turmoil (as in 2009) followed by a slow recovery, bonuses may not be added. See in Table 2.2 an example of the approach to the smoothing policy.

Table 2.2   An example of the smoothing policy

Types of policies	Time horizon of smoothing	Operator
Conventional with-profit policies	Previous five years	The geometric average of the actual investment returns
Unitised wit-profit policies	Previous two years	The geometric average of the actual monthly investment returns

Source: Liverpool Victoria Friendly Society Limited, 2009. *Principles and Practices of Financial Management.*

In the UK, when investment returns have been low, the insurer/bancassurer may also apply a Market Value Reduction (MVR) to ensure that the policyholder does not leave the fund with more than the fair share of his assets. This mechanism protects policyholders who remain in the fund. It is necessary to strike a balance between policyholders whose investments start at different times, policyholders remaining in the fund, those leaving the fund and the insurance company/bancassurer's shareholders. The insurance undertaking/bancassurer often allocates at least 80 per cent of returns to policyholders with the remaining 20 per cent going to its own shareholders. But how does the intermediary estimate MVR? The decision of whether or not to apply MVR takes into account the level of expected surrenders and the expected cost of not applying a market value reduction. Some policies may also have MVR-free dates in which the policyholder can end his policy earlier without paying the MVR, for example at the retirement age.

The use of the smoothing policy with the market value reduction implies the assessment of the inherited estate. This is part of a with-profit fund which consists of several generations of retained with-profits policyholders' investments or of past injections of money from shareholders. The insurer/bancassurer shares the inherited estate or cuts the management expenses when market conditions are bad. The inherited estate management is controlled by advocate policyholders, appointed actuaries, independent experts and the relevant authority. In particular, the policyholder's advocate estimates the value of the one-off cash payment offered to all policyholders in exchange for the rights and interests they are asked to give up. Some insurance companies/bancassurers offer the with-profit policies with a bonus set at a predetermined level or with a guaranteed annuity rate for pension. At the retirement time, the insurer/bancassurer will pay the pension at a predetermined rate which may be higher than the rates available in the market in that moment.

When the policyholder terminates the policy early he loses the financial guarantees, the annual bonuses and any life cover. The policyholder can sell the with-profit endowment in the second-hand market. For the other types of with-profit policies he must assess the surrender value.

The risk associated with the with-profit policy is an investment risk while the actuarial risk is linked to life cover if it is offered. The insurer/bancassurer has an obligation to report on the investment strategy, smoothing and bonuses policy and how the market value reductions, if any, the charges and the expenses are calculated. In Italy the insurance undertakings/bancassurers have to publish the following information every year: (a) the asset allocation of the with-profit fund;

(b) the average amount of investments; (c) the rate of return; (d) the rate of policyholders' participation; and (e) the management fee. In the UK each insurer/bancassurer produces a publicly available document (Principles and Practices of Financial Management), from which it is possible to draw all of the key information. This annual report contains the actuary assessment on the compliance of issuer with his Principles and Practices of Financial Management and his policyholders' interests. The authority for financial services (FSA) requires some kind of safeguard to be put in place for with-profits policyholders, such as a with-profit committee. The with-profit committee assesses the compliance with principles and practises of good management predefined by the insurance company/bancassurer and the way the intermediary has handled conflicts of interest among different generations of policyholders and between policyholders and his shareholders.

2.4 The recent development of bancassurance

In this section we analyze the products linked to needs different from investment and pension. This group embraces any kind of policy which can provide financial support in the event of certain unexpected events. The customer could protect himself and his family against unexpected events such as accidents, disablement, critical illness, redundancy, unemployment, and so on. The most common types of protection that the customer and his family need throughout their life are: life insurance (term insurance and whole of life), critical illness insurance, income protection insurance, mortgage/loan protection (also with decreasing term assurance), home insurance, car insurance, travel insurance, ... One reason people do not have protection is because they think they cannot afford it.[6] The bancassurers can have a role to increase the sensibility to cover the gap of protection.

With the aim of analysing the recent interest of bancassurers for products linked to needs different from investment and pension, we first identify three phases of the relation between the policyholder and his intermediary:

- the assessment of the gap protection. From the intermediary viewpoint the questionnaire is the first element to avoid the adverse selection problem. This instrument is necessary to understand the exact extension of the cover and its limits. For example, life insurance or critical illness cover imply collecting information about: the presence of any pre-existing protection covers the policyholder has in place, medical history (treatments), policyholder's family medical history, ... Not providing relevant information and all the material facts is known as a non-disclosure attitude and it is the most common reason for the non-payment of a claim. The policy documentation explains what is covered and what is not, how the intermediary settles claims, the limits and the sublimits to the cover and the premium. Each year before renewal the intermediary will send the customer a new schedule to point out any changes to the insurance and to check that the cover still meets the customers' needs;

- the control of the policyholder's behaviour. At this stage, it is important for the intermediary to control the moral hazard of the policyholder: during the contract the policyholder will need to meet the terms and conditions of the insurance. Alternatively, the claim may be rejected or payment could be reduced. The policyholder must take all reasonable steps to avoid any accident and prevent loss or damage to everything which is covered by the insurance. Every policy of this kind is linked to an annual contract and may be renewed each year according to the terms and conditions then applicable;

- the claim process. Events that may give right to a claim under the insurance contract must be notified as soon as possible. When an accident occurs, the customer should take immediate action with a claim notification. Any information concerning the cause and the value of any claim is necessary: this information will enable the intermediary to make an initial evaluation of the policy liability and claim value. The intermediary often requires additional information depending on specific circumstances.

Bancassurers have an advantage in the first phase: thanks to the trust of the mass-market clients they can easily understand the insurance and life cover needs and could propose non-life products. Bancassurers' claim processes, instead, are less efficient than those of insurance undertakings.

Bancassurers started to enter into this business with the help of reinsurers to overrun the insurance companies but have now gained the knowledge that allows them to build their own products without the help of reinsurance companies. The success of bancassurers in this business is dependent on a number of factors:

- the products proposed are still easy to understand for the customer and for the sellers (!);[7]
- the guarantees are standardized with few options (for example, capital on death);

- the tariff system is very simple (for example, travel insurance is linked to the policyholder's age);
- the application processes are easy and quick.

These characteristics permit lower fees on premiums and a simplified subscription in comparison with offerings from insurance companies.

We now underline the basic cover for each product and the possibility of including other benefits to customize the policy: the efforts of bancassurers focus on the non-life basic products whereas the policies of insurance undertakings are richer in extra benefits. First we analyze the policies directly linked to banking products (life insurance and payment protection insurance), secondly we focus on the policies packaged with banking products (home insurance and car insurance) and, finally, we analyse policies not related to banking products but more standardized and with limited underwriting risk (travel insurance and pet insurance) or more interesting in the next future (health insurance) (see Figure 2.2).

It is worth remembering that life insurance falls into the life business sector, but in order to identify the gap of protection we consider life insurance (assurance on death: term insurance and whole of life insurance) as an opportunity directly linked to banking products. Payment

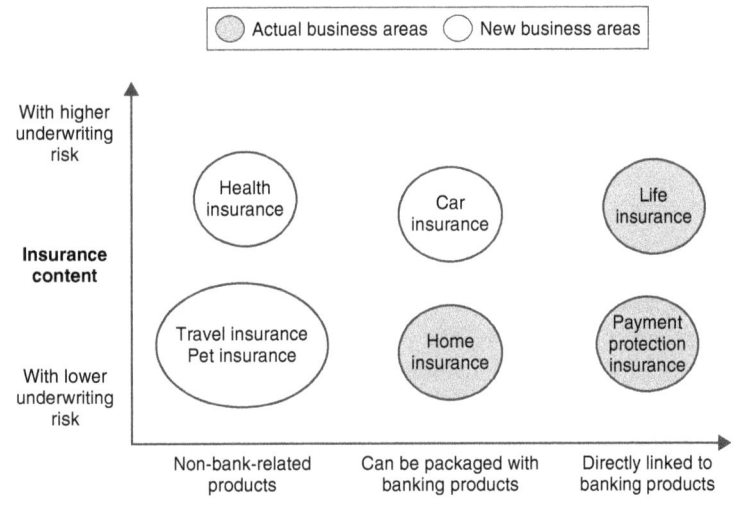

Figure 2.2 Bancassurance business areas: the link between banking products and insurance content
Source: Our processing on Milliman data (Milliman, 2008).

protection insurance (PPI), also known as credit protection insurance or loan repayment insurance, covers mortgage payments, rent and generally the cost of living when the policyholder has had an accident or suffers from an illness and consequently is not able to work. Box 2.4 reports an example of a PPI policy linked to the cover of a mortgage.

In difficult times, these policies can also cover unemployment but in this case the cover generally has a minimum length (usually 12 months) and a maximum length (usually 36 months). When the cover is in place the cash-in values of the policy substitutes for the work income. The level of the cover can be fixed or inflation-linked (generally when it leads living expenses protection). If the cover is inflation-linked, the premiums rise each year in line with inflation.[8]

The payment protection policies (PPI) should not be confused with the income protection insurance (IPI): the cash-in values of IPI are inferior to those of PPI as the latter provides for a series of cash flows for leading mortgage and general expenses whereas the IPI can only lead the general expenses. In other words the IPI protects the policyholder when he is unable to work due to an accident or an illness and provides for regular payments. In most cases the worker or the self-worker can insure up to 50 per cent of the gross earned premium and he can add the cover for career breaks (option available). The premium depends on

Box 2.4 Payment protection insurance

name of product: Mutuo Sicuro Persona

bancassurer: AXA MPS Assicurazione Vita

premium: the premium depends on: (1) the residual value of mortgage; (2) the age of the policyholder; (3) the health of the policyholder (all material facts must be disclosed); and (4) the work of the policyholder (temporary workers are not eligible)

maturity: maturity of mortgage

insurance cover: the payment on death of policyholder is equal to the residual value of mortgage

conditions: regular payments

fees and charges: 19.5 per cent of the premium

Source: AXA MPS Assicurazione Vita SpA, 2010. Mutuo Sicuro Persona – Policy terms and conditions (*Fascicolo informativo*).

the age, the health condition of the policyholder and, finally, the type of work because there are no limits to the number of claims.

In France the borrower must subscribe to a payment protection insurance policy if he wants to grant a mortgage. Often the borrower underwrites the bank's payment protection insurance rather than an insurer's policy. In Spain and Italy, the bancassurers cross-sell creditor insurance as well as home insurance with mortgages. In Italy the bancassurer is simultaneously the provider of the life cover and the beneficiary of the policy: the authority (ISVAP) is regulating this practice.

Life insurance is designed to provide a one-off cash payment if the policyholder dies before the end date of the policy. The cash goes to estate (or trust if any) and could be used to pay off a mortgage or to provide a lump sum to ease the financial worries (other debts, such as the outstanding credit card bill) of the policyholder's family or the policy's owner.[9] The premium depends on the level of the cover (fixed or decreasing), the age of the insured and other circumstances (health conditions, for example if the policyholder smokes). Generally, the intermediary defines the cover that the policyholder can apply for in accordance with his age, as in the example in Box 2.5.

Box 2.5 Life insurance

name of product: Vita protetta

bancassurer: CNP Unicredit Vita SpA

premium: payments can be monthly or annually. The premium is function of the age at the start date (from 18 years to 60 years) and the sex of policyholder.

maturity: ten years

insurance cover: €50,000 on death

conditions: a statement about the health conditions and a period of deferment of 6 months

fees and charges: the acquisition cost is 31 per cent of the premium while the management charge is 10 per cent of the premium. The distribution channel keeps 71.3 per cent of these charges

Source: CNP Unicredit Vita SpA, 2010. Vita Protetta – Policy terms and conditions (*Fascicolo informativo*).

In the joint life plan the age limit applies to the oldest of policyholders, while if the policyholder has more than one life insurance plan the limits apply to the amount of the cover under all plans added together.[10]

Thanks to their limited insurance content, life insurance or payment protection insurance are often included in bank account packages and sometimes in the basic bank account. Consequently, these policies have become a fundamental product in the bancassurer's activity.

It is straightforward for home insurance to be packaged with mortgages. There are at least three versions of this policy: buildings and contents, buildings only or contents only. The basic version (new for old) covers the contents in the policyholder's home against loss or damage by fire, flood, storm, theft, flooding and other similar causes. If the sum insured is less than the full replacement value, the claim may be reduced. Intermediaries often supply a discount for taking both buildings cover and contents cover. The home insurance is frequently the instrument to obtain a special discount on new policies. The average cover for building is generally up to €1,000,000 as in the example of Box 2.6.

Car insurance covers accidental damage caused to the policyholder's car as well as damage and/or injury the policyholder causes in an accident to another vehicle or to its driver. It also covers the policyholder's

Box 2.6 Home insurance

---

name of product: Casa Sicura

bancassurer: AXA MPS Assicurazione Danni SpA

premium: the premium depends on the type of cover chosen. The policyholder can choose to pay by lump sum or by installments

maturity: one year

insurance cover: the policy provides new for old cover for buildings (sum insured is €500,000 or €1,000,000) and/or contents (sum insured is €65,000 or €85,000)

fees and charges: not disclosed

options: the policyholder can add the cover of accident damage, the home assistance, the family legal protection, the identity theft, the bicycle cover, the student cover and the personal possession cover

Source: AXA MPS Assicurazione Danni SpA, 2010. Casa Sicura – Policy terms and conditions (*Fascicolo informativo*).

car if it is damaged by fire or stolen. The basic cover generally includes third party injury liability, damage to third party property, loss or damage to the policyholder's car as a result of fire or theft, and accidental damage to the policyholder's car. Generally the additional covers are: cover for up to 180 days in EU countries, legal expenses up to a certain limit, personal accident benefit from a minimum to a maximum, new car replacement if the policyholder's car is less than 12 months old, window replacement in case of theft, and so on. The car insurance provided by an insurance undertaking offers an extensive range of features and benefits, whereas the car insurance linked to banking accounts is often a basic cover, shown in Box 2.7.

In formulating car insurance premiums some providers use information obtained from a number of sources, including credit reference agencies. This helps the intermediary to give a quote and to

Box 2.7 Car insurance

name of the product: Santander Car Insurance
bancassurer: Santander
premium: the premium depends on: (1) the characteristics of the vehicle; (2) the policyholder's driving experience; (3) the type of policy (third party only; third party, fire and theft; comprehensive version)
maturity: one year. Renewal will be subject to the terms and conditions that apply at the time of renewal
insurance cover (for third party only): the most the bancassurer will pay for property damage is £20,000,000 for any one claim or claims arising out of one incident while the most the bancassurer will pay for costs and expenses arising from property damage is £5,000,000 for any claim or claims arising out of the incident
charges: not disclosed
options: legal expenses insurance; personal accident and road cover; boomerang tag-key protection service
gift: TomTom Sat Nav (this offer is subject to availability and can be withdrawn at any time)
Source: Santander, 2010. Santander Car Insurance – Policy Summary.

decide on the kind of payment. Car insurance has more insurance content than home insurance but it can be easily packaged with banking products.

Travel insurance pays out if certain adverse events occur either before or during a period of travel. Most travel insurance policies cover the damage to or loss of baggage and other mishaps such as emergency medical bills, legal expenses and flight delays. For example, the travel insurance covers the necessary emergency expenses incurring during the journey. A single trip policy covers up to 30 days whereas a multi-trip policy covers up to 90 days in one year (see Box 2.8 for an example).

There are a large number of factors behind the growth in travel insurance: travel covers is included as a benefit in many packaged bank accounts; people make more journeys per year and consequently prefer multi-trip policies; there are a number of channels that provide for travel insurance (bancassurers, for example). The management of these policies is less difficult than in other areas (especially home insurance) because of the limited levels of cover. Travel insurance, in fact, does not cover any events that are known before the taking out of the policy or the booking of the trip (for example, travel disruption caused by volcanic ash). The application process is extremely rapid: the travel insurance quote only requires the details of all of the people to be insured (date of birth and some elements of their medical history).

Pet insurance[11] generally covers the medical care that a family pet (usually a dog or a cat) may need in a crisis. The basic cover is linked to veterinary fees (for a maximum of 12 months and up to a limit per condition). The other covers are: third party liability (only applicable in the case of dogs); death of a pet; boarding fees if the customer has to go to hospital; and so on. Pet insurance can be considered to be a non-bank-related product but thanks to its restricted insurance content it can also be packaged with banking products.

Health insurance is not a bank-related product and has a high underwriting content. Nevertheless, it will become a target of bancassurance in future years because of the restrictions on the treatments offered by the National Health Service. Health insurance covers private medical treatment for short-term illness and injuries[12] and normally excludes all conditions suffered before the start of the policies and during the deferment period. The most important exclusions are health problems in the past (so-called 'pre-existing conditions');[13] chronic medical conditions such as long-standing or incurable illness; treatment for HIV/AIDS or cosmetic surgery and so on. The extension of the cover depends on

Box 2.8 Travel insurance

name of product: AXA MPS Vacanza Sicura

bancassurer: AXA MPS Assicurazioni Danni SpA

premium: the premium depends on the type of cover. The policy offers the following types of cover:

- personal baggage;
- personal accident (accident bodily injury which results in death, loss of limb, loss of sight, hearing or speech, permanent total disablement);
- personal liability (an insured person becomes legally liable to pay for accidental damage to material property, accidental bodily injury to any person, obstruction trespass nuisance wrongful arrest detention or false imprisonment);
- medical emergency travel expenses;
- legal expenses;
- cancellation curtailment or rearrangement expenses;
- missed departure.

maturity: trip must not last longer than 90 days

insurance cover: the cover is:

- €500 for Italy, €1,000 for Europe and €1,500 for personal baggage;
- €75,000 for personal accident;
- €500,000 for personal liability;
- €300 for Italy, €10,000 for Europe, €15,000 for world for medical emergency travel expenses;
- €2,500 for legal expenses;
- for the cover is £5,000 each insured person; for loss of passport the cover is £250 each insured person;
- from €250 to €5,000 for missed departure.

The cover for cancellation curtailment or rearrangement expenses depends of the type of policy

fees and charges: not disclosed

exclusions: hazardous activities

Source: AXA MPS Assicurazioni Danni SpA, 2010. AXA MPS Vacanza Sicura – Policy terms and conditions (*Fascicolo informativo*).

the type of treatments. It is possible to identify at least three different types of treatments:

- in-patient treatment. This treatment is referred to the core set of in-patient fees, such as diagnostic procedures, radiotherapy and chemo-therapy, physiotherapy, and of daycare surgery (in-patient drugs and dressings), accommodation costs. This treatment is usually covered by private medical insurance (PMI);[14]
- out-patient treatment. This treatment refers to home nursing, private ambulance transport, specialists, consultants, ... and is covered by a health cash plan. The health cash plan provides a limited series of payouts towards everyday healthcare bills;
- other treatment. Normally this treatment refers to dental care, optical care or physiotherapy ... The dental insurance covers all normal routine dental care and supplementary treatment as a result of accidents.

In the example of Box 2.9 the treatment depends on the reference rate appointed by social security.

Box 2.9 Health insurance

---

name of the product: BNP Paribas Protection Santè – La Formule Essentielle

bancassurer: BNP Paribas

premium: the minimum amount of the monthly premium is €19.62 for unmarried young employees. The premium is function of: (1) the age of the policyholder; (2) the health conditions of the policyholder family; (3) the type of treatment chosen.

maturity: one year

insurance cover: the insurance content depends on the reference rate of social security. The reference rate is the basic rate appointed by social security to make its repayments. La Formule Essentielle cov-ers 100 per cent of the reference rate, while the other policies cover up to 250 per cent of the reference rate

charges: not disclosed

conditions: no health questionnaire

options: Dental care

Source: BNP Paribas, 2010. BNP Protection Santè – Policy terms and conditions (*Documentation*).

The choice of health insurance depends upon the cover offered by the company-sponsored scheme. If the company does not offer this treatment or if the policyholder is retired or self-employed the choice of health insurance depends on the health conditions and on the age of the policyholder.

2.5 Conclusions

This chapter has provided an analysis of bancassurance products based on their saving content for life business and their ability to satisfy cover needs for non-life business. The second section has shown the spectrum of financial needs and the potential supply of bancassurers for each service required by customers. The third section has analyzed the traditional bancassurance products that are mainly life products with a relevant saving content. The risk profile and the asset allocation strategy of these products are strictly linked to the reference entity and to the type of relation with the reference entity. The performance of the unit-linked policies depends on the value of UCITSs/internal funds to which they are linked and the relation between the policy and the reference entity is direct. The performance of the index-linked policies is linked to a share index or a basket of share indexes and the relation with the reference entity depends on an (exotic) option. The rate of return of with-profit policies depends on the characteristics of the pool of investments and on the acquisition cost of these investments. The fourth section has analyzed the opportunities of bancassurance in the non-life business. It is possible to identify the actual and new business areas of bancassurance through the analysis of the link between bancassurance products with the banking products and the measurement of the insurance content of the bancassurance products. The actual areas concern the life insurance, the payment protection insurance and the home insurance whereas the new areas are represented by the car insurance, the travel insurance, the pet insurance and the health insurance.

Notes

1. In some markets the policyholders have access to self-estimation made by the asset managers and to the rating given by independent advisers.
2. To this aim it is interesting to analyze the index-linked policies issued in Italy and linked to Lehman Brothers bonds.
3. Some companies offer help to consumers to pursue their complaints with financial services firms and with the Ombusdman.

4. The with-profit endowment policies include the option of trading the policy as well as surrendering it, if it has been running for at least five years. The endowment policies linked to a share index do not have this characteristic.
5. The annual bonus is shown in the annual statement.
6. For example the average life cover premium for a 35-year-old, non-smoker male, 25-year term, €110,000 sum assured is €12 a month (see Lloyd's TSB's website – quote at August 2010).
7. The growth of online aggregator sites allows easy comparison among channels.
8. See the FSA report (FSA, 2005) on the level of compliance with rules by firms selling PPI with credit arrangements (revolving cards, unsecured loans, ...).
9. In the UK if the doctor has diagnosed a terminal illness between the start date and 12 months or more before the end date, the policyholder can ask the insurance undertaking to advance the payment of the amount of the cover. Generally, the company reduces the amount of the cover.
10. Especially in the UK policies include the plans designed to help pay for funeral expenses, any loans or bills or to leave a gift for the loved ones.
11. This type of insurance is more common in the UK. The Pet Travel Scheme allows individuals to take their pet abroad to certain specified countries and re-enter the UK without the need for the pet to go into quarantine.
12. Health insurance does not cover critical illnesses such as heart attack.
13. Moratorium policies cover the 'pre-existing conditions': each treatment in the deferment period is excluded.
14. Normally each PMI is linked to a list of approved hospitals graded into 'bands': a high band reflects a high quality of accommodation.

References

AXA MPS Assicurazioni Danni SpA (2010), AXA MPS Vacanza Sicura – Policy terms and conditions (*Foglio informativo*).
AXA MPS Assicurazione Danni SpA (2010), Casa Sicura – Policy terms and conditions (*Foglio informativo*).
AXA MPS Assicurazione Vita SpA (2010), Mutuo Sicuro Persona – Policy terms and conditions (*Foglio informativo*).
BNP Paribas (2010), BNP Protection Santè – Policy terms and conditions (*Documentation*).
CEA (2010), Insurance Distribution Channels in Europe, CEA Statistics No. 39. www.cea.eu.
CNP Unicredit Vita SpA (2010), Vita Protetta – Policy terms and conditions (*Foglio informativo*).
EurizonVita (2010), Eurizon Valore Garanzia – Policy terms and conditions (*Foglio informativo*).
FSA (2005), The Sale of Payment Protection Insurance – Results of thematic works. www.fsa.gov.uk.
Liverpool Victoria Friendly Society Limited (2009), Principles and Practices of Financial Management. www.lv.com.
Lusardi, A. and O. Mitchell (2007), 'Baby Boomer Retirement Security: The Roles of Planning, Financial Literacy, and Housing Wealth', *Journal of Monetary Economics*, LIV, 1, 205–24.

Milliman (2008), European Bancassurance Benchmark, Research Report. www.milliman.com.

Mitchell, O. and J. Moore (1998), 'Can Americans Afford to Retire? New Evidence on Retirement Saving Adequacy', *Journal of Risk and Insurance*, LXV, 3, 371–400.

PosteVita (2009), Programma Garantito Terra – Policy terms and conditions (*Foglio informativo*). www.postevita.it.

PosteVita (2008), Stereo – Policy terms and conditions (*Foglio informativo*). www.postevita.it.

Santander (2010), Santander Car Insurance – Policy Summary.

3
The Bancassurance Market in Europe

Massimo Caratelli

3.1 Introduction

Bancassurance, the provision of policies by banks or lending institutions, represents one of the most significant changes to have occurred in the insurance industry over recent years. This practice originated in France in the mid-1980s, and spread rapidly, particularly in Europe, Australia, and emerging markets; however, it is applied heterogeneously around the world. The present chapter draws on these appraisals, outlining the use of bank branches in insurance distribution. The aim is to identify the reasons for the pervasiveness of bancassurance in markets and business lines. In particular, differences among countries and type of products are examined on the basis of public statistical data and available reports. Special attention is given to the European area, consistent with the purpose of this volume.

The rest of the chapter is organized as follows:

- section 3.2 presents an overview of the insurance industry;
- section 3.3 describes the development of bancassurance in the life and non-life sectors;
- section 3.4 identifies the role of traditional channels in policy distribution;
- section 3.5 discusses the most representative business models adopted to implement bancassurance operations. Examples are introduced with a view to refining the comprehension of the models, using information available on the web sites of financial intermediaries;
- section 3.6 summarizes the principal findings.

3.2   An overview of the insurance industry

According to Swiss Re (2010), worldwide premiums amounted to US$4,102 billion (€2,941 billion) in 2009. This volume of activity was reached through the distinct expansion of the two sectors into which insurance has traditionally been classified: life and non-life sectors. The former industry contributed to global insurance, generating more than 57 per cent of all premiums, see Table 3.1. The same table shows income separated by region. It shows that the European area is the leading continental market with a share of 39 per cent.

North America is the second largest international market, but has continued its downward trend (Figure 3.1). In 2009, its share decreased to 30 per cent. Conversely, Asia has experienced growth originating 25 per cent of the world's gross written premium and is in third place.

With regards to Europe, insurance has weathered the economic crisis since 2007 (Figure 3.2). In 2009, total premiums returned to growth driven by the life sector, which accounts for about 60 per cent of all regional premiums. The holding of the guaranteedreturn policies offered by life insurers could explain the favourable results. These instruments benefited households' increasing demand for savings.

The highest level of insurance activity was observed in north-western Europe, where the penetration of policies exceeded the degree registered in industrialized countries such as the United States and Canada. Figure 3.3 supports this appraisal. The graph exhibits total gross written premiums as a percentage of gross domestic product (GDP). This ratio reveals the vast growth potential of local insurance markets such as Turkey and Romania, where specific insurance contracts are still under-developed and recent bank failures have penalized financial activities (Swiss Re, 2007).

The top four life insurance markets in Europe are, in order of size, the UK, France, Germany and Italy, which together represent more than 70 per cent of the European life industry (Table 3.2).

Regarding the structure of life premiums, Figure 3.4 shows the percentage of premiums collected through a unit-linked contract. The latter expresses the amount of coverage and premiums in terms of investment units such as shares in trusts or building societies. Unit-linked policies are 18 per cent of the total European life premiums, with a market share ranging from 5 per cent in Bulgaria to 42 per cent in the United Kingdom (CEA, 2010b).

In the last decade, several markets have exhibited a significant increase in the share of unit-linked premiums (Figure 3.5). Obviously, the success

Table 3.1 Premium volume by region (direct business in force)[1]

	Premium volume (in millions of USD)		Share of world market (in %)	Premiums (1) in % of GDP	Premiums (1) per capita (in USD)		
	2009	2008	2009	2009	2009	Life (% of total)	Non-life
America	1 359 081	1 450 909	33.13	6.95	1 480.7	642.1 (43.36%)	838.6
North America	1 249 254	1 344 105	30.46	8.02	3 665.8	1 604.6 (43.77%)	2 061.2
Latin America and Caribbean	109 827	106 804	2.68	2.77	190.3	73.7 (38.73%)	116.6
Europe	1 617 597	1 701 480	39.44	7.59	1 860.9	1 108.0 (59.54%)	752.9
Western Europe	1 532 710	1 603 387	37.37	8.47	2 920.8	1 805.9 (61.83%)	1 114.9
Central and Eastern Europe	84 888	98 094	2.07	2.76	263.4	56.0 (21.26%)	207.4
Asia	1 008 132	935 428	24.58	6.08	247.4	184.2 (74.45%)	63.2
Japan and newly industrialized Asian economies	716 068	677 495	17.46	10.58	3 384.0	2 627.8 (77.65%)	756.2
South and East Asia	262 309	229 407	6.40	3.34	74.1	52.9 (71.39%)	21.1
Middle East and Central Asia	29 755	28 526	0.73	1.55	95.9	23.4 (24.40%)	72.5
Africa	49 502	52 625	1.21	3.30	49.1	32.3 (65.78%)	16.7
Oceania	67 346	78 536	1.64	6.04	1 865.8	931.3 (49.91%)	934.5
World (2)	4 101 658	4 218 979	100.00	7.01	600.3	345.3 (57.52%)	255.0
Industrialized countries (3)	3 567 597	3 705 078	86.98	8.68	3 431.1	2 003.8 (58.40%)	1 427.3
Emerging markets (4)	534 062	513 901	13.02	2.85	91.7	48.7 (53.11%)	42.9

Notes: (1) Excluding cross-border business; (2) Insurance penetration (premiums as a percentage of GDP) and density (premiums per capita) include cross-border business; (3) North America, Western Europe (w/o Turkey), Japan, Hong Kong, Singapore, South Korea, Taiwan (counted as an emerging market in earlier editions), Oceania, Israel; (4) Latin America, Central and Eastern Europe, South and East Asia, the Middle East (w/o Israel) and Central Asia, Turkey, Africa.
Source: Author's elaboration on data from Swiss Re (2010), p. 5.

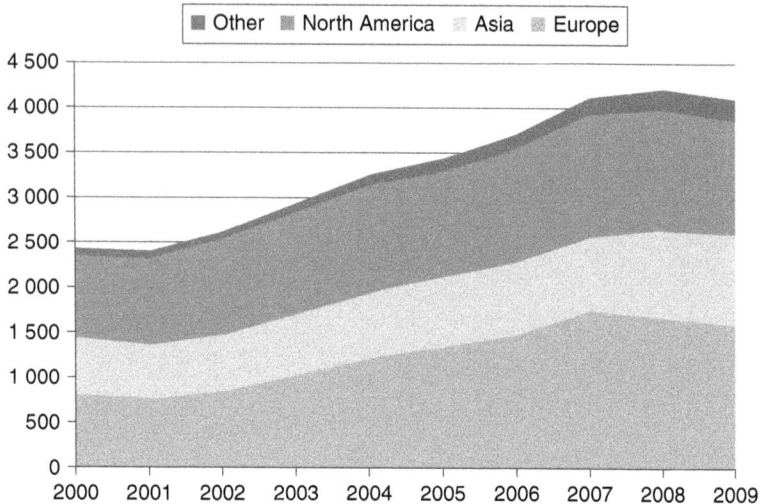

Figure 3.1 Premium volume by year (in billions of US$)
Source: Author's elaboration on data from CEA (2010a); Swiss Re (2010), p. 5.

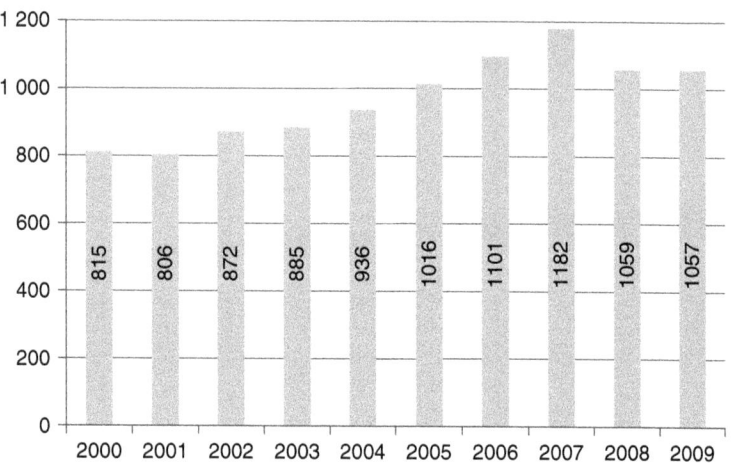

Figure 3.2 European premium volume by year (direct business in force; in € billion)
Source: Author's elaboration on data from CEA (2010a); CEA (2010b), p. 34.

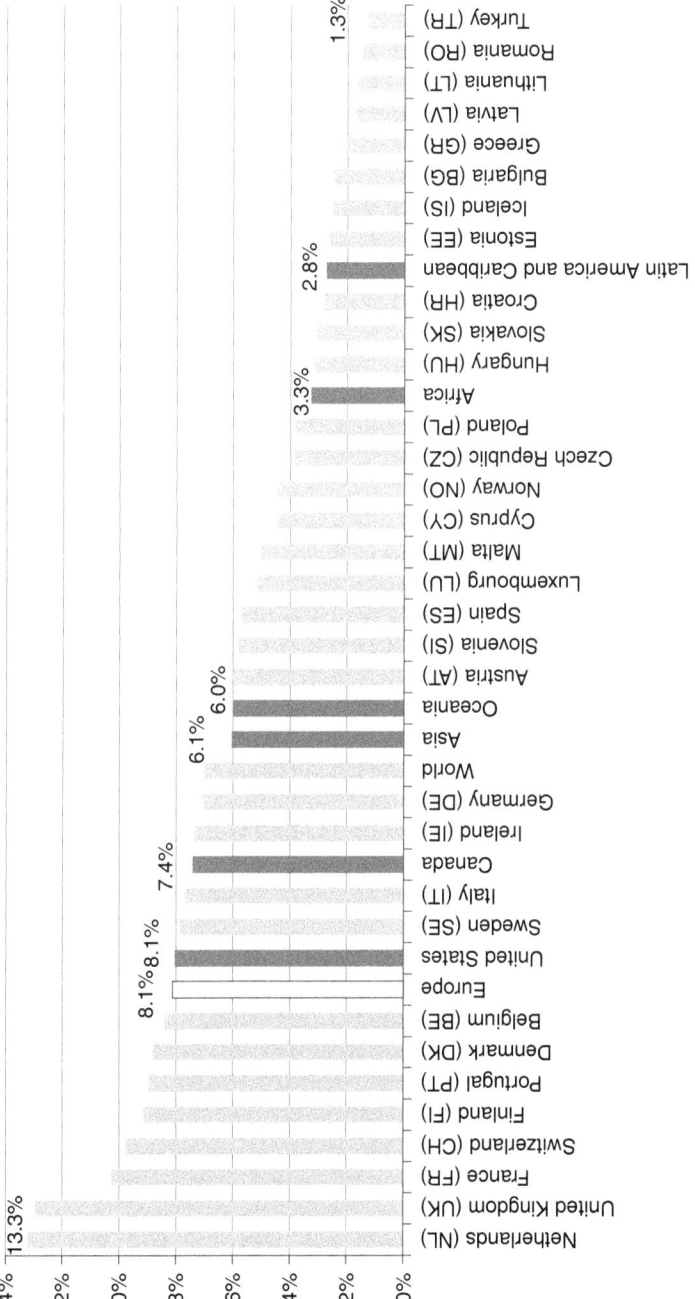

Figure 3.3 Insurance penetration. Premiums as a percentage of GDP in 2009
Source: Author's elaboration on data from CEA (2010b), pp. 34 and 50; Swiss Re (2010), p. 13.

Table 3.2 Life premium volume by region and year. First ten European markets

Country	Share of life market (in %) 2009	Premium volume (in millions of EUR)								
		2009	2008	2007	2006	2005	2004	2003	2002	2001
United Kingdom (UK)	23.16	149 850	185 734	295 249	222 918	193 979	176 560	166 375	186 570	166 844
France (FR)	21.37	138 278	122 368	137 080	140 203	120 668	105 341	92 022	85 500	84 635
Germany (DE)	13.17	85 250	79 586	78 967	78 455	75 244	70 343	68 574	65 301	62 565
Italy (IT)	12.53	81 120	54 565	61 439	69 377	73 471	65 627	62 780	55 294	46 329
Spain (ES)	4.41	28 538	27 489	23 241	23 341	21 004	19 530	17 799	26 531	22 864
Netherlands (NL)	3.75	24 277	26 446	26 367	26 143	25 085	25 560	25 338	24 052	25 879
Switzerland (CH)	2.97	19 243	18 651	17 477	17 847	19 229	19 585	21 154	23 612	21 944
Belgium (BE)	2.83	18 328	19 352	21 658	20 382	25 177	19 891	17 524	14 431	13 170
Sweden (SE)	2.78	17 963	17 723	17 508	15 452	15 059	12 314	12 503	11 749	13 112
Denmark (DK)	2.14	13 870	14 540	13 617	12 471	11 007	10 143	9 676	8 891	8 132
Other	10.88	70 436	75 186	72 889	66 349	59 153	48 113	42 275	40 030	38 022

Source: Author's elaboration on data from CEA (2010b), p. 36.

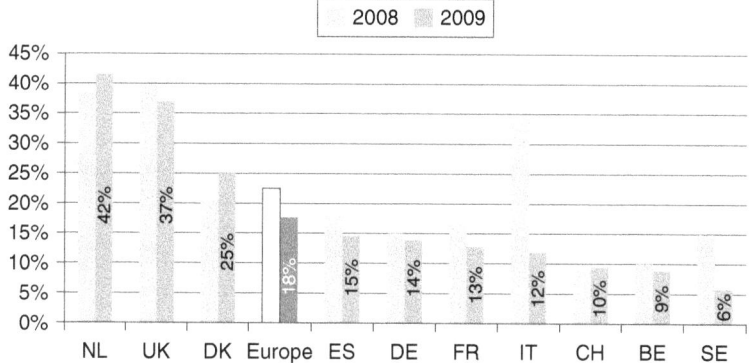

Figure 3.4 Unit-linked premiums to total life volume (in %; year: 2009)
Notes: for ES, the unit-linked premiums to total life premiums ratio is not available in 2008.
It was substituted by the ratio of 2007.
Source: Author's elaboration on data from CEA (2010c).

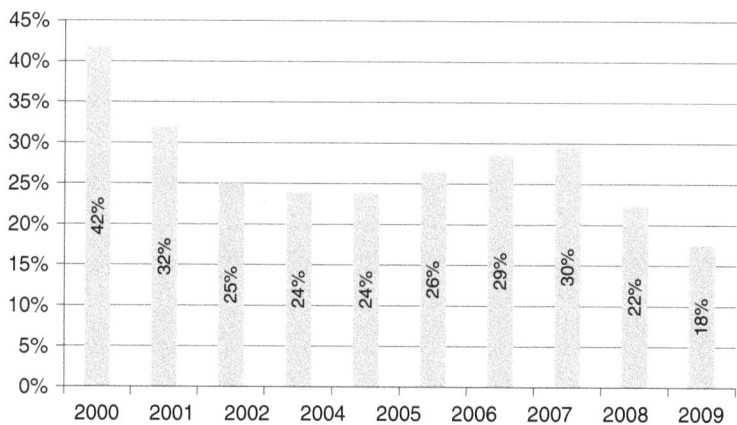

Figure 3.5 Unit-linked premiums to total life volume during the last decade (in %)
Notes: for ES, the unit-linked premiums to total life premiums ratio is not available for 2008.
It was substituted by the ratio of 2007.
Source: Author's elaboration on data from CEA (2010c).

of these instruments was associated with the growth of the stock market. Other life contracts commonly commercialized by insurers are term policies, permanent life agreements and index-linked instruments. For more details on these products, see Chapter 2. Unfortunately, no accurate data are available on the penetration of these contracts in European countries.

The non-life industry embodies about 40 per cent of overall European insurance. The top five non-life markets are, in order of size, Germany, France, the UK, the Netherlands and Italy, which together represent more than 70 per cent of the non-life sector (Table 3.3).

Motor and health insurance are the two largest non-life business lines in Europe, with respective market shares of 30 per cent and 25 per cent (Figure 3.6). Remaining premiums are gathered through property policies (20 per cent), general liability agreements (8 per cent), accident instruments (7 per cent), and other non-life contracts (10 per cent), including legal expenses and credit policies. The motor insurance market is dominant in Italy (55 per cent), Spain (36 per cent), and Belgium (32 per cent), whilst a low penetration was observed in Eastern Europe (CEA, 2010b). In the three years up to 2010, the motor business experienced a decline in premium income. The main reason is the recent fall in the registration of new motor vehicles. Conversely, health insurance has been rising as a result of the ageing population and increasing medical costs. In Europe, this line of business is led by the Dutch and German markets respectively, which together collect a little less than 70 per cent of health insurance's premiums (CEA, 2010b).

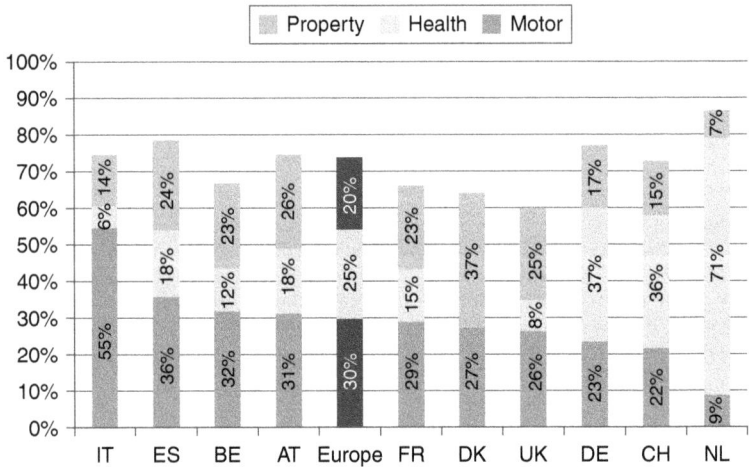

Figure 3.6 Breakdown of non-life insurance premiums by business (in %; year: 2009)
Source: Author's elaboration on data from CEA (2010b), pp. 38–41.

Table 3.3 Non-life premium volume by region and year. First ten European markets

Country	Share of life market (in %) 2009	Premium volume (in millions of EUR)								
		2009	2008	2007	2006	2005	2004	2003	2002	2001
Germany (DE)	21.02	86080	84937	83956	83490	82740	81823	79155	75707	72528
France (FR)	15.09	61779	60826	58652	56889	55216	52885	50006	46498	43424
United Kingdom (UK)	13.18	53960	61289	71323	71351	72607	69652	70371	68656	61847
Netherlands (NL)	12.73	52118	50113	48551	47243	23160	23256	21444	19943	16456
Italy (IT)	8.97	36746	37454	37656	37125	36309	35411	34213	32414	29925
Spain (ES)	7.18	31836	32597	31056	29495	27775	25888	22832	21530	18152
Switzerland (CH)	3.88	15895	15015	12655	13504	13428	13232	12753	12539	11658
Belgium (BE)	2.46	10058	9927	9535	9107	8655	8526	8250	7873	7401
Austria (AT)	2.20	9004	8852	8668	8406	8171	7809	7424	6998	6639
Denmark (DK)	1.47	6032	6271	5952	6231	5980	5747	5362	4535	4138
Other	11.22	45957	50192	48308	45129	42529	38798	36985	33816	30092

Source: Author's elaboration on data from CEA (2010b), p. 37.

3.3 Bancassurance in practice

Premiums are distributed by insurance companies through different channels. In Europe, bancassurance is the most significant means of marketing for the life sector and is a growing vehicle for the non-life industry (Figure 3.7). Specifically, bancassurance is defined as the provision of insurance products by banks or lending institutions (including national post offices). For more details about the definition of bancassurance, refer to Swiss Re (2002) and Chapter 1. The other channels commonly used to promote insurance policies are direct writing, agents and brokers. These three means embody traditional vehicles for insurance companies. For details of direct writing, agents, and brokers, consult section 3.4.

Bancassurance originated in France in the mid-1980s. Its level of penetration, after having increased sharply between 1985 and 2000, has stabilized in most markets in recent years (Figure 3.8). Life bancassurance now accounts for more than half of premium income in many Western European countries. In particular, banks represent the dominant channel in Portugal (82 per cent), Spain (72 per cent), Italy (63 per cent) and France (60 per cent). In order to evaluate life bancassurance's premium structure, unit-linked are the largest written contracts in many markets, with a penetration rate reaching more than 50 per cent in Italy, Belgium, and France (CEA, 2010d).

At the same time, banks gather about 5–10 per cent of non-life business. Notably, high market shares were observed in Turkey (12 per cent), Spain (12 per cent) and France (10 per cent), whilst in many Central and Eastern European countries the presence of this channel does not exceed 2 per cent. Lending institutions are widespread in property insurance with observed penetration rates higher than in the other non-life sectors for the majority of the European markets. Conversely, placement by banks of motor policies is limited: less than 5 per cent in all countries. Similar rates were observed in health contracts; only Portugal exhibits a penetration rate in this insurance business line of about 30 per cent.

Opportunities generated for insurers and banks allows the interpretation of the pervasiveness of bancassurance in local markets and business lines. By making use of banks' structures, insurance companies gained access not only to well-established distribution networks and customer bases, but also to areas in which they were not previously present – for example, in Portugal and Turkey. With bancassurance, companies could have expanded market share quickly in bank-dominated countries,

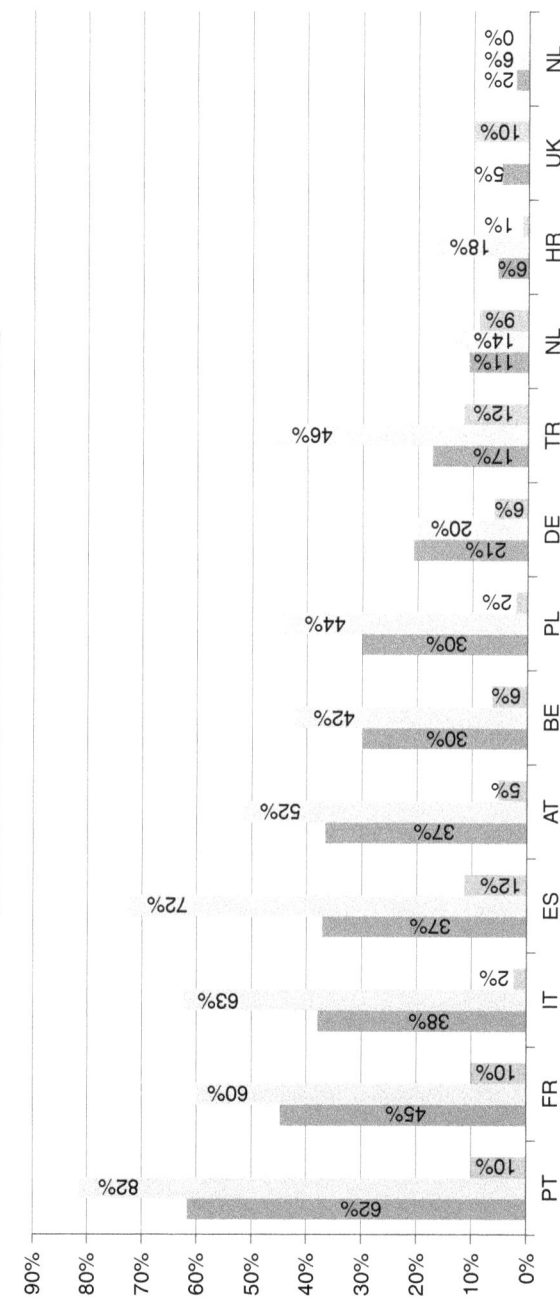

Figure 3.7 Premiums distributed through the bancassurance channel in 2008

Notes: Data for ES is from 2007; Data for DE is from 2007; Data for DE refers to new business[2]; ■ Total insurance: Data for the UK is not available.

Source: Author's elaboration on data from CEA (2010b), pp. 48–9.

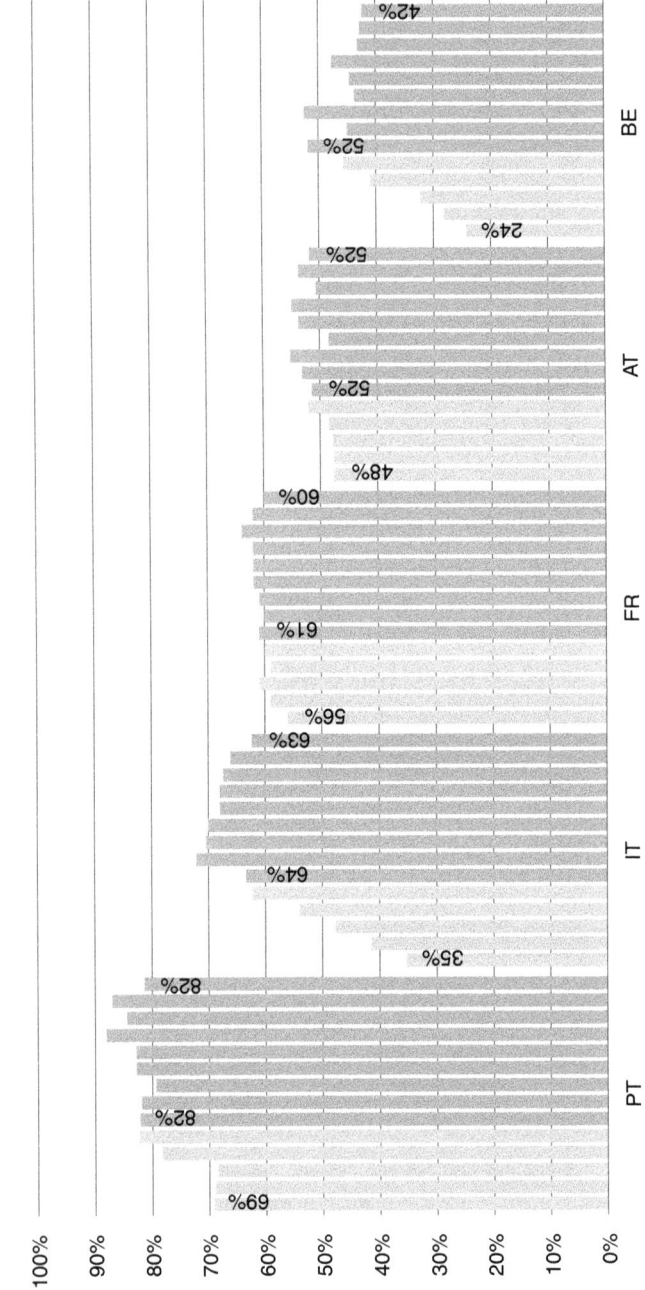

Figure 3.8 Life premiums distributed through the bancassurance channel since 1998
Source: Author's elaboration on data from CEA statistics (various years).

like France and Spain; concurrently, insurers diversified their customer relationship and took advantage of the marginal distribution cost of bank branches, as in Italy and France (Figure 3.9).

Furthermore, many life insurance products are, by nature, similar to the investment and savings contracts sold by banks and hence fairly easy to commercialize for their sales personnel. This phenomenon allowed insurers, for example in Portugal, to benefit from the strong and increasing household demand for savings, multiplying their sales opportunities. The same phenomenon should explain the success of the distribution through banks especially of simple deposit-substitutes such as unit-linked policies. Life instruments are also frequently guaranteed and supported by favourable tax treatment to encourage private provision for protection or retirement planning. In recent years, favourable treatments were provided by the French, Spanish, and Italian governments. These special terms made life policies particularly attractive for bank customers. This broadening of product offering brought banks a new source of income and helped lending firms to increase their levels of customer loyalty. Additionally, events that trigger the sales of banking instruments, like mortgage applications, generated contacts that allowed lending institutions to cross-sell insurance products such as property agreements. This practice enhanced productivity.

Notably, bancassurance is underdeveloped in two of the largest European markets: specifically, Germany and the UK. In Germany, the low level of penetration (21 per cent) may be related to a lack of selling

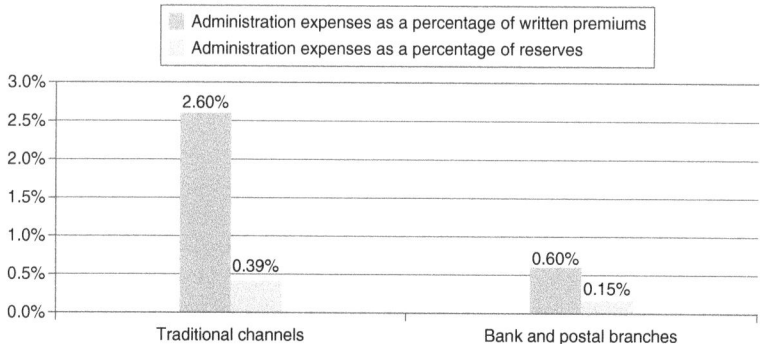

Figure 3.9 Administration expenses for distribution channel in 2009 (sector: life insurance; Italian companies)
Source: Author's elaboration on data from ANIA (2010), pp. 35 and 37.

culture in lending firms (Davis, 2007). Another possible deterrent could have been the fragmentation of the national banking system. The large number of small and regional banks could have impeded the widespread distribution of simple standardized products, typical of the bancassurance marketing (CEA, 2010d). In the UK, the provision of policies by banks is estimated to account for about 15–20 per cent of the new life business (CEA, 2010b; Accenture, 2010), and 20 per cent of the non-life direct business in force. In the UK, the presence of strong traditional distribution channels (such as brokers and direct writing) has limited the scope for bancassurance. The Netherlands had a similar experience. In general, the pervasiveness of traditional channels characterizes the non-life sector and explains the difficulties bancassurers found in reaching significant market shares.

A favourable regulatory environment is critically important for the development of bancassurance. Liberal regulations on ownership of insurance companies by banks, and on sales of policies through banking networks, are clearly a precondition for the success of this channel. In Italy, for example, the 1990 Amato Law made it possible for banks to invest in insurance companies and enabled bancassurance to develop. More recently, the liberalization in India, China, and South Korea has facilitated the growth of bancassurance in Asia where new domestic and foreign insurers used banks' structures to nullify the competitive advantage of incumbents provided with large traditional networks (Swiss Re, 2002). Noticeably, the Australian deregulation program led to a high level of bancassurance penetration through the acquisition of many life companies by banking groups. In contrast, in the UK and the Netherlands, a heavily regulated sales process for long-term products has promoted strong independent broker channels and limited the success of bancassurance. Additionally, in North America, the restrictive regulations on banks' distribution penalized the involvement of lending firms in the insurance industry. Specifically, in Canada banks are to date prevented from selling policies through branches, even though they are allowed to own insurance companies. In the United States, the Glass–Steagall Act, passed in 1933, blocked ownership ties between banks and insurers, as well as sales of insurance instruments through branches. Banks reacted by developing their asset management resources and commercializing investment products that were much more competitive than those offered by insurers. In 1999, the Gramm–Leach–Bliley Act removed restrictions on banks engaging in insurance activities. The deregulation, however, has not promoted the development of bancassurance in the USA. Banks were not

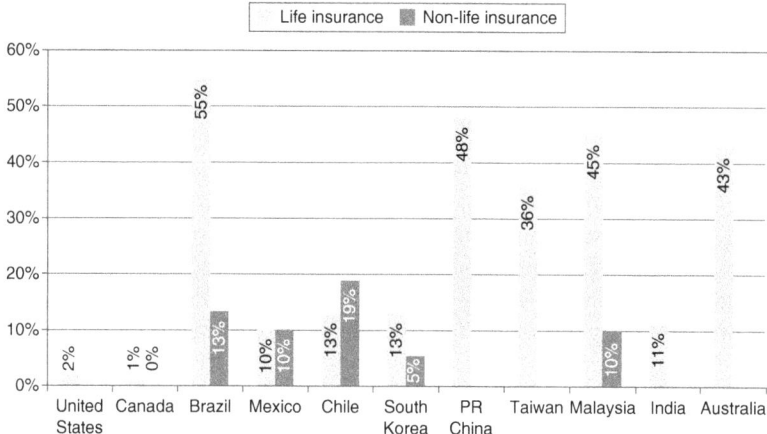

Figure 3.10 Share of premiums distributed through bancassurance outside Europe (in %)

Notes: The latest data quoted for the United States and Taiwan are for 2006, 2007 for India, and 2008 for China and South Korea (non-life business). The other data shown are 2005 figures, expect for South Korea life business where 2009 data are used.

Source: Author's elaboration on data from Swiss Re (2007); LIMRA (2007); BCG (2009); KLIA (2010); KNIA (2009); TII (2007).

interested in selling traditional insurance products, perceived to be at lower margins than investments (Swiss Re, 2007). Consequently, they did not buy product providers; instead, they bought insurance brokers reinforcing their service component and protecting their market share in the savings sector, where they were already dominant (Davis, 2007). For an overview of bancassurance penetration outside Europe, see Figure 3.10.

3.4 The traditional channels

In the insurance market, the other channels commonly used by companies to distribute premiums are direct writing, agents and brokers. These three means embody traditional channels. With regard to direct writing, it is conventionally split into insurance employees and distance selling. The former consists in the insurer's own sales force operating from branch networks. With distance selling, no face-to-face contact occurs between consumer and seller. Clients purchase products directly from the insurer by responding to the company's advertisement, mailing or telephone offers. Customers can also use the Internet to buy insurance policies directly. In most countries direct sales are carried out mainly through company employees. Distance selling is frequently used for the diffusion of simple products which can be easily understood by clients an dnned little extra explanation.

Notably, several Eastern European countries, such as Slovakia (64 per cent) and Croatia (61 per cent), manifest high penetration rates for distribution by direct writing. This condition is linked to the dominant role played in Eastern markets by former state-owned companies, which often commercialize insurance through their networks of employees (Figure 3.11). Direct writing is also particularly widespread in the Netherlands (41 per cent), where the use of distance selling is common between customers. In the UK, the broad recourse to the Internet and telephone, particularly for acquiring motor policies, explains the high ratio observed in the non-life sector (22 per cent).

The second traditional channel which is examined in this section corresponds to agents. These are intermediaries who represent the interest of the insurer. Agents are full-time commissioned sales personnel, holding an agency contract. They are rarely paid on a salary basis, instead receiving incentive compensation for their sales. According to their contract, agents could be either 'tied' or 'multi-tied'. Tied agents have an exclusive agreement with the insurer and they can promote only its policies. Multi-tied agents have arrangements with several insurance providers and can make recommendations about any of the products from those companies. Unfortunately, no accurate data are available on the subdivision between tied and multi-tied agents in Europe; however, their presence is influenced by local practice and national legislation (CEA, 2010d).

Agents show a high level of penetration in several countries due to the existence of embedded networks that traditionally distribute life and non-life policies to customers (Figure 3.12). With regards to the Netherlands, the large presence of this channel (57 per cent) is explained in part by the absence of distinction between agents and brokers in statistical data; the latter should be prevalent. Agents now gather more than half of life premium income in Germany (55 per cent) and Slovenia (53 per cent). In Germany, the unavailability of simple standardized policies has obstructed the provision of insurance products by lending institutions. Accordingly, traditional channels have been protected from bancassurance development. In the non-life industry, agents are absolutely dominant in Italy (84 per cent), Turkey (72 per cent), Slovenia (68 per cent) and Portugal (61 per cent). Recent trends suggest that there has been a slight decline in agents' market share.

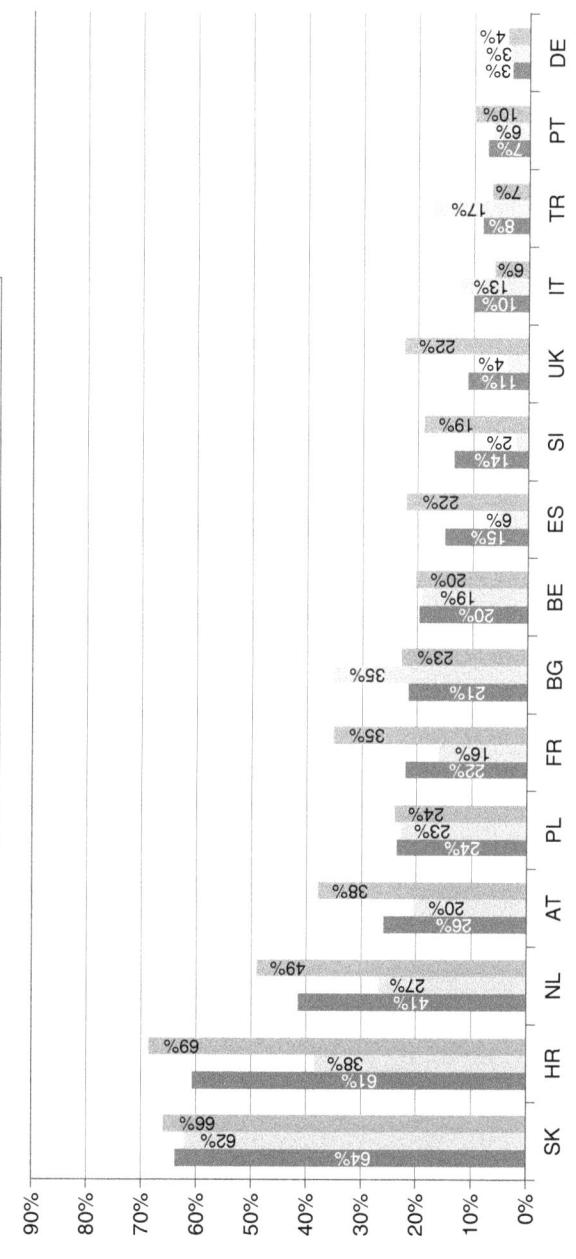

Figure 3.11 Premiums distributed through direct writing in 2008

Notes: Data for ES is from 2007; Data for DE refers to new business; ■ Total insurance: Data for DE are from 2007; ■ Life insurance: Data for the UK are not available.

Source: Author's elaboration on data from CEA (2010b), pp. 48–9.

70

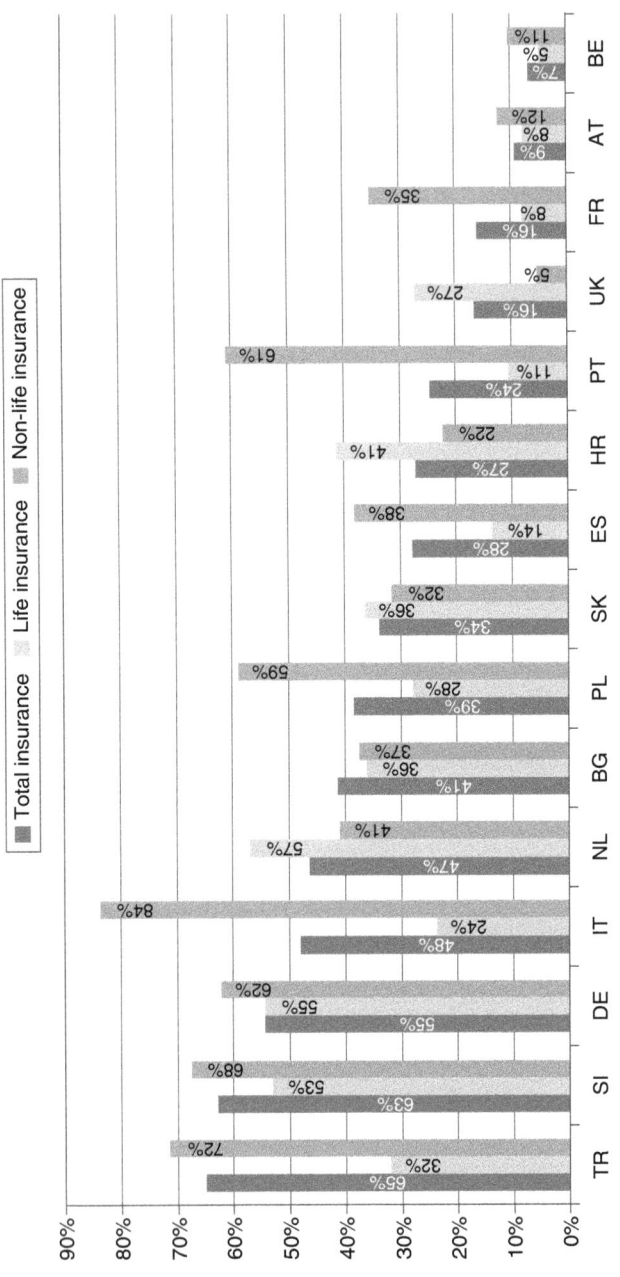

Figure 3.12 Premiums distributed through agents (tied and multi-tied) in 2008

Notes: Data for ES is from 2007; Data for DE refer to new business; For NL, there is no distinction between agents and brokers ■ Total insurance: Data for DE are from 2007; ■ Life insurance: Data for the UK is not available.

Source: Author's elaboration on data from CEA (2010b), pp. 48–9.

This phenomenon is closely associated to a strategy of commercial diversification implemented by insurers. One exception is represented by Bulgaria where, in 2008, there was a significant shift from agents to direct sales and – to a lesser extent – to brokers.

Agents are different from brokers, who are intermediaries who represent the interest of the insured (Figure 3.13). They have a deal with the customer (rather than with the provider of the policies) and are remunerated by commissions paid on an advice basis. Brokers are fully independent of insurance companies. They can recommend any products which could improve the trust of their clients. In the UK and the Netherlands, regulatory requirements have promoted a strong independent broker channel. Brokers also play an important role in the non-life industry of Belgium (62 per cent), Bulgaria (40 per cent), and Austria (38 per cent).

Other intermediaries involved in the distribution of premiums are affinity groups, estate agents and travel agencies. Figure 3.14 exhibits the diffusion of these channels in Europe.

3.5 Bancassurance models

Bancassurance developed in the last two decades, giving birth to a wide range of organizational structures, according to the relationship existing between the banks and the insurers involved. The most common models adopted in Europe and in the rest of the world were partnerships, joint ventures and captives (Fitch Ratings, 2006; EY, 2010). The specific socio-economic, cultural and regulatory environment of the host country, as well as the market framework and consumer preferences, affected the choice of the models (Swiss Re, 2007). There is no country in which bancassurance relied on a single form. Moreover, several operators adopted concurrently different solutions to diversify their strategies, often internationally.

The partnership model requires that an insurance company distributes its products through banking channels on the basis of a deal. The banks involved are remunerated with selling commissions paid by the insurer, and sometimes by entry and management fees charged to policyholders. There is no dedicated legal entity to underwrite the business, and the sales directly affect the insurer's balance sheet. A cross-shareholding can strengthen the link between the subscribers of the agreement. For details on the interests which move an insurer to take part in a partnership, see section 3.3 and Chapter 1. Usually, a bank accepts a commercial agreement when it recognizes the opportunity

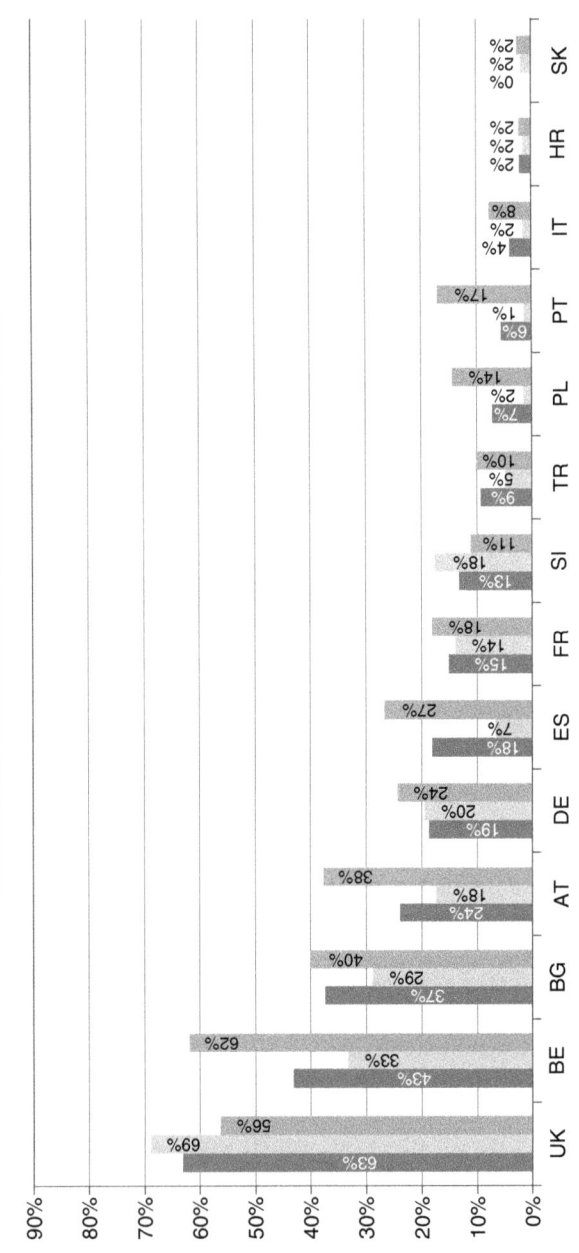

Figure 3.13 Premiums distributed through brokers in 2008

Notes: NL is not included according to the absence of distinction between brokers and agents; Data for ES are from 2007; Data for DE refer to new business; ▪ Total insurance: Data for DE are from 2007; ▪ Life insurance: Data for the UK are not available.

Source: Author's elaboration on data from CEA (2010b), pp. 48–9.

73

Figure 3.14 Premiums distributed through affinity groups, estate agents, and travel agencies in 2008

Notes: Data for ES are from 2007; Data for DE refer to new business; Total insurance: Data for DE are from 2007; ■ Life insurance: Data for the UK are not available.

Source: Author's elaboration on data from CEA (2010b), pp. 48-9.

to offer insurance instruments to its clients (mostly life policies) being unable or unwilling to develop the relative expertise internally. In some cases, a partnership can be the occasion on which to create competition among various insurance providers in order to attract customers interested in the distribution capabilities of the bank.

Box 3.1 The partnership model. The case of Generali Deutschland

Generali Deutschland (GD), originally AMB Generali, is the management holding company of the second largest insurance group in Germany (after Allianz). The firm is 85 per cent owned by the Italian group Assicurazioni Generali, which has worldwide activities. GD, with its headquarters in Cologne, now controls 22 financial intermediaries working in life, health, and property insurance (Figure 3.15).

At December 2009, the Generali Deutschland Group originated a gross written premium of €12.4 billion, with net profits of €340.5 million. The number of employees amounted to 14,957 individuals; of these, 23 per cent worked in the field, and 77 per cent were engaged in administrative services.

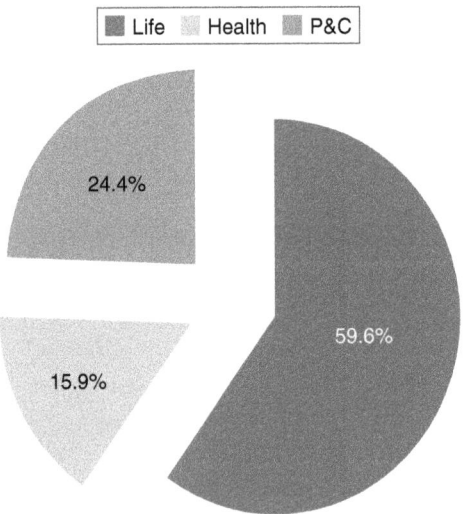

Figure 3.15 Total premium by insurance business line for 2009 (in %)
Source: Author's elaboration on data from GD (2010), p. 35.

GD affirmed its role in the national market operating through a multi-channel organization. Specifically, it relied on (Figures 3.16 and 3.17):

• exclusive strategic distribution partnerships with primary intermediaries, such as Commerzbank – the second largest credit institution in Germany – and the investment firm Deutsche Vermögensberatung;
• the company's own sales force, consisting of more than 5,200 agents;
• direct selling, by means of the brand CosmosDirekt.

CosmosDirekt is a one-stop shop for all private risk provision instruments. With a premium income of €1.4 billion, it is the first direct-selling insurer in Germany and the biggest in the European life sector. Its main focus is on providing cover for surviving dependants and occupational disability. CosmosDirekt also deals with retirement provisions.

In 1999, Generali Deutschland subscribed a commercial agreement in order to market its insurance instruments through the sales

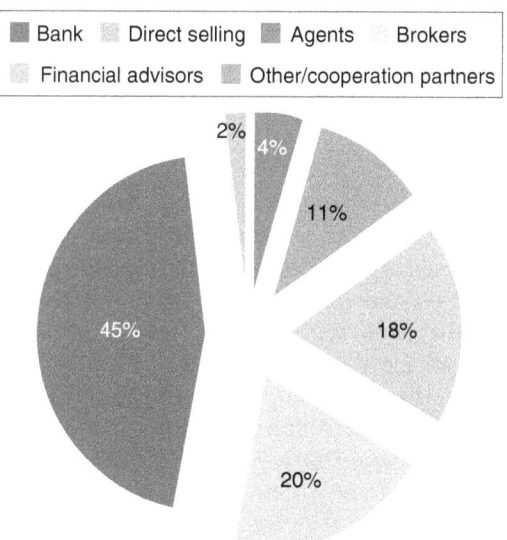

Figure 3.16 New business in the life sector by distribution channels for 2009 (in %)

Source: Author's elaboration on data from GD (2010), p. 36.

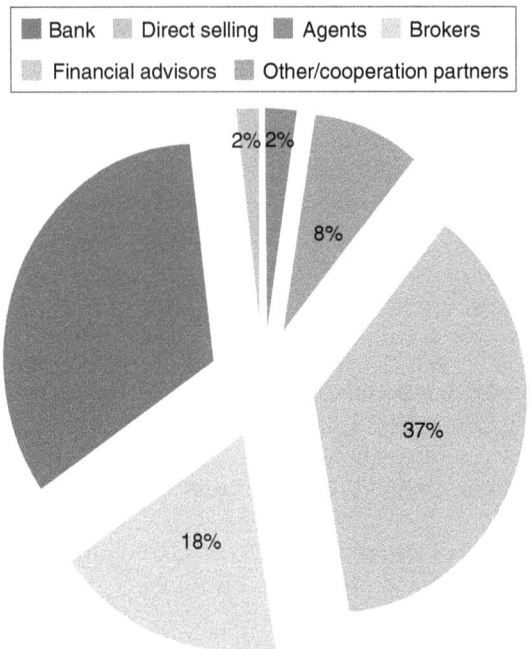

■ Bank   ▨ Direct selling   ■ Agents   ▨ Brokers
▨ Financial advisors   ▨ Other/cooperation partners

2% 2%

8%

37%

18%

Figure 3.17   New business in the non-life sector by distribution channels for 2009 (in %)
Source: Author's elaboration on data from GD (2010), p. 36.

personnel of Commerzbank, in which Assicurazioni Generali assumed a 5 per cent stake in return for 2.5 per cent of its equity capital. The partnership also contemplated Commerzbank's banking products would be sold through the network of Deutsche Badenia Bausparkasse, the bank subsidiary of Generali Deutschland. The deal accounted for more than 3 per cent of the new business of the insurance group. The partnership expired in 2010 when the German bank achieved a deal with Allianz. The latter sold its Dresdner Bank participation to Commerzbank in 2009, becoming its first share-holder after the merger of the two giants. Since October 2010, the new Commerzbank has offered Allianz's insurance instruments through an exclusive sales agreement.

Deutsche Vermögensberatung (DVAG) is the biggest autonomous sales organization for financial services in Germany with 5.4 million customers and more than 37,000 financial advisors. Since 2002, DVAG has had a strategic agreement with Generali Deutschland to distribute polices for residential property and retirement. The premium volume generated up to now by the deal exceeds €5.7 billion. On the one hand, the success of the partnership is based on the enormous distribution strength of the investment company. On the other hand, the commercial agreement represents a persistently creative element for GD in the development of new and performance-oriented products.

The presence of a policy provider possessed by banking and insurance partners characterizes the joint venture model. The will to enlarge the product offering and build up expertise in insurance production justifies the banks' engagement. The company distributes its policies only through the affiliated banking network affiliated, which is remunerated by selling commissions, and sometimes by the entry and management fees charged to policyholders. Typically, the property of the provider is balanced between the bank and the insurance partners, which benefit from the dividends paid. The agreement is sometimes reinforced by a strategic cross-shareholding. On several occasions, the bank or the insurer participating in the joint venture have tried to gain full control of the provider after few years.

Box 3.2 The joint venture model. The case of Barclays–CNP Assurances

In 2009 Barclays, a global bank headquartered in London, and CNP Assurances, the leading personal insurer in France with operations in the rest of Europe and in South America, established a long-term life joint venture in Spain and Portugal. Under the terms of this agreement:

• CNP acquired 50 per cent shareholding in the life insurance company owned by Barclays 'Vida y Pensiones' (BVP), which operates in Spain and Portugal;

- the life and pension products offered by the joint venture firm would be distributed exclusively through Barclays retail network in Spain and Portugal, which included 1,000 branches at the end of 2008.

  As a result of the agreement, CNP paid Barclays Bank an initial upfront consideration of €140 million in cash. Additional fees could be payable over a period of 12 years according to the volume achieved and margin thresholds. The amount of the disbursements is affected by Barclays branch openings in order to maintain a balanced sharing of the value created through the joint venture between the two partners.

  In 2010, CNP BVP gathered premiums of €608 million, mainly from operations in Spain (70 per cent) but also in Portugal (15 per cent). A number of milestones were reached during the first year of work, including the launch of 18 new products and the start-up of Italian operations in the first half. In Italy, CNP BVP introduced an innovative savings product with a unit-linked formula which generated new volumes of activity valued at €90 million.

In the captive structure, an insurance company provides its instruments through the distribution channels of a banking parent. The latter controls the insurance company with a share ownership typically very high, often 100 per cent. The captive firm may be a direct subsidiary of the bank or a sister corporation, with both being owned by the same holding company. The sister corporation, rather than the direct subsidiary, often engages third-party distributors, in addition to the network of the owner. The provider pays selling commissions to the banking parent. The bank also benefits from the dividends disbursed by the insurance company. Frequently, several banks, cooperative in nature, participate in a common exclusive captive firm. The ownership is split among the various banks distributing the products, and sometimes with the involvement of an external insurance company. A bank accepts participation in a captive model when it recognizes the opportunity to offer insurance products to its clients (mostly life policies) but also to keep the full know-how and profitability of the business in-house. For the success of the initiative, it is decisive that the management of the banks manifests its insurance capabilities.

Box 3.3 The captive model – The case of Sogécap

Sogécap is the life insurance subsidiary of Société Générale, a leading banking group in Europe. It has over 30 years' experience in France, where, at the end of 2009 – with a business production of EUR 9 billion – it was the seventh largest life insurer and the fourth largest bancassurer in premium income terms (Figure 3.18). At December 2010, Société Générale owned 100 per cent of the voting rights of Sogécap.

The technical reserves of the company consisted of €71 billion in 2009, whilst its contribution to Société Générale's gross operating result amounted to €283 million (Figure 3.19).

Sogécap today employs 1,210 people worldwide, including 642 individuals in France (Figure 3.20). In Europe, it is present in ten countries, with the Czech Republic, Serbia and Luxembourg embody the most significant markets outside France. Subsidiaries are also established in Morocco, Egypt and the Lebanon. Without a doubt Sogécap's major competitive advantage is the effectiveness of the integrated model developed with Société Générale's international distribution network.

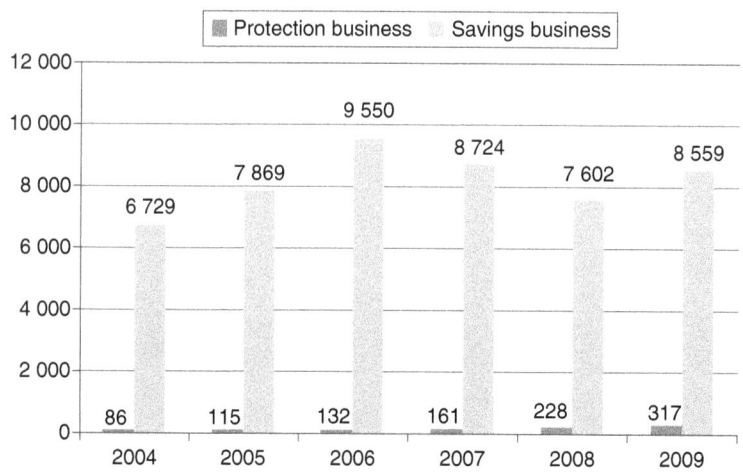

Figure 3.18 Premium income (in millions of euros)
Source: Author's elaboration on data from SOGECAP (2010), page 30.

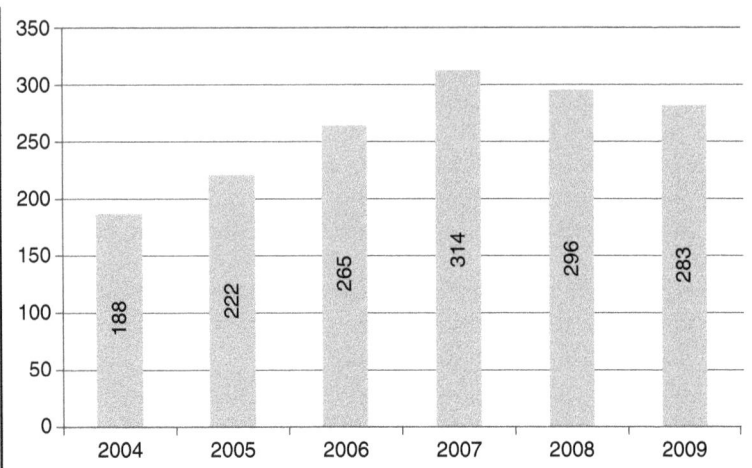

Figure 3.19 Sogécap's contribution to Société Générale's gross operating result (in millions of euros)
Source: Author's elaboration on data from SOGECAP (2010), p. 29.

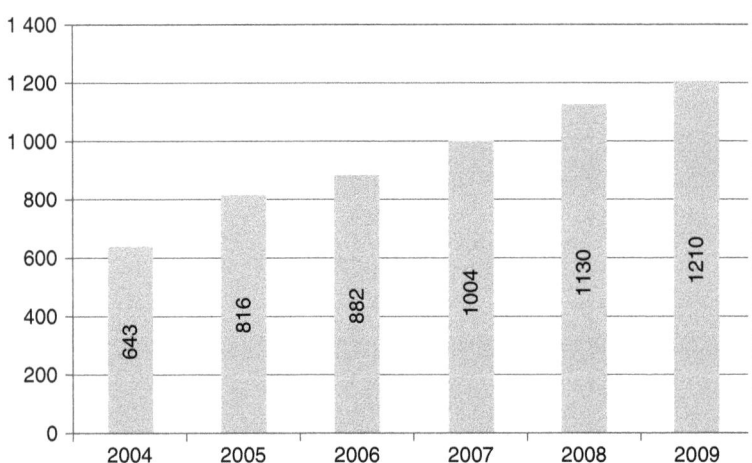

Figure 3.20 Worldwide staff numbers
Source: Author's elaboration on data from SOGECAP (2010), p. 29.

At the beginning of 2011, this company presented a wide range of customizable solutions composed of eight policies to meet the requirements of its individual and professional clientele in response to their medium- and long-term savings plan. Each policy had its own special features, even if they were built on a common base, that offered the following benefits:

- solutions available from €50 a month;
- different income payment plans to choose from;
- possibility of saving using various asset management strategies depending on personal ambitions;
- access to more than 80 eligible investment funds, also realized outside the Société Générale Group.

In addition, Sogécap marketed five different instruments to protect private individuals against accidents and provide finance for funeral expenses. The product offering also included coverage for consumer and mortgage loans in the event of death, permanent or temporary disablement. Contemporaneously, the life insurance provider of Société Générale designed contracts to suit the savings requirements of corporate clients proposing tailor-made support in pension planning for staff. Solutions were available also to cover the risk of losing one of the organization's 'key men'. A key man – as clarified by the same insurance provider – is a person whose temporary or permanent absence would generate severe financial, commercial or industrial difficulties for the client firm. The key man may be a company director, officer or staff member. For more details upon the proposals, consult the property site of the company (www.societegenerale-insurance.com).

All of these instruments are distributed exclusively through the Société Générale's retail and private banking networks, which comprises:

- 2,300 branches, managing and advising corporate, professional, and individual clients;
- four private banking offices in Paris and also branches the provinces of Lyon, Marseille, and Bordeaux.

As an added feature, Sogécap has implemented an Internet service for life insurance policyholders by offering administration functions via the web. Clients can now manage their policies entirely on-line:

- making voluntary payments;
- carrying out fund switching;

- managing installments;
- accessing transaction statements.

At the same time, Sogécap offered a broad range of solutions for independent wealth management consultants and distribution platforms via its life insurance and savings subsidiary specialized in outside alliances, Oradéa Vie. The latter has been 100 per cent controlled since 2001. Oradéa Vie posted premium income of €138 million in 2009, whilst its technical reserves on business in force reached €842 million. A feature of 2009 for Oradéa Vie was the launching of a multi-fund policy at the beginning of the year. This is a highly flexible individual life insurance product aimed at a high net worth clientele. This new product won awards from specialist media, in particular the Gold Wealth Management Trophy assigned by Agefi Actifis, one of the major French professional magazines (www.agefifr). Sogécap also works in close synergy with Sogessur, the non-life insurance company of Société Générale dedicated to development of motor, home and accident contracts. At December 2010, Société Générale owned 100 per cent of the voting rights of Sogessur, after the acquisition of a 35 per cent stake held by Aviva, the largest insurance group in the UK. Sogessur posted premium income of €184 million in 2009, whilst its net profits reached €1.6 million.

3.6   Conclusion

The chapter has delineated the use of bank branches in insurance distribution, with a specific focus on Europe. The aim was to draw on the realities of the market to identify the reasons for the pervasiveness of bancassurance.

Life bancassurance now accounts for more than half of premium income in many Western European countries. In particular, banks represent the dominant channel in Portugal, Spain, Italy and France. Unit-linked are the largest written contracts in many markets. At the same time, banks gather about 5–10 per cent of non-life volume. It is noteworthy that high market shares were observed in Turkey, Spain and France, whilst in many Central and Eastern Europe countries the presence of this channel does not exceed 2 per cent. Lending institutions are widespread in property insurance with observed penetration rates higher than in the other non-life sectors for most of the European markets.

Opportunities generated for insurers and banks allow an analysis of the pervasiveness of bancassurance in markets and business lines. By making use of banks' structures, insurance companies gained access to well-established distribution networks and customer bases, and also to areas in which they did not already have a presence. With bancassurance, companies could have expanded market share quickly in bank-dominated countries; concurrently, insurers diversified their customer relationship and took advantage of the marginal distribution cost of bank branches. Furthermore, many life insurance products are, by nature, similar to the investment and savings contracts sold by banks and hence fairly easy to commercialize for their sales personnel. This phenomenon allowed insurers to benefit from the strong and increasing household demand for savings, multiplying the sales opportunities. The same phenomenon should explain the success of the distribution through banks, especially of simple deposit substitutes such as unit-linked policies. Life instruments are also frequently guaranteed and supported by favourable tax treatment to encourage private provision for protection or retirement planning. These special terms made life policies particularly attractive to bank customers. The broadening of product offering brought banks a new source of income and helped lending firms to increase their customer loyalty. Additionally, events that trigger sales of banking instruments, like mortgage applications, generated contacts that allowed lending institutions to cross-sell insurance products such as property agreements. This practice contributed to an enhancement of staff productivity.

A favourable regulatory environment has been shown to be critically important for the expansion of bancassurance. Liberal regulations in relation to the ownership of insurance companies by banks, and to the sales of policies through banking networks, were clearly a precondition for the success of this channel. In Italy, for example, the 1990 Amato Law made it possible for banks to invest in insurance companies and enabled bancassurance to take off. In contrast, in the UK and the Netherlands, a heavily regulated sales process for long-term products has promoted strong independent broker channels and limited the success of bancassurance.

The provision of insurance products by lending institutions has developed in the past two decades, leading to a wide variety of organizational structures, which reflected the different relationships existing between the banks and the insurers involved. The most common models adopted in Europe and in the rest of the world were partnership, joint venture and captive. The specific socioeconomic, cultural and regulatory environment of the host country, and also the market framework and consumer preferences, affected the choice of model. There is no country in which bancassurance relied on a single form. Moreover, several operators adopted concurrently different solutions to diversify their strategies, often internationally.

Notes

1. The *direct business in force* corresponds to the total premiums written by insurers before deductions for reinsurance and ceding commissions.
2. The *new business* represents insurance contracts written during the year. Premiums are paid at subscription. For periodic payments, data correspond to the annual amount. Supplementary payments made on already existing policies are not included.

References

Accenture (2010) *How Bancassurance can Dominate the UK Life Insurance Industry*, London.
ANIA (2010) *Fact Pack 2010. Life Sector*, December, Rome.
BCG (2009) *Bancassurance in China. Reaching the Next Level*, December.
CEA (2010a) 'European Insurance in Figures: Data 1999–2008', *CEA Statistics*, No. 40, July, Brussels.
CEA (2010b) 'European Insurance in Figures', *CEA Statistics*, No. 42, November, Brussels.
CEA (2010c) 'The European Life Insurance Markets: Data 2000–2009', *CEA Statistics*, No. 43, December, Brussels.
CEA (2010d) 'Insurance Distribution Channels in Europe', *CEA Statistics*, No. 39, March, Brussels.
Davis, S. I. (2007) *Bancassurance: The Lessons of Global Experience in Banking and Insurance Collaboration*, June, London.
EY (2010) *Bancassurance: A Winning Formula*, July, London.
GD (2010) 'Generali Deutschland Full Year 2009 Results', *Investor Relations*, March, Cologne.
KLIA (2010) 'Annual Statistics FY2009: Premium Income by Distribution Channel', *KLIA Annual Report*, Seoul.
KNIA (2009) 'Fact Book 2009: Distribution Channels', *KNIA Annual Report*, Seoul.
LIMRA (2007) 'Bancassurance Around the World', *LIMRA Global Research*, Windsor.
Munich Re (2001) *Bancassurance in Practice*, Munich.
SOGECAP (2010) *Annual Report 2009*, Paris.

Swiss Re (2002) 'Bancassurance Developments in Asia – Shifting into a Higher Gear', *Sigma*, No. 7, October, Zurich.

Swiss Re (2007) 'Bancassurance: emerging trends, opportunities and challenges', *Sigma*, No. 5, August, Zurich.

Swiss Re (2010) 'World Insurance in 2009. Premiums dipped, but industry capital improved: Statistical Appendix', *Sigma*, No. 2, December, Zurich.

TII (2007) 'Taiwan Life Insurance', *TII Market Report*, Taiwan.

4
The Regulatory Framework

Maria Grazia Starita

4.1 Introduction

The aim of this chapter is to analyze the regulatory framework for diversified financial institutions, considering its main evolution overtime and the drivers of future change. The opportunity to develop the bancassurance model was offered by the Second Banking Directive (89/646/EEC) which removed the existing barriers between different sectors of the financial services industry, so that a credit institution can become a distribution channel of financial and insurance services, if this complies with its strategy.

According to the literature and the European legislation there are two alternative models through which a bank can obtain the benefits of bancassurance: the universal bank and the banking group models.

In the universal bank model the bank is the holding company of the group. It entrusts the ancillary activities to separate individual entities. This model presents some factors of strength: on the side of the risk, a universal bank has the maximum degree of risk control and a high degree of effectiveness of the risk control activity whereas on the side of pricing policy, a universal bank has the maximum degree of flexibility thanks to the income-smoothing activity among several business units. Moreover, a universal bank has the possibility of defining a systemic and consistent strategy without any constraints linked to the framework. The main factors of weakness are linked to the time needed to respond to the changes in the financial system: there is a low degree of differentiation within the organisational structure and consequently a high degree of cultural uniformity (from the point of view of culture). *According to this model what are the opportunities for bancassurance?* The banking and the insurance activities are completely integrated. The bank establishes an entity which is completely dedicated to the insurance business, or buys an insurance company already operating in the market.

A banking group is composed of a holding company and some entities. The aim of the holding company is to coordinate the various activities and to define the objectives of the group in terms of the characteristics of the financial services it offers. Each entity can engage in a product/ service or different kinds of activities and can be legally separated from the holding company. In the banking group, the holding company is the bank or a mixed financial company which participates in the ownership of the bank. This model presents some factors of strength: the high degree of flexibility among the intermediaries and the growth of the specific knowledge directly linked to the distinctive feature of each sector. Thanks to the specific knowledge it is possible to develop innovation, to pursue a variety of policies and to offer specific services. Each intermediary maintains a good reputation of provider of a specific financial service. The major factor of weakness of a banking group corresponds to the major factor of strength of a universal bank: the difficulties linked to the effectiveness of the strategic control. In fact, a banking group suffers from the lack of coordination between the entities engaged in the back office and the sales entities, and there is a risk of duplicating some common activities and of a limited promptness. *According to this model what are the opportunities for bancassurance?* The holding company could control an insurance company, or cooperate with insurance entities through a joint venture which is in charge of product design (financial and actuarial characteristics), or sells the policies of several insurance companies by means of a simple agreement with them.

Banks which lead a universal bank or belong to a banking group take advantage of the knowledge of the financial characteristics of their clients, merging the information about the financial products with the insurance needs (for example, the mortgage with the need of a payment protection insurance or the personal loan with the need of the indemnity policy) for stand-alone clients (see Chapter 2). A bank can offer an integrated 'package' to new clients and automatically match financial and insurance needs.

The next section (4.2) analyzes the financial conglomerates from an economic and regulatory point of view whereas the aim of section 4.3 is to describe the characteristics of the so-called lead supervisor and the methodologies to measure the degree of capital adequacy of financial conglomerates. Section 4.4 analyzes all the characteristics of the supplementary supervision, whereas section 4.5 offers some conclusions and remarks.

4.2   The financial conglomerates

The abolition of institutional segregation among the sectors of the financial intermediation has promoted the M&A process within the financial sectors, the increase of financial groups, the achievement of financial regulation with the aim of obtaining the benefits of diversification.

From an economic point of view, financial conglomerates are financial groups that operate *in at least two* of the different sectors of financial intermediation (banking, securities and insurance) and are active in one or more country. From a regulatory point of view financial conglomerates are financial groups that operate *in both* the insurance and banking business and are active in one or more countries.

The literature has identified the risks of financial conglomerates from an economic standpoint. The system of risks of a financial conglomerate depends on the risks of the entities within the group and on the risk pertaining to the group as a whole (Figure 4.1).

Among the risks at the conglomerate level, the activities of the sectoral supervisors and regulators may be obstructed through the circumvention

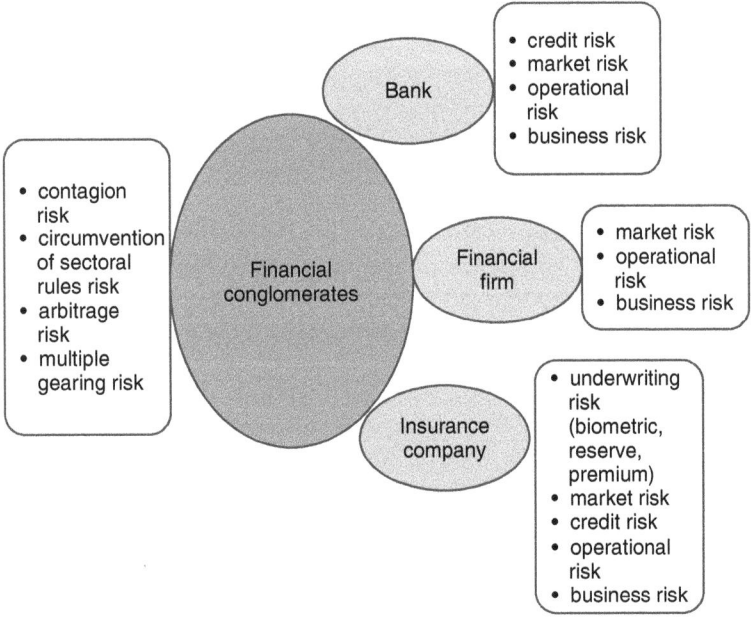

Figure 4.1   System of risks of the financial conglomerate
Source: Author's elaboration on Lelyveld and Schilder (2002).

of sectoral rules (Lelyveld and Schilder, 2003). From a regulatory point of view the supervision of financial conglomerates implies different levels of supervision:

- *at the single entity level*, the intermediary needs to be authorized as an insurance company or bank and must comply with the insurance or banking regulation. The solo supervision of individual intermediary continues to be a primary source of control, but it needs to be integrated through group-wide control;
- *at the group level*, the group of authorised banking and/or insurance entities is subject to consolidated banking or insurance group supervision;
- *at the conglomerate level*, the financial conglomerate is subject to supplementary supervision in addition to the specific banking and insurance supervision. While a parent entity can be a regulated entity itself, such as a bank or an insurance company, it can also take the form of a holding company. The parent entity defines the business strategies, the governance framework and the drivers of risk management processes for all the entities.

The degree of capital adequacy is crucial for the effectiveness of the supervisory control. From a theoretical point of view it is possible to identify criteria, approaches and techniques to assess the capital adequacy of financial conglomerates. Two **criteria** have been identified to measure the capital requirements of financial conglomerates: consolidation supervision and solo-plus supervision (Joint Forum, 1999). The first criterion focuses on the parent or holding company whereas the second focuses on individual entities. According to the first criterion the capital requirements are applied to the consolidated entity at the parent level after the consolidation of the assets and liabilities of the individual entities. According to the second criterion, the capital requirements are applied on the basis of the individual entities and this assessment is complemented by a general qualitative and quantitative group-wide assessment. Once the criterion to apply is established, it is necessary to identify the *approach* according to the type of group. In homogeneous groups the supervisors can apply the accounting-based consolidation of assets and liabilities for the application of capital adequacy rules, whereas in heterogeneous groups it is necessary to classify and to aggregate the assets and liabilities according to the type of underlying risk (so-called 'block capital adequacy'). The literature has identified four different **techniques**: the building-block prudential approach; the risk-based aggregation; the risk-based deduction; and the total deduction technique. Both the approaches and the techniques of financial conglomerates depend on the type and the structure of the group. The first technique is based on the consolidated accounts at the level of the parent entity whereas the second is based on a simplified method of risk assessment. The third technique is based on the diversification effects resulting from the low correlation of different business risks (for example, credit risk versus underwriting risk). The 'total deduction' technique is based on an effective and conservative treatment of the double gearing.

With a view to describe criteria, approaches and techniques suggested by the EU Directive on Financial Conglomerates in the paragraphs that follow, it is necessary to clarify the rules on the *degree of control* (full control, significant influence and effective control) and consequently the use of the surplus of each entity.

The minority shareholdings over which the parent entity has neither control nor significant influence (that is, less than 20 per cent of the shares or voting rights owned) are not taken into account in the assessment of capital adequacy. When the group has an ownership between 20 and 50 per cent of the shares or voting rights over a group's entity, it is necessary to apply a pro rata approach: any capital deficits and any capital surplus is attributed to the group over pro rata approach. From an operating point of view there are no obstacles to the free movement of capital surpluses within the group from a 'going concern' perspective.

From the supervisory point of view the financial conglomerates behaviour could modify the 'normal' link between capital and risks. The same funds may not be included in the calculation of capital at both the single entity and the parent entity level. The *level of capital* should be adjusted with respect to number of factors: group risk; risks of contagion among group entities due to intra-group exposures; concentration risk when a risk is present in several entities of the group at the same time; and the conflict of interest risk.

According to the EU Directive 2002/87/EC, a financial conglomerate has to satisfy the following conditions:

a) the presence of regulated entities. The regulated entity can be the head of the financial conglomerate or a subsidiary of the group. According to sectoral rules, there must be at least a regulated entity inside the group;

b) the relevance of the financial sector. The regulated entity at the head of the group is either a parent undertaking of an entity operating in the financial sector, an entity which holds a participation in an entity in the financial sector, or an entity linked to an entity in the financial sector in compliance with Directive 83/349/EEC;

c) the relevant weight of the financial activities. When the head of the financial conglomerate is not a regulated entity, it is necessary to identify the weight of the financial sector through a ratio:[1]

$$activities\ in\ the\ sector = \frac{\sum_i total\ assets_i}{\sum_j total\ assets_j}$$

i = regulated and unregulated entities of the financial sector

j = entities with in the group

The group's activities mainly occur in the financial sector if the ratio exceeds 40 per cent.

d) the type of business mix: at least one of the entities in the group is within the insurance sector and at least one is within the banking and investment services sector.[2] The Directive considers only banking institutions entering the insurance business or insurance undertakings entering the banking and investment services sector. Consequently, only two combinations need to be analysed: banking entering in the insurance sector and insurance undertakings entering banking activities.

e) the relevance of the business mix: the activities of the entities in the group within the insurance sector and the activities of the entities within the banking and investment services sector are both significant. *But what is the meaning of 'significant'?* To avoid the cost of supplementary supervision, the Directive identifies the instruments to measure the weight of banking activity, investment services activity and insurance activity. If the average of the following two ratios:

$$ratio\ of\ total\ assets = \frac{total\ assets_i}{\sum_j total\ assets_j}$$

i = banking and investment services or insurance activities

j = banking, investment services, insurance activities

$$ratio\ of\ solvency\ requirement = \frac{solvency\ requirement_i}{\sum_j solvency\ requirement_j}$$

i = banking and investment services or insurance activities

j = banking, investment services, insurance activities

exceeds 10 per cent, the activities in different financial sectors are significant. All of the calculations referring to the ratios and the thresholds shall be made on the basis of the aggregated balance sheet total of the entities of the group according to their annual accounts and their accounting principles or on consolidated accounts where available. The solvency requirement shall be calculated in accordance with the provision of the relevant sectoral rules. These two ratios do not consider the cross-sectoral activities of the financial conglomerates. These activities are significant when the balance sheet total of the smallest financial sector in the group exceeds €6 billion.

To apply these conditions, the relevant competent authorities may:

- exclude an entity when it calculates the ratios of solvency requirements;
- identify the thresholds by calculating the average of three consecutive years to avoid regime shifts or consequences linked to the group's structure;
- substitute or add the criterion based on the balance sheet total with data on the income statement and/or data on off-balance activities;
- take into account: a lower ratio of activities in the financial sector (35 per cent); a lower ratio of total asset and solvency requirement (8 per cent); a lower figure of €5 billion for the smallest financial sector in the group for financial conglomerates already subject to supplementary supervision;
- agree with other relevant competent authorities to cease to apply the lower ratios or the lower amount;
- not to regard the group as financial conglomerates or not to apply the provision with reference to risk concentration, intra-group transactions and internal control and risk management processes.

A group is not considered a financial conglomerate if the application of the Directive rules is not necessary or would be inappropriate or misleading. The basic philosophy of the Directive is that the solo supervision of individually regulated entities should continue to be the foundation for effective supervision, and accordingly if either the relative size of the smallest financial sector does not exceed 5 per cent in terms of balance sheet or solvency requirement, or the market share does not exceed 5 per cent in any Member State measured in terms of balance sheet in the banking or investment services sector or in terms of gross premiums written by the insurance sector.

4.3   The supplementary supervision

Over the past few years, it has been recognised that many of the problems encountered in the supervision of financial conglomerates have been approached from the perspective of a particular sector – the supervision of banks, or of insurance companies, or of securities firms (Boot and Schmeits, 2000; Freixas, Loranth, Morrisona, 2005; National Bank of Belgium, 2002).

In an attempt to achieve the Single Market for Financial Services, the European Commission has identified a series of actions to undertake, including the development of supplementary prudential legislation for financial conglomerates. In particular, this legislation concerns the solvency position, the risk concentration and the risk management processes at the level of the conglomerate, the fit and proper characters of management and the intra-group transactions. These objectives were not better achieved at the Member State level, consequently the European Parliament and the Council issued Directive 2002/87 and the Commission performed technical guidance and implemented measures to take into account the new developments in financial markets. This Directive represents the first comprehensive implementation of international recommendations of the Joint Forum on Financial Conglomerates.[3] The Joint Forum is an international group made up of representatives of the Basel Committee on Banking Supervision, the International Association of Insurance Supervisors and the International Organization of Securities Commissions (Tripartite Group, 1995; Joint Forum of Financial Conglomerates, 1999; Basel Committee, 2001).

Directive 2002/87/EC identifies five pillars of the supplementary supervision:

1. the capital adequacy of the financial conglomerate, to ensure that own funds are always available at the level of the financial conglomerate (the calculation of the degree of capital adequacy must be carried out at least once a year according to the rules of the coordinator);
2. the monitoring of the risk concentration at the level of the financial conglomerate to ensure the capital adequacy;
3. the monitoring of the relevant intra-group transactions (when this transaction exceeds at least 5 per cent of the capital requirements at the level of the financial conglomerate);

4. the internal control mechanisms, to identify all material risks and their impact on own funds through sound reporting and accounting procedures;
5. the risk management processes to ensure that the risk monitoring systems are well integrated into the conglomerate organisation.

In the following paragraphs we analyze the role and the tasks of the coordinator and then we describe the five pillars of the supplementary supervision with specific reference to the methodologies used to calculate capital adequacy requirements.

4.3.1   The role and the tasks of the coordinator

Section 3 of the Directive identifies the measures necessary to facilitate supplementary supervision: the criteria for the appointment of the coordinator – the supervisor who is responsible for the supplementary supervision; the tasks of the coordinator; the duties of cooperation and exchange of information between competent authorities; the access to information; the powers of verification; the range of enforcement measures; and, finally, the additional powers of the competent authorities in the light of the circumvention risk of sectoral rules.

The coordinator is responsible for the coordination of the competent authorities and the exercise of supplementary supervision. The Directive prescribes a general principle of cooperation between the competent authority appointed as the coordinator and the competent authorities responsible for the supervision of regulated entities within the financial conglomerates. This principle is linked strictly to the duty to provide any information which is 'essential' or 'relevant' for the exercise of the authorities' supervisory tasks according to the Directive and the sectoral rules. This duty implies the communication on request of all 'relevant' information and also the transmission of all 'essential' information about the own initiatives under prudential supervision. But *what exactly constitutes the 'essential' and 'relevant' information*? The Directive provides a list of this kind of information: some of the information is linked to the characteristics of the financial conglomerates such as the group structure, the strategic policies, the financial position in terms of capital adequacy, intra-group transactions, risk concentration and also profitability; the organization and the framework of controls (risk management and internal control system). Other information is linked to stress situations, financial crises and every adverse development in regulated entities or in other entities of the conglomerate which could affect the conglomerate as a whole, the exceptional measures taken by the competent authorities under sectoral rules or by the coordinator under the Directive, the major sanctions against each entity within the financial conglomerates. From a procedural point of view, the coordinator and the competent authorities must share the procedures for the collection of information and the verification of that information. It could be difficult to collect information from the parent undertaking:[4] each Member State asks the parent entity any information related to the tasks of the coordinator.

Some of this information is gathered for solo supervision and/or for consolidated supervision under sectoral rules. In that case a coordinator wanting to control the financial conglomerate requests information directly from the competent authorities without duplicating the cost of reporting.

The Directive also sets out the power of verifying the information concerning an entity situated in another Member State. Each competent authority can ask the authority of another Member State to carry out the verification or participate in the verification process, even if the entity is a non-regulated entity. To remove any existing obstacles to the verification process, the competent authority which receives the request may carry out the verification or allow an auditor/expert to do it or allow the authority which made the request to carry it out itself.

Among the 'essential' and 'relevant' information there are two cases for which any decision taken by the competent authority must be shared with other competent authorities: the decision to approve or authorise changes in the shareholder structure or in the organisational or management structure of regulated entities can be taken only after consulting all competent authorities involved in the control of the regulated entities in the financial conglomerate. This is because any changes in the shareholder structure has a series of effects in the ownership configuration of the entities within the group. In addition, major sanction decisions must be shared in the light of the effect they have on the reputation of the financial conglomerate. However, the other important decision to be shared with other competent authorities concerns exceptional events such as the event which is less likely to occur (for example, the financial turmoil). Under no circumstance the exchange of information should compromise the exercise of control and, above all, the responsibility of control by any competent authority. Only in the case of urgency or when the time needed for consultation may jeopardise the effectiveness and the promptness of the decisions, the competent authority may decide not to consult the other competent authorities and inform them afterwards.

What are the duties of the competent authorities when they use the information provided by the entities? The Directive sets out the provisions on professional secrecy and the communication of confidential information laid down in the sectoral rules. It is therefore important to highlight the fact that in the case of non-regulated entities the competent authorities do not play a supervisory role on a stand-alone basis when it comes to collecting and holding information about non-regulated entities within the conglomerate.

On the other hand, the Member State ensures that any information which would be relevant for the purposes of supplementary supervision is accessible. In addition, information about good reputation and experience of people who effectively direct the business of a mixed financial holding company is protected by professional secrecy. Each Member State ensures that there are no legal impediments within their jurisdiction to the exchange of any information about natural and legal persons within the scope of the supplementary supervision.

With the aim to ensure proper supplementary supervision of the regulated entities in the financial conglomerate, the coordinator is appointed among the competent authorities of the Member State concerned. The appointment process is complicated when a mixed financial holding company is at the head of the financial conglomerate (Table 4.1).

When the application of these criteria is inappropriate because of the structure of the conglomerate or of the relative importance of its activities in different countries, the competent authorities concerned can appoint a different coordinator on the basis of a common agreement upon the conglomerate's advice.

What are the tasks of the coordinator (the so-called 'lead supervisor')? The coordinator always works in close collaboration with the relevant competent authorities involved and plans and organizes the activities of supervisors in going concern circumstances and, above all, in emergency situations. The coordinator has a fundamental role in monitoring the behaviour of financial conglomerates: it engages in the gathering of information (not only public information) and the dissemination of data relative to ordinary situations and to emergency situations. It is necessary to coordinate this task with the role of the competent authorities under sectoral rules: the coordinator must share the information with the competent authorities.[5] If the information needed has already been given under sectoral rule, the coordinator contacts the competent authority directly in order to avoid the duplication of supervisory costs and reporting costs for supervised intermediaries.

The most important task of the 'lead supervisor' is to assess the financial conglomerate from the supervisors' point of view. As described in the next subsection three aspects of the financial conglomerates are strictly supervised by the coordinator: the financial position, the capital adequacy

Table 4.1   Criteria to appoint the coordinator

Head of conglomerate	Regulated entities	*Coordinator is the authority that authorised:*
Regulated entity	Regulated entity at the head of the financial conglomerate	Regulated entity at the head of the financial conglomerate
Mixed financial holding company	More than one regulated entities	Regulated entity who operates in the Member State of the mixed financial holding company at the head of conglomerate
Mixed financial holding company	More than one regulated entities who operate in different sectors	Regulated entity who operates in the most important sector
Mixed financial holding company	More than one regulated entities who operate in the same sector	Regulated entity with the largest balance sheet total
More than one mixed financial holding company	More than one regulated entities who operate in different sectors	Regulated entity who operates in the most important sector
More than one mixed financial holding company	More than one regulated entities who operate in the same sector	Regulated entity with the largest balance sheet total
Not regulated entity Not mixed financial company	One regulated entity	Regulated entity in the group
Not regulated entity Not mixed financial company	More than one regulated entities	Regulated entity with the largest balance sheet total in the most important sector

Source: Author's elaboration on Directive 87/2002/EC.

and the conglomerate's characteristics (structure, organization and internal control system). In particular, the assessment of capital adequacy and the effects of risk concentration and of intra-group transactions on capital adequacy implies the use of criteria and algorithms described in the Directive while the assessment and overview of the financial situation of the conglomerate depends on the activities of the coordinator. In order to facilitate the exercise of the supplementary supervision by the coordinator it is possible to make a coordination agreement in which the coordinator and the other relevant competent authorities define the guidelines to assess the financial position of the conglomerate and above all the procedures for the decision-making process. With reference to the European Union, see the Memorandum of Understanding on cooperation between the financial services authorities, central banks and finance ministers of the European Union on cross-border financial stability (European Commission, 2008). This Memorandum includes a template for a systemic assessment framework through which the authorities describe the procedure to adopt in case of an emergency situation. This procedure provides for supporting elements for the assessment of the critical nature of: the financial institutions (shortage in liquidity, market confidence,...); the financial markets (bid–ask spread, market volatility,...); the financial infrastructure (recovery time, pending transactions,...); the contagion channels (main financial institutions, markets and infrastructures affected); the real economy (market losses on assets of non-financial economic agents and their restricted access to financial services).

With reference to a single country, see, for example, the agreement among the supervisor of the Italian banking system (Banca d'Italia), the supervisor of financial firms (Consob) and the supervisor of the insurance sector (ISVAP) (Banca d'Italia, Consob, Isvap, 2006). With reference to two countries, see the 1993 agreement, prior to the Directive on Financial Conglomerates, between the Italian banking supervisor (Banca d'Italia) and the Deutsche banking supervisor (BaFin) to assess the financial stability of Unicredit group (Banca d'Italia, BaFin, 1993).

The Directive sets out some enforcement measures but it does not describe enforcement measures. Therefore, *under what circumstances could the coordinator or the other supervisor authorities adopt an enforcement measure? And what is the competent authority appointed to adopt the enforcement measure?*

Four situations have been identified in which the enforcements measures should be adopted immediately:

1. the regulated entity does not comply with the requirements provided for capital adequacy, risk concentration, intra-group transactions or corporate governance of the financial conglomerate;
2. the regulated entity meets the requirements provided for the financial stability of conglomerates but solvency position may be jeopardized;
3. the effects of intra-groups transactions threaten the financial position of conglomerates;
4. the risk concentration threatens the financial position of conglomerates.

The enforcement measures are adopted by the competent authorities of regulated entities. When the financial conglomerate is headed by a mixed financial holding company there are two levels of enforcement: the coordinator adopts enforcement measures at the level of the mixed financial holding company while the competent authorities act on the regulated entities.

4.3.2 The methodologies to calculate capital adequacy requirements

A European financial conglomerate is subject to supplementary supervision on capital adequacy requirement, risk concentration, intra-group transaction and internal control.

The most important aspect of the group's financial position is capital adequacy. Annex I to the European Directive explains four *technical principles* and four *technical calculation methods*[6] to identify capital requirements.

To explain the first **technical principle** we analyse the case of a solvency deficit of an entity within the group or a notional solvency deficit of a non-regulated financial sector entity within the group. To this aim we report three hypothetic structures of financial conglomerate (Figure 4.2).

The notional solvency requirement of a non-regulated entity is equal to the capital requirement with which such an entity would have to comply under the relevant sectoral rules if it were a regulated entity of that particular financial sector (see the ancillary banking service organisation in Diagram A of Figure 4.2). The notional solvency requirement of a mixed financial holding company is equal to the capital requirement of the most important financial sector within the financial conglomerate (see Diagram B in Figure 4.2). According to the European Directive, the solvency deficit or the notional solvency deficit has to be taken into account but *what is the parent's responsibility in this situation*? In the non-financial sector, the responsibility of the parent undertaking owing share of the capital is normally limited to that share of capital, whereas in the financial sector the responsibility of the parent towards the financial conglomerate is not necessarily limited: an increase in the probability of failure of each entity could threaten the financial stability of the financial conglomerate because of the contagion risk.[7] Only in certain cases can the coordinator give permission to take into account the proportional basis in the solvency deficit. In the horizontal conglomerates (see Diagram C in Figure 4.2) where there are no capital ties between entities in a financial conglomerate, the coordinator normally identifies the proportional share of each entity to cover the solvency deficit of another entity.

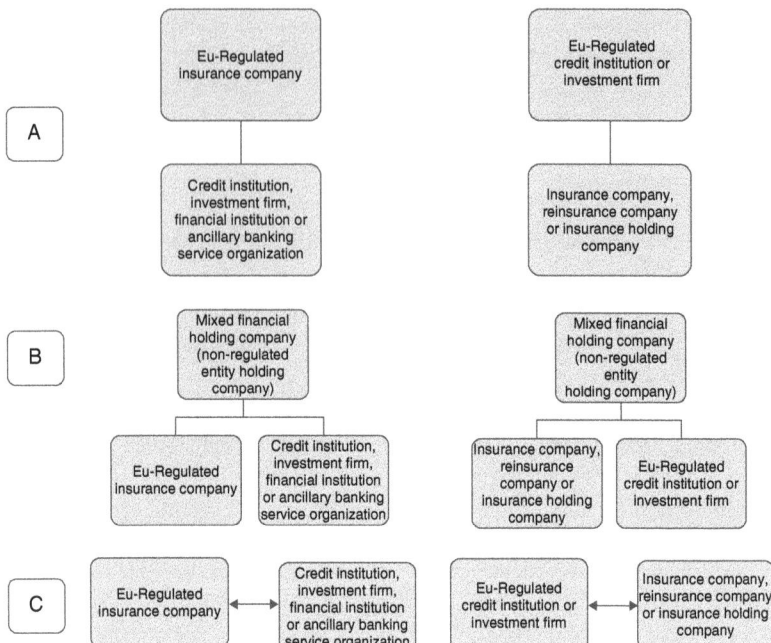

Figure 4.2 Structures of financial conglomerates subject to supplementary supervision
Source: Gruson (2004).

The other technical principles are linked to the qualities of the own funds of financial conglomerates. The capital needed to meet the solvency requirement could ensure: the elimination of multiple use of elements eligible for the calculation of own funds at the financial conglomerate level (through double or multiple gearing); the elimination of the inappropriate intra-group creation of own funds (through the double leveraging); the consistency of eligible elements across the sector rules (cross-sector capital) when there is a deficit of own funds at the financial conglomerates level;[8] the effectiveness of the transferability and availability of the own funds across the different legal entities within the group.[9]

The *methods* to identify the solvency requirement of the financial conglomerates are three, to which the Directive adds the combination of these three methods. The aim of each method is to preserve the integrity of capital in the financial conglomerate and to ensure that it captures the risk of the group as a whole. The methods identified by the European

Commission are: (1) the 'accounting consolidation' method; (2) the 'deduction and aggregation' method; (3) the 'book value/requirement deduction' method. All of the methods identify the supplementary capital adequacy requirements on the basis of the comparison between the own funds of a specified entity or some predefined entities and the solvency requirement calculated according to the sectoral rules. The increase of this difference implies a new depreciation of the own funds.

1. According to the 'accounting consolidation' method the supplementary capital requirement is equal to:

$$SupCAR = OF_{group} - \sum_i SR_{financial\ sector_i}$$

where: *SupCAR* = Supplementary Capital Adequacy Requirement; *OF* = Own Funds; *SR* = Solvency Requirement (or Notional Solvency Requirement for non-regulated financial sector entities); *i* = entities of the financial sector within the group.

The basis for the application of this method is the data of the consolidated balance sheet and the solvency requirements calculated according to the corresponding sector rules (Directive 2002/12/EC for credit institutions, 93/6/EEC for credit institutions and investment firms and 98/78/EC for insurance undertaking). Thanks to the consolidated accounts it is possible to eliminate the effects of multiple gearing and excessive leverage. From the coordinator's point of view, this method is simple to apply when the financial conglomerate is headed by a regulated entity and the other regulated entities belong to other sectors of the financial system, whereas it is difficult to apply when the financial conglomerate is headed by a mixed financial holding company and when there are a lot of non-regulated entities.

2. The 'deduction and aggregation' method calculates the supplementary capital adequacy as:

$$SupCAR = \sum_i OF_{reg\ and\ unreg} - \left(\sum_i SR_{reg\ and\ unreg} + \sum_j BV_{other} \right)$$

where: *SupCAR* = Supplementary Capital Adequacy Requirement; *OF* = Own Funds; *SR* = Solvency Requirement (or Notional Solvency Requirement for non-regulated financial sector entities); *BV* = Book Value of the participation; *i* = entities of the financial sector within the group; *j* = entities not belonging to the financial sector within the group.

This method is based on the accounts of each entity in the group. It simulates the situation of consolidated accounts with reference to the solvency requirement/book value of each entity. From the coordinator point of view, this method could be applied in financial conglomerates with a high degree of heterogeneity since it eliminates multiple gearing and excessive leverage.

3. According to the 'Book value/Requirement deduction' method the solvency requirement of the financial conglomerate corresponds to:

$$SupCAR = OF_{parent} - \left[SR_{parent} + \max (BV_k ; SR_k) \right]$$

where: *SupCAR* = Supplementary Capital Adequacy Requirement; *OF* = Own Funds; *SR* = Solvency Requirement; *BV* = Book Value of the participation; *k* = entities within the group.

Like the previous method, this calculation is based on the accounts of each entity within the group. The solvency requirement of each entity, other than the parent entity, shall be taken into account for their proportional share. This method underlines the role of the parent entity or the entity at the head of the financial conglomerate within the group and it is effective in the case of financial conglomerates with a low level of financial intermediation. Thanks to this method it is possible to identify the solvency requirement of each subsidiary within the group through the book value instead of the own funds: it is an easy way to assess potential multiple gearing in the group (Joint Forum, 1999).

One additional method consists of a combination of all the methods mentioned above. The competent authority may also allow the use of a combination of two of them.

Each financial conglomerate must have an adequate *capital requirement policy* in place. The objective of this policy is primarily to guarantee the accomplishment of solvency requirements as defined by the law of each sector where the entities operate and secondly to safeguard the going concern activity. This policy is strictly linked to capital management policy. The main objective of the capital management policy is to continue to guarantee adequate remuneration of the shareholders' capital. Consequently, the capital management implies a trade-off problem between the supervisor's objective and the shareholders' objective: when the financial conglomerate maximizes the capital allocation for solvency purposes, it waives the maximization of shareholders' interest of each entity within the group. At the same time when the financial conglomerate prefers to maximize the shareholders' interest it waives the supervisors' interest and consequently the rights of depositors, investors and policyholders.

The monitoring of the coordinator on financial conglomerates is also based on the *risk concentration* and intra-group transactions. Every year the coordinator has the right to receive a specific report on any significant risk concentration and any significant intra-group transactions. The law of each Member States of the European Union may set quantitative limits or may allow their competent authorities to set quantitative limits at the level of financial conglomerates. These quantitative limits can be substituted with other supervisory measures with the aim to satisfy the objective of supplementary supervision. The necessary information on risk concentration and on intra-group transactions is submitted to the coordinator by the regulated entity at the head of the financial conglomerate or by the mixed financial holding company or by the regulated entity identified by the coordinator after consultation with the other relevant competent authorities and with the financial conglomerate for homogeneous conglomerates.

The *risk policy* (risk strategy and risk appetite) is linked directly to the degree of diversification within the group. This degree depends not only on the correlation between the risks of the different financial sector (between underwriting risk[10] and credit risk[11] or between market risk[12] and underwriting risk), but also on the level of relative concentration of those risks. The aim of the risk policy is to maintain a balanced risk profile without any risk concentration. The presence of one or more disproportionately large risks or large exposures to single creditors or group of creditors could amplify the effects of the risk concentration: these situations can produce substantial losses at both the operating entities level and conglomerate level.

It is possible to identify the risk concentration through the allocation of the capital at risk for each risk category, the assessment of the benefit of diversification, the calculation of risk concentration in terms of non-diversified internal risk capital across the group (see, for example, Table 4.2 with reference to the Allianz Group).

The first part of Table 4.2 shows the capital at risk allocated without taking into account the benefit of diversification among business areas and among risks. Data in the second part of Table 4.2 show a systemic decrease of the capital absorption at the group level. The decrease is drastic for underwriting risk and for business risk.

The *intra-group transactions* could modify the consistency of the supplementary capital adequacy of the financial conglomerate or the level of risk sharing within the group. It is for this reason that on at least an annual basis the regulated entity or the head of the financial conglomerate reports to the coordinator on the state of intra-group transactions. The Directive presumes an intra-group transaction to be

Table 4.2   The allocation of capital at risk in the Allianz Group[13]

2009 € mn	Credit risk	Market risk	Underwriting risk	Business risk	Total risk capital
Non-diversified					
Property-casualty	2,770	8,387	22,149	6,055	39,361
Life/Health	1,908	10,623	3,017	5,519	21,067
Asset Management	—	—	—	4,194	4,194
Banking and other segment	825	3,858	410	681	5,774
Total Group	5,503	22,868	25,576	16,449	70,396
Share of total Group internal risk capital in%	9	32	36	23	100
Group diversified					
Property-casualty	1,927	4,385	7,406	1,921	15,639
Life/Health	1,141	5,132	310	2,133	8,716
Asset Management	—	—	—	1,948	1,948
Banking and other segment	481	3,318	130	159	4,088
Total Group	3,549	12,835	7,846	6,161	30,391
Share of total Group internal risk capital in%	12	42	26	20	100

Source: Author's elaboration on Allianz Group data (Allianz, 2010).

significant if it exceeds at least 5 per cent of the total amount of capital adequacy requirements at the level of a financial conglomerate. The coordinator, following consultation with other competent authorities and also with the group itself, can identify the type of transactions and the significant threshold for intra-group transactions. The infra-group policies as well as the internal-dealing policy for each listed entity must be inspired by the principles of consistency, integrity and sustainability.

A financial conglomerate has in place a **risk management process** and an internal control mechanism. The risk management process focuses on the system of risks of the financial conglomerate and consequently on the adequacy of the capital policy and the effectiveness of the cor-porate governance. The main aim of the **internal control system** of the financial conglomerate is to identify all material risks that could threaten the stability of the conglomerate.

In Annex 2 of the Directive, the European Legislator identifies some basic elements of the monitoring activity of the coordinator. When overviewing the risk concentration and the intra-group transactions, the coordinator shall monitor at least:

1 the risk of contagion in the group;
2 the risk of a conflict of interests. The literature has identified some typical situations which can be treated as conflict of interests: between investment banking and asset management (advisory and underwriting services), between lending and asset management activities, between lending activities and analyst activities belonging to the group;
3 the risk of circumvention of sectoral rules. The literature has identified two phenomena linked to this risk: the double gearing and the regulatory arbitrage. They are due to the lack of regulation or, on the contrary, an overlap of sectoral regulations;
4 the level or volume of risks. This prediction refers to each type of risk but in particular to the risk at the level of the financial conglomerate. Again the risk of contagion is a specific risk of the financial conglomerate.

4.4 Drivers of regulatory framework

The regulatory framework shown in the previous section is changing. This section reviews the main drivers of regulatory scenario for banks, insurance undertakings and financial conglomerates. We can identify at least four extensive changes that will modify the regulatory framework of the financial system in the next years (see Figure 4.3).

Some of these changes depend on the process of revision of the legislation in force (Solvency II and the revision of the Directive on financial conglomerates), whereas others are directly linked to the effects of the financial crisis (the new framework of supervision and Basel III). The scope and the objectives of these changes are different. The Solvency II Directive will modify the capital management of insurance companies and bancassurers (it will be in force at the end of 2012), while Basel III will change the liquidity risk management and the sources of the available capital to comply with banking solvency requirements. The institution of European authorities has the aim of constructing the supervision on the European financial system and on European financial intermediaries while the revision of the financial conglomerates Directive has the aim of modifying the supplementary capital requirement and the

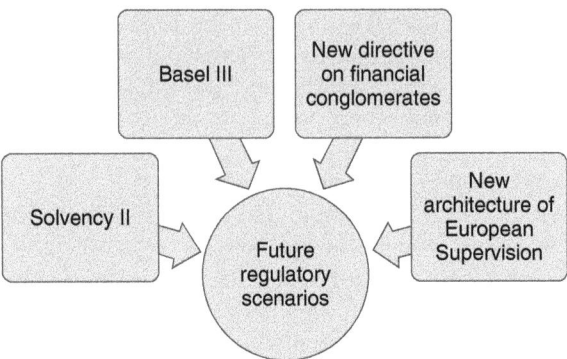

Figure 4.3   The drivers of regulatory scenarios
Source: Author's elaboration.

supplementary supervision on European financial conglomerates and on third countries financial conglomerates authorised.

4.4.1   Solvency II

This section does not take into account all of the characteristics of the new regulation; it focuses only on the risks from which the capital requirements are derived. The aim of the Solvency II project is to create a capital requirement strictly linked to the risks underlying the insurance business. Under Solvency I, the life minimum capital requirement depends on predefined coefficients, technical provisions and capital under risk, while the non-life minimum capital requirement is strictly linked to predefined coefficients, volumes of written premiums or claims.[14] It is clear that the capital requirement under Solvency I is more simple to apply, but it is not directly linked to the effective risks underlying the insurance business. The new solvency requirement described in the EU Directive 2009/138/EC wants to be more appropriate to the risk faced by insurance companies. Each insurance company can adopt the standard model (essentially a factor-based approach) or an internal model previously authorised by the national supervisor. The solvency requirement under the standard model of Solvency II depends on:

- four types of risks: credit risk, market risk, operational risk and obviously underwriting risk. Credit risk (counterparty default risk) is linked to exposures at the reinsurance companies and in relation to the derivatives. Market risk is the risk arising from the level and volatility of market prices of financial instruments which have an impact upon the value of assets and liabilities and their degree of mismatching: it depends on interest rates, exchange rates, real estate, equities, spreads and on the degree of concentration. Operational risk is linked to unpredictable external events and/or internal errors. Underwriting risk is the specific risk of the insurance business that are life underwriting risk, non-life underwriting risk and health underwriting risk. Life underwriting risk is the risk arising from the perils covered and the processes used in the conduct of business and consequently its sub-risks are: mortality risk, longevity risk, morbidity/disability risk, life expense risk, revision risk linked to annuities rates, lapse risk and, finally, catastrophe risk linked to extreme and irregular events. The sub-risks of non-life underwriting risk are: premium and reserve risk, arising from fluctuations in the timing, frequency and severity of insured events and in the timing and amount of claim settlement, and catastrophe risk, related to extreme and exceptional events. For health business managed differently by life business, the health underwriting risk is linked to premium and reserve;[15]

• the degree of diversification/correlation among the underlying risk. The solvency capital requirement is calibrated so as to ensure that all quantifiable risks to which the entity is exposed are taken into account with reference to the existing business and the new business. The aggregation of the capital requirement, as the aggregation of sub-risks into each risk, depends on the correlation matrix. Table 4.3 shows the correlation matrix of lines of business as defined by CEIOPS for the application of the standard formula. For example, the correlation between non-life underwriting risk and default risk is set at 0.5 because of the resort to reinsurance contracts.

• the degree of profit sharing as a risk mitigation technique and the adjustment for the loss-absorbing capacity of technical provisions and deferred taxes. The 'discretionary participation features' are additional benefits linked to the performance of a specified pool of contracts or the realized/unrealized investment return of a specified pool of assets or the profit/loss of the company. Under adverse circumstances the entity can use future discretionary benefits to cover unexpected losses when they arise. This reflects potential compensation of unexpected loss through a simultaneous decrease in technical provisions or deferred taxes.

Table 4.3 The correlation matrix among risks of pillar I (according to the standard formula of Solvency II)[16]

	Market risk	Default risk	Life underwriting risk	Health underwriting risk	Non-life underwriting risk
Market risk	1				
Default risk	0.25	1			
Life under-writing risk	0.25	0.25	1		
Health under-writing risk	0.25	0.25	0.25	1	
Non-life underwriting risk	0.25	0.50	0	0	1

Source: CEIOPS (2009a).

According to the standard formula, the capital requirement for market risk depends on predefined scenarios.[17] For example for the interest rate risk, a sub-risk of market risk, it is necessary to analyse the effects of two scenarios (upward shock and downward shock) on the net asset value calculated as assets minus liabilities: the capital charge is the maximum of the capital charge calculated in an upward scenario and of the capital charge calculated in a downward scenario, subject to a minimum of zero. The capital requirement for mortality risk is calculated as the change in net asset value following a permanent 15 per cent increase in the mortality rate and its effect on the amount payable of death exceeding the technical provisions held by the insurance company. The capital requirement for premium and reserve risk of non-life business merges the information about premiums and reserves: the premium risk is linked to existing business and to the new contracts written during the year, while the reserve risk depends on the misestimation of the claim provisions and on its volatility around the mean value. Consequently, the capital requirement of non-life underwriting risk depends on a predefined volume measure for each line of business and a measure of the combination of volatility of reserve risk and premium risk. Also, for health underwriting risk managed as non-life underwriting risk the capital requirement depends on the reserve and premium for three lines of business (accident, sickness and worker compensation). The capital requirement for operational risk takes into account the amount of annual expenses incurred in respect of the life insurance contracts and the volumes of non-life contracts in terms of earned premiums and technical provisions.[18]

4.4.2 Basel III

Basel III is a comprehensive project to reform the regulation and supervision of the banking sector following the financial crisis. The first suggestions of the Basel Committee on banking supervision imply a focus on business risk and on system-wide risk, rather than internal processes and structures, with an increase of the power to constrain the risky cross-border activities.

On the side of capital, Basel III recommends an increase in the quality of bank capital and the development of cyclical buffers above the minimum capital requirement. On the side of liquidity risk, Basel III suggests a more intrusive liquidity regulation such as liquidity lines and credit lines provided for off-balance-sheet entities and a stronger capital requirement for trading book exposures and re-securitisations.

4.4.3 EU Directive on financial conglomerates

In the light of the financial crisis, the European Commission has proposed a revision of the Financial Conglomerates Directive. The objective of this revision is to restore the full spectrum of tools and powers of supervisors. In practice, national financial supervisors are almost obliged to choose between banking and insurance supervision under the sector-specific Directives and supplementary supervision under the Financial Conglomerates Directive. In fact, the definition for banking and insurance holding companies in the sector-specific Directives excludes the definition for mixed holdings in the Financial Conglomerates Directive: the effectiveness of supplementary supervision depends on the legal structure of financial conglomerates (groups or holding company). The European Commission defines this 'difference' as an 'unintended consequence of the current rules'. Consequently, the aim of the proposed amendments is an enforcement of the conglomerates' identification process and of the effectiveness of supervision.

Under current rules, financial conglomerates identification depends on the balance sheet figures. Group risk is risk that arises from the group structure and which is not related to the balance sheet indicators. The identification process of financial conglomerates should be a risk-based assessment in addition to existing definition of quantitative indicators.

Under current rules, the supplementary supervision excludes the sector-specific rules. The proposal intends to promote the application of sector-specific supervision and supplementary supervision on the conglomerate's parent entity, even if it is a holding company. This approach implies the resolution of the problem of the supervisory arbitrage.

To obtain efficient allocation of the supervisors' resources, the European Commission promotes the concentration on the larger and systemically important conglomerates, although smaller than €60 billion total assets and when the group risk is negligible.

The Commission hopes to see these changes enter into force in 2011 but this implies: (i) the amendment of the Capital Requirement Directives (2006/48/EC and 2006/49/EC) and the Directive on Supplementary Supervision of Insurance Undertakings in Insurance Groups (98/78/EC); (ii) the coordination with the Directive on Supervisory Rules for Insurance and Reinsurance (Solvency II) and its implementation process; (iii) the link with the new European supervisory structure. The new European Banking Authority (EBA) and the new European Insurance and Occupational Pension Authority (EIOPA) have formed a Joint Committee to restore the coordination among national supervisors in the case of financial conglomerates.

4.4.4   The new European supervision architecture

What is the relationship between systemic risk within the financial system and contagion risk within the financial conglomerate? When a financial conglomerate has a large market share in all the sectors of financial intermediation or has a systematic presence in each sector, its contagion risk could be a driver of systemic risk.

The de Larosière group report was published in February 2009. It aims to define a new European regulatory approach in the light of the financial crisis. The report argued for:

1. the creation of a European Systemic Risk Board (ESRB) led by the European Central Bank with the help of the European System of Financial Supervisors (ESFS). ESRB will be responsible for the macroprudential supervision of the European financial system. Its aim is to contribute to the prevention and the mitigation of systemic risk through the smoothing of the policies pursued by the competent authorities. In fact, the systemic risk arises from the collective behaviour of financial intermediaries, also from their interactions through the activity of financial conglomeration, and, finally, from interlinkages between the financial system and the real economy. The European Supervisor Authorities (ESAs) will cooperate closely with ESRB and will provide for all information on systemic risk needed to fulfil its tasks. An Advisory Technical Committee arranged by supervisory authorities will provide assistance on technical issues.

Table 4.4   The new European authorities

The committee established in the context of the Level 3 of the Lamfalussy procedure	The new authorities – European Supervisory Authorities (ESAs)
The Committee of European Banking Supervisors (CEBS)	The European Banking Authority (EBA)
The Committee of European Securities Regulators (CESR)	The European Securities and Markets Authority (ESMA)
The Committee of European Insurance and Occupational Pensions Supervisors (CEIOPS)	The European Insurance and Occupational Pensions Authority (EIOPA)

2. an enhancement of the degree of coordination among European financial regulators and supervisors through the transformation of the existing three Lamfalussy Committee into regulatory authorities with significant powers to foster good supervisory practice (Table 4.4).

The main task of these new authorities is to establish a set of high-quality regulatory and supervisory standards to promote the consistency in European legislation application and in supervisory outcomes. To this aim it is important to underline the conduction of the peer reviews of supervisory authorities to take actions in emergency situations.

4.5   Conclusions

This chapter has analyzed the main regulatory issues of bancassurance, analyzing the cooperation between banks and insurance companies from the supervisor's perspective.

From an economic point of view the presence of underwriting risk among the risks of financial conglomerate can affect the exercise of control by the supervisor and the degree of capital adequacy. From a regulatory point of view the supervision of financial conglomerates implies three different levels of control: at the single entity level, at the group level and at the conglomerate level. According to EU Directive 2002/87/EC, these three levels of supervision are strictly linked to the presence of regulated entities, the relevance and the weight of the financial sector within the conglomerate, the type and the weight of business mix within the conglomerate. The choice of the methodology to calculate the capital requirement depends on the structure of the conglomerate. If the supervisors want to prevent the multiple gearing and the excessive use of leverage, they have to adopt: (i) the 'accounting consolidation' method when the financial conglomerate is headed by a regulated entity and the other regulated entities belong to other sectors of financial conglomerate; (ii) the 'deduction and aggregation' method when the financial conglomerates has a high degree of heterogeneity; or (iii) the 'book valued/requirement deduction' when the parent entity has the most important role within the conglomerate.

The regulatory framework will be affected by the innovations in the legislation of bank capital adequacy (Basel III) and the solvency of insurance undertakings (Solvency II). The new recommendations of Basel Committee and the Solvency II Directive have introduced new risks for which it is necessary to create a bearing fund. The revision of the Directive on Financial Conglomerates is necessary to strengthen the supervisor's control of financial conglomerates: actually national supervisors are obliged to choose between banking and insurance supervision under a sector-specific Directive and supplementary supervision under the financial conglomerates Directive. The functioning of the new supervisory system will increase the effectiveness of the supervisory control within the financial entities of the conglomerate.

Notes

1. 'Total assets' here means 'balance sheet total' (see Joint Forum 1999).
2. With the aim of identifying the threshold the banking and investment services sector are considered together. See Gruson (2004).
3. The European Commission placed the draft of a Directive on the supplementary supervision of financial conglomerates at the end of 1999, in consultation with the Mixed Technical Group (MTG) formed by the predecessors of the committees of the second and the third level of Lamfalussy framework.
4. See the next subsection.
5. See, for example, the dissemination of the results of the stress tests on the European Banking sector after the financial turmoil firstly among the supervisor authorities. See ECB (2010).
6. We do not take into account those financial conglomerates which have a head of the group outside of the European Union; as in the latest identification of financial conglomerates at 30 June 2010 there are four of them.
7. See for example, the behaviour of AIG in the recent financial turmoil and its responsibility towards the entities within the group.
8. According to the sectoral rules, the issued and fully paid ordinary stocks are the most important element among the eligible elements. See, for example, Basel Committee on Banking Supervision (2006).

9. For example, some local laws and regulations establish restrictions on the amount of dividends that may be paid to shareholders. Insurance entities located in the US are subject to limitation on payment of dividends to their parent companies under applicable State insurance laws.
10. Unexpected financial losses caused by the inadequacy of premiums and reserves for non-life business or by the unpredictability of mortality and longevity for life business.
11. Possible losses due to the failure of debtors, bond issuers, counterparties but also reinsurance partners.
12. Possible losses caused by changes in interest rates, equity prices, foreign exchange rate and real estate values.
13. Data on own funds are not available for each sector.
14. See KPMG (2002).
15. CEIOPS distinguishes the sub-risks of health underwriting risk on the basis of the similarity with the techniques used for life business: SLT (Similar to Life Techniques) Health sub-risk, non-SLT Health sub-risks and Cat (Catastrophe) Health sub-risk. See CEIOPS (2010).
16. The capital requirement for operational risk is added to basic solvency capital requirement. The basic solvency capital requirement takes into account all the risks in Table 4.3.
17. Assets which are allocated to policies where policyholders bear the investment risk are excluded from the quantification of the capital requirement of market risk. See CEIOPS (2009a).
18. The capital requirement for operational risk cannot exceed 30 per cent of the Basic Solvency Capital Requirement (CEIOPS, 2009b).

References

Allianz Group (2010) Annual Report. www.allianz.com.
Banca d'Italia, BaFin (1993) Memorandum of understanding of 16 August 1993. www.bancaditalia.it.
Banca d'Italia, Consob, Isvap (2006) Accordo di Coordinamento in materia di Identificazione e Adeguatezza Patrimoniale dei Conglomerati Finanziari. www.bancaditalia.it.
Basel Committee on Banking Supervision (2001) Compendium of Documents produced by the Joint Forum. www.bis.org.
Basel Committee on Banking Supervision (2006) International Convergence of Capital Measurement and Capital Standard. www.bis.org.
Boot, A. and A. Schmeits (2000) 'Market Discipline and Incentive Problems in Conglomerate Firms With Applications to Banking', *Journal of Financial Intermediation*, IX, 3, 240–73.
CEIOPS (2009a) CEIOPS's Advice for Level 2 Implementing Measures on Solvency II: Standard Formula SCR – Loss-Absorbing Capacity of Technical Provisions and Deferred Taxes. eiopa.europa.eu.
CEIOPS (2009b) CEIOPS's Advice for Level 2 Implementing Measures on Solvency II: Standard Formula SCR – Art 111 (f) – Operational Risk. eiopa.europa.eu.
CEIOPS (2010) CEIOPS's Advice for Level 2 Implementing Measures on Solvency II: Standard Formula SCR – Calibration of Health Underwriting Risk. eiopa.europa.eu.

ECB (2010) Annual Report. www.ecb.int.

European Commission (2008) Memorandum of Understanding on Cooperation between the Financial Supervisory Authorities, Central Banks and Finance Ministries of the European Union on Cross-border Financial Stability. ASvailable online at ec.europa.eu.

Freixas, X., G. Loranth and A. D. Morrisona (2005) 'Regulating Financial Conglomerates', *Cambridge Endowment for Research in Finance*, Working Paper no. 19. Available online at www-cfap.jbs.cam.ac.uk.

Gruson, M. (2004) Supervision on Financial Conglomerates in the European Union, unpublished paper available at http://imf.org/external/np/leg/sem/2004/cdmfl/eng/gruson.pdf.

Joint Forum on Financial Conglomerates (1999) Supervision of Financial Conglomerate. www.bis.org.

KPMG (2002) Study into the methodologies to assess the overall financial position of an insurance undertaking from the perspective of prudential supervision – Study commissioned by Internal Market Directorate General of the European Commission. ec.europa.eu.

Lelyveld, I. and A. Schilder (2002) 'Risk in Financial Conglomerates', *Brookings-Wharton Papers on Financial Services*. ideas.repec.org.

National Bank of Belgium (2002) 'Financial Conglomerates', *Financial Stability Review*, 1, 61–80.

Tripartite Group (1995) The Supervision of Financial Conglomerates. www.bis.org.

5
Insurance Financial Statements

Sabrina Pucci

5.1 Introduction

The aim of this chapter is to describe the evolution of accounting rules and financial statements for insurance companies, focusing on the evolution of the IFRS discipline. Current provisions and their prospective evolutions are particularly relevant for all financial institutions providing insurance contracts. The chapter is organized as follows:

- section 5.2 begins with a general introductory framework for insurance accounting: section 5.2.1 reviews the main provisions of the accounting directive for insurance companies and section 5.2.2 analyzes the rules introduced by the IFRS 4 on insurance contracts;
- section 5.3 examines the main evolution of the IFRS discipline on insurance accounting: section 5.3.1 summarizes the basic ideas contained in the 2007 Discussion Paper, while section 5.3.2 describes the structure of the 2010 Exposure Draft;
- section 5.4 provides some first comments on the most relevant aspects of the Exposure Draft: the measurement model (section 5.4.1), the acquisition costs of insurance contracts (section 5.4.2) and the proposal for a new income statement for insurance companies (5.4.3);
- section 5.5 presents some final remarks.

5.2 The financial statements of insurance companies: some general remarks

Accounting rules and financial statements for insurance companies have been characterized for a long time by specific solutions, sometimes

115

different – even for identical items – from those adopted for the financial statements of manufacturing and commercial firms. This happens, both in European accounting rules and in international accounting principles, because of particularities in the activity of insurers that are not present in the manufacturing and commercial sector – for example, the inversion of the business cycle (in the insurance sector companies obtain premiums – revenues – before costs); the necessity to create technical liabilities that are covered by specific assets in front of the risks assumed and the existence of Supervisory Authorities interested in evaluating the solvency and access requirements of these firms in the public interest.

The European Union, despite having adopted the general Annual Accounts Directive (Directive 78/660/EEC) and the Directive on Consolidated Accounts (83/349/EEC), has issued the 91/674/EEC Directive for the preparation of annual and consolidated accounts of insurance firms.

The Directive, which is examined in some detail in the following section, leaves to Member States a great number of options in evaluating assets and liabilities. One of the most important refers to the possibility of discounting or not discounting the property and casualty technical reserves. However, in the following years, the necessity to compare in a better way the financial statement of companies makes especially important the use of similar accounting principles.

With EC Regulation no. 1606/2002[1] on the application of international accounting standards, the European Parliament states that, 'in order to contribute to a better functioning of the internal market, publicly traded companies must be required to apply a single set of high quality international accounting standards for the preparation of their consolidated financial statements'. In detail:

- European listed companies, for each financial year starting after 1 January 2005, have to prepare their consolidated financial statements in accordance with the principles adopted by the European Community of those issued by IASB (art. 4);
- Member States may permit or require extensive adoption of those principles (consolidated accounts of unlisted companies, annual accounts) (art. 5);

IFRS 4 for insurance contracts is adopted by the European Community and this applies in the insurance sector as the previously mentioned directive.

From these few elements, it can easily be inferred that, at this stage, insurance companies may have different situations with annual and consolidated accounts referring to the decision adopted by the single State member regarding the options left by art. 5 of EC Regulation no. 1606/2002. It is possible that the States have adopted international accounting standards both for consolidated accounts and for annual accounts, either for listed or unlisted companies. It is possible at the same time that another State decided to apply two kinds of accounting rules, even if this causes difficulties for managers who must evaluate the same asset in a different manner, determining in fact the existence of a double accounting system. Individual financial statements and consolidated financial statements can differ in terms of relevant information, classification and measurement referring to the same item. Sometimes the reconciliation of values can be very difficult and the work of the analyst is very hard. For example, the main differences include: the definition of assets and liabilities; the classification of financial instruments; and, consequently, their measurement, allocation of tangible assets and their measurement and liabilities evaluation.

5.2.1 The accounting directive for insurance companies

The 91/674/EEC Directive of 19 December 1991 on the annual and consolidated accounts of insurance companies points out the special nature of the insurance sector and that certain changes are necessary in the structure, evaluation criteria and notes in annual and consolidated accounts. For this reason the Directive requires a specific structure for balance sheets (art. 6) and for profit and loss accounts (art. 34). There are also disclosure rules necessary for preparing the notes properly.

Section 7 contains **valuation rules**. For investments, the principle of purchase price or production cost should be applied. It is, however, possible to use current value in the evaluation of investments, following the criteria defined in arts 48–9 of the Directive but 'the same valuation method shall be applied to all investments included in any item denoted by an Arabic numeral or shown as assets under C (I)' Investments (art. 46, point 5).

Another important choice given to State Members from the Directive concerns the possibility of whether to amortize or not the *acquisition costs* deriving from policies (art. 18 and art. 54), with an immediate effect on profit and loss accounts.

Referring to *technical liabilities*, the Directive states that 'the amount of technical provisions must at all times be such that an undertaking can meet any liabilities arising out of insurance contracts as far as can reasonably be foreseen' (art. 56). Some specific principles are also fixed for the estimate of single reserves: provision for unearned premium (art. 57), provision for unexpired risks (art. 58), life assurance provision (art. 59) and provision for outstanding claims (art. 60).

Actuarial methods, commonly applied in the market or accepted by the insurance supervisory authorities, should be used in the evaluation of life assurance provisions; these methods may be implemented by any actuary or any expert in accordance with the conditions which may be laid down in national law and with due regard for the actuarial principles recognized in the framework of the Directive. In the calculation of the provision for outstanding claims, any implicit discounting or deduction is prohibited, and precise conditions for recourse to explicit discounting or deduction are defined.

In every part of the 91/674/EEC Directive, the concept of prudent and transparent evaluation of technical provisions emerges. As will be seen in the following section, the concept of prudence is less strong in International Accounting Principles, where it refers only to the necessity for prudence in estimates.

5.2.2 The current IFRS 4

IFRS 4 and all IAS-IFRS principles should apply in every European country to consolidated financial statements of listed companies and may apply in other cases.

First of all, it must be remembered that IFRS 4 concerns insurance contracts and not insurance companies. This choice made by IASB determines that, from a theoretical point of view, it is possible that some other firms may apply these prescriptions.

The scope of IFRS 4, currently in force, referring to paragraph 2, is to fix accounting principles for all insurance and reinsurance contracts issued in conjunction with the financial instruments which provide for a discretionary participation feature.[2] The rules for the accounting of financial assets and financial liabilities held by the insurer do not fall within the scope of the principle. In IFRS 4 a series of exclusions is also defined, the details of which can be found in paragraph 4.[3]

The definition of an insurance contract, given in Appendix A of IFRS 4, is: 'a contract under which one party (the insurer) accepts significant insurance risk from another party (the policyholder) by agreeing to compensate the policyholder if a specified uncertain future event (the insured event) adversely affects the policyholder'.

From the above definition, some important concepts for insurance contracts emerge such as: *'significant insurance risk'* which defines the line between financial contracts, for which it applies IAS 39 (IFRS 9 when approved by EC), and insurance policies; the definition of uncertainty as an integral part of each company 'offset'; the negative effects caused by the risk through the payment of a sum of money.

The definition of *significant insurance risk* can be found in the Appendix in paragraph B23, where it is described as follows:

> Insurance risk is significant if, and only if, an **insured event** could cause an **insurer** to pay significant additional benefits in any scenario, excluding scenarios that lack commercial substance (i.e., have no discernible effect on the economics of the transaction). If significant additional benefits would be payable in scenarios that have commercial substance, the condition in the previous sentence may be met even if the insured event is extremely unlikely or even if the expected (i.e., probability-weighted) present value of contingent cash flows is a small proportion of the expected present value of all the remaining contractual cash flows'.

This definition, involving the concept of commercial substance of the transaction, is the basis for identifying a contract as an insurance policy.

The current version of IFRS 4 does not fix specific criteria for the evaluation of technical provisions and refers to the so-called *local GAAP for the quantification of insurance liabilities*: this leads to negative effects in terms of comparability of insurance industry financial statements, given the importance that this item has on total liabilities and to the numerous methods that can be used to evaluate technical provisions in relation to similar contracts.

IFRS 4, however, has introduced an element of security with the aim of ensuring that technical provisions will always be sufficient to meet insurer obligations, regardless of how they are calculated. IFRS 4 paragraph 15 states that every company must carry out a *Liability Adequacy Test* (LAT)[4] in relation to their technical reserves. This consists of a check on the adequacy of provisions for existing contracts. If the sum of the discounted expected cash flows deriving from insurer obligations – determined according to the principles defined in IFRS 4 – exceeds the amount defined as a technical reserve in financial statements, the difference between the two values must be immediately entered in the income statement as operating cost.

IFRS 4, in describing the principles that must be followed in the implementation of the LAT, states that the test should consider the estimated present value of all future contractual cash flows including those arising from claim management, from embedded options and guarantees issued for any reason by the insurer. The analysis can be carried out on a single contract or on a portfolio of homogeneous contracts. The effects arising from the purchase of capitalized commissions and effects in relation to intangibles acquired as a result of business combination (for example, the value of the policy portfolio) must also be considered in the evaluation process.

5.3 The reform project of IFRS 4

IFRS 4 in its current version allows only the limited harmonization of accounting principles for insurance contracts because, as we have seen in the previous section, there is no single model to measure the technical provisions. Therefore, for several years the IASB has been trying to complete and improve the contents of IFRS 4 in order to make them cohere more closely with the economic reality of insurance companies and to achieve greater comparability of financial and economic results. The IASB itself defines the current IFRS 4 as 'an "interim standard" that permits a wide variety of previous accounting practices for insurance contracts to continue until phase II is complete. Users of insurers' financial statements find it difficult to understand and compare those practices. The IASB, jointly with the FASB, is undertaking Phase II of this project to develop a standard that will replace IFRS 4'.[5]

Here is a short history of the project. In May 2004, the IASB took up Phase II of the insurance contract project and issued a Discussion Paper named *Preliminary Views on Insurance Contracts;* in September 2004, the IASB created a working group to advise it on the project; in May 2007, the IASB issued the new Discussion Paper *Preliminary Views on Insurance Contracts* with a comment period ending on 16 November 2007. In August 2007, the US Financial Accounting Standards Board (FASB) issued an invitation to comment on whether the FASB should add to its agenda a joint project with the IASB to develop a comprehensive standard on accounting for insurance contracts. In February 2008, the IASB began its review of responses to the discussion paper Preliminary Views on Insurance Contracts. In October 2008 the FASB added a project on insurance contracts to its agenda and the boards agreed to undertake it jointly. In July 2010, the IASB issued the Exposure Draft *Insurance Contracts* with a comment period ending on 30 November 2010 and in September 2010 the FASB issued the Discussion Paper Preliminary Views on Insurance Contracts with a comment period ending on 15 December 2010.[6]

5.3.1 The 2007 Discussion Paper: basis idea

In August 2007 the IASB issued the *Exposure Draft* about *Insurance Contracts.* This paper is divided into nine parts: background, objective, recognition and derecognition, measurement – core issues, policyholder behaviour, relationship and acquisition costs; measurement – other issues; policyholder participation; disclosure, effective date and transition. There are also seven Appendixes: the first contains the questions for respondents; the second concerns a comparison with IAS 39 (initial and subsequent measurement presentation); the third examines other IASB projects that could be relevant for an insurance company (conceptual framework, revenue recognition, fair value measurements, financial instruments ...); the fourth summarizes the issues not covered in the Discussion Paper (such as catastrophe and equalization reserves, deferred tax, ...), the fifth is guidance on the estimates of future cash flows (and defines consistency with current market price); the sixth concerns risk margin evaluation; the seventh contains examples (referring to compensation for bearing risk or shock absorber, service margin, and so on).

Although the Discussion Paper offers many interesting points for debate, in this section only some aspects are considered particularly relevant for understanding the main difficulties in evaluating an insurance contract and the evolution of IASB accounting principles concerning insurance contracts.

The measurement model for technical liabilities is based on the definition of the *current exit value*,[7] which is 'the amount the insurer would expect to pay at the reporting date to transfer its remaining contractual rights and obligations immediately to another entity'.[8] The IASB clarifies that determining a current exit value in practice does not mean the 'real' transfer of the portfolio to another company but the criterion that appears the best to give users and stakeholders useful information about the insurer's economic and financial results. The model gives important information 'about the amount, timing and uncertainty of the future cash flows resulting from the contractual rights and contractual obligations created by insurance contracts'.[9]

The Discussion Paper defines in paragraph IN18 the 'three building blocks' of the measurement model: '(a) explicit, unbiased, market-consistent, probability-weighted and current estimates of the contractual cash flows; (b) current market discount rates that adjust the estimated future cash flows for the time value of money; (c) an explicit and unbiased estimate of the margin that market participants require for bearing risk (a risk margin) and for providing other services, if any (a service margin)'.[10]

Examining these three building blocks more deeply, some possible problems emerge regarding the business model of insurance companies. The Discussion Paper proposes that in measuring technical liabilities, the insurer should determine future contractual cash flows that:

'(a) are explicit;
(b) are as consistent as possible with observable market prices;
(c) incorporate, in an unbiased way, all available information about the amount, timing and uncertainty of all cash flows arising from the contractual obligation;
(d) are current, in other words they correspond to conditions at the end of the reporting period;
(e) exclude entity-specific cash flows. Cash flows are entity-specific if they would not arise for other entities holding an identical obligation'.[11]

A delicate aspect is constituted by the hypotheses that must be used in the evaluation of future cash flows. The problem concerns whether to use market-consistent assumptions or, especially for demographic and insurance assumptions, to use entity-specific data. The IASB affirms that

'a measurement of an insurance liability should represent faithfully the economic characteristics of that liability. Therefore, that measurement should reflect the cash flows generated by that liability. It should not capture cash flows generated by other assets and liabilities or arising from synergies between the insurance liability and other assets or liabilities. In other words, the measurement should not capture cash flows that are specific to the insurer and would not arise for other market participants holding an obligation that is identical in all respects (entity-specific cash flows)'.[12]

This IASB position has been criticized by most respondents because of the importance that the characteristics of a single portfolio has in the evaluation of insurance liabilities. Policies of the same branch may be very different because of geographical reasons, demographic assumptions, different types of population, and so on. In addition, insurance liabilities do not have a regulated market and the trading of groups of policies is not sufficiently frequent to make the hypothetical market values representative.

Referring to **discount rate**, the Discussion Paper clarifies that:

'the objective of the discount rate is to adjust estimated future cash flows for the time value of money in a way that captures the characteristics of the liability, not the characteristics of the assets viewed as backing those liabilities. Therefore, the discount rate should be consistent with observable current market prices for cash flows whose characteristics match those of the insurance liability, in terms of, for example, timing, currency and liquidity. It should exclude any factors that influence the observed rate but are not relevant to the liability (for example, risks not present in the liability but present in the instrument for which the market prices are observed)?.[13]

The choice of adopting a discount rate that is closer to a risk-free rate, rather than a rate that takes into account the evaluation of existing assets backing insurance reserves, is a choice that, as discussed below, has been retained by IASB also in the 2010 Exposure Draft except for certain specific types of policy. This choice is based on a strong assumption which first requires incorporation of all the elements of variability in future cash flows, second, the creation of an explicit margin for the risks assumed by contracts (risk margin).

Referring to **margins**, the Discussion Paper states that two types of margins exist: a risk margin and a service margin. The main contents of this subject are summarized in the following part of this section. The 'risk margins are compensation for bearing risk' (para. 75). 'At each reporting date an insurer would assess how much risk remains in the liabilities and would adjust the risk margin accordingly' (para. 73). 'The objective of a risk margin is to convey decision-useful information to users about the uncertainty associated with future cash flows. The objective is not to provide a shock absorber for the unexpected, nor is it to enhance the insurer's solvency' (para. 86a). 'The Board does not intend to prescribe specific techniques for developing risk margins. Instead, the Board intends to explain the attributes of techniques that will enable risk margins to convey useful information to users about the uncertainty associated with risk margins.'[14]

The *risk margin* must be determined both at inception and subsequently. IASB have decided not to fix specific techniques to evaluate this margin but to give indications that must be considered in the choice. The factors which must be used for the quantification of risk are the following: to consider in what manner market operators should have determined the risk and how many units they have used to quantify the risk; the use of cash flow scenarios to estimate the existing risk unit; the adoption of observed market prices, pricing models and other inputs to determine the margin for units of risk; to do tests for errors at the end of the valuation process. The overall margin is the product of unit margins multiplied by the number of units subject to risk. The annual change in margin represents a cost or a gain in the income statement. For IASB this margin is not a shock absorber.

In relation to *service margin*, the paper argues that:

'many insurance contracts require an insurer to provide other services as well. An important example is when the contract requires the insurer to provide investment management services, such as in many unit-linked contracts or universal life contracts and some participating contracts. An investment manager would not take on an obligation to provide investment management services without adequate compensation. Similarly, presumably an insurer would not willingly provide the same services within an insurance contract without adequate compensation'.[15] ...

This suggests that the measurement of an insurance liability should include a service margin if market participants typically require such a margin.

The presence of this margin is linked to the IASB perception that, in some cases, insurance companies provide customers with other services in addition to the hedging of risk, such as investment management services (especially for unit-linked and participating contracts).

The IASB receives a lot of comments in relation to this Discussion Paper and some of these comments disagree completely with the current exit value as a measurement model while appreciating the building blocks idea. The large number of criticisms of the Discussion Paper contents by the main players in the global insurance market has made the IASB reconsider some aspects of valuing technical provisions. For example, for most respondents: it is not possible to apply a market consistent approach to all of the assumptions used in the evaluation process; the current exit approach does not consider the fact that in most cases the policies are not transferred to third subjects bur remain in the company; the service margin is not clearly defined by IASB and is very difficult to evaluate because of the methods generally adopted for the calculation of policy premiums.

These criticisms, as will be seen in the next section, have determined that the Exposure Draft differs significantly from the Discussion Paper in certain important aspects.

5.3.2 The 2010 Exposure Draft: the structure

On 30 July 2010, the IASB issued the Exposure Draft on Insurance Contracts. This document is divided into eight parts: objective, scope, recognition, measurement, derecognition, disclosure, effective date and transition. There are also three important Appendices: the first one concerns the meaning of the main terms used in the Exposure Draft, the second is application guidance that clarifies for instance: the notion of insurance risk (different from financial), the criteria and the assumptions that must be used to measure insurance and reinsurance contracts (for example, the principles that it is necessary to remember in the estimate of future cash flows), the notion of risk adjustment and the permitted techniques; the third concerns the amendments to other IFRSs.

There are a lot of important points in the Exposure Draft and also some problems to solve. The main characteristic is the measurement model created to determine the liabilities value and based on a current fulfillment value estimated by three building blocks (expected present value of future cash flows, risk adjustment, residual margin).

It must be clarified that the definition of insurance contracts presented in the Exposure Draft applies equally to life, property and accident/casualty insurance. This is an important decision made by the IASB; a choice already made in the 2007 Discussion Paper that has been maintained in the new Exposure Draft. The IASB also makes no distinction in terms of measurement model of technical provisions (which look the same regardless of whether the contracts are life or non-life). The only exception is for short term contracts for which there are specific rules for evaluation and inclusion in the income statement.

The evaluation model for technical liabilities is based on the definition of the **current fulfillment value**. The present value of the fulfillment cash flow is defined as 'the expected present value of the future cash outflows less future cash inflows that will arise as the insurer fulfils the insurance contract, adjusted for the effects of uncertainty about the amount and timing of those future cash flows'.[16] The insurer should determine the liabilities using these three building blocks:

'(a) an explicit, unbiased and probability-weighted estimate (i.e., expected value) of the future cash outflows less the future cash inflows that will arise as the insurer fulfils the insurance contract;
(b) a discount rate that adjusts those cash flows for the time value of money; and
(c) an explicit estimate of the effects of uncertainty about the amount and timing of those future cash flows (risk adjustment)'.[17]

The future cash flows must be determined following these criteria:

(a) be explicit (i.e., separate from estimates of discount rates that adjust those cash flows for the time value of money and the risk adjustment that adjusts those cash flows for the effects of uncertainty about the amount and timing of those future cash flows).

(b) reflect the perspective of the entity but, for market variables, be consistent with observable market prices.

(c) incorporate, in an unbiased way, all available information about the amount, timing and uncertainty of all cash flows that will arise as the insurer fulfils the insurance contract.

(d) be current (i.e., the estimates shall reflect all available information at the measurement date).

(e) include only those cash flows that arise from existing contracts (i.e., cash inflows and cash outflows that arise within the boundary of those contracts – see paragraphs 26 and 27).

As may easily be seen, the Exposure Draft criteria to estimate future cash flows are similar to those defined by the previous Discussion Paper but some important aspects have been changed. For example:

• referring to point (b), in the Exposure Draft the cash flows are based on an entity specific evaluation ('reflect the perspective of an entity'), in the Discussion Paper they are 'as consistent as possible with observable market price': the change is done to issue an Exposure Draft more consistent with the insurance business practice where demographic and insurance assumptions are generally entity specific and financial assumptions are market consistent;

• referring to point (e) the exclusion of entity-specific cash flows presented in the Discussion Paper is deleted and there is the insertion of the theme of contract boundary.

The definition of discount rate is the same as the Discussion Paper; in fact:

'an insurer shall adjust the future cash flows for the time value of money, using discount rates that:

(a) are consistent with observable current market prices for instruments with cash flows whose characteristics reflect those of the insurance contract liability, in terms of, for example, timing, currency and liquidity;

(b) exclude any factors that influence the observed rates but are not relevant to the insurance contract liability (e.g. risks not present in the liability but present in the instrument for which the market prices are observed)'.[18]

However, there is clarification regarding the cash flows arising from policies in which the results depend wholly or partially on the performance of specific assets: in this case, the discount rate must consider this linkage (the Exposure Draft referring to replicating portfolio technique).

The last building block is the *risk adjustment*: 'the risk adjustment shall be the maximum amount the insurer would rationally pay to be relieved of the risk that the ultimate fulfillment cash flows exceed those expected'.[19] Some important details are fixed referring to this margin. In Appendix B to the Exposure Draft, may be found some guidance to risk margin evaluation. Some specific techniques are identified to determine the adjustment amount: confidence level, conditional tail expectation and cost of capital.[20] These three are the only solutions admitted by the IASB. The Appendix gives some details about these techniques and also some warnings about the conditions in which one or the other may be used. For example, for the confidence level, the Exposure Draft argues:

'The use of confidence levels for estimating a risk adjustment has the benefits of being relatively easy to communicate to users and relatively easy to calculate. However, the usefulness of confidence level diminishes when the probability distribution is not statistically normal (which is often the case for insurance contracts). When the probability distribution is not normal (in which case, the probability distribution may be skewed and the mean may not equal the median), the selection of the confidence level must take into account additional factors, such as the skewness of the probability distribution. In addition, this technique ignores outliers (i.e., extreme losses in the tail of the distribution beyond the specified confidence level)'.[21]

The solution adopted is therefore quite different from the one in the Discussion Paper, in that case in fact the IASB have decided not to define any evaluation criteria.

One new important concept introduced by the Exposure Draft is the residual margin. This margin is defined as the amount 'that eliminates any gain at inception of the contract. A residual margin arises when the amount in (a) is less than zero (i.e., when the expected present value of the future cash outflows plus the risk adjustment is less than the expected present value of the future cash inflows)'.[22] In the Exposure Draft, the accounting nature of this margin is of a liability, even if it contains the future profits that will arise from the insurance contracts issued by the company. One of the main problems referring to the residual margin, according to the IASB, is its release in the coming years. IASB states that this margin should not be updated in the life period of the contract.

5.4 First comments on relevant aspects in the Exposure Draft

After having summarized in the previous paragraph the main evaluation principles of the Exposure Draft, in this paragraph some specific points that are particularly interesting for a group composed of insurance companies and banks are further analyzed.

5.4.1 Measurement model

Only two or three considerations of the Exposure Draft measurement model are presented. The first refers to the **change of the reference model**: in the Discussion Paper the estimates of technical liabilities are based on the definition of the current exit value, in the Exposure Draft on the definition of the current fulfillment value. Both definitions refer to a fair value approach but the implication of the two models are different: the first definition (current exit value) refers to a transfer value of insurance contracts, the second one (current fulfillment value) considers the contractual terms and the obligations that the insurer has with the policyholder. Although the current fulfillment value represents a choice nearer to the insurance business model,[23] its adoption may create some problems for European insurers. For example some contents of the Solvency II Directive adopted in the period immediately following the issue of the Discussion Paper can determine problems. Indeed this Directive in order not to create a dual model of assessment of technical provisions – one valid for the purposes of the financial statements, the other for of solvency purposes – has taken the current exit value as a fundamental parameter. Art. 76, par. 2, states that: 'the value of technical provisions shall correspond to the current amount insurance and reinsurance undertakings would have to pay if they were to transfer their insurance and reinsurance obligations immediately to another insurance or reinsurance undertaking ...'.[24] This article of the Directive and the approach followed in the QIS preparation, together with the actual prescriptions of the Insurance Exposure Draft create the conditions for a double measurement of technical liabilities. It could also happen that technical reserves evaluated for solvency purposes are lower than the provisions presented in the financial statements.

Another consideration refers to the *unit of account*. In the previous Discussion Paper, the unit of account is the contract, in the Exposure Draft all the building blocks are evaluated referring to a portfolio of policies. The solution adopted in the ED is an important step forward compared with the 2007 solution: the portfolio approach permits a better representation of the principle of mutuality, typical of insurance companies.

Another important point that emerges from the analysis refers to discount rate and it is represented by the evaluation of a *liquidity or illiquidity premium* in this rate. The Exposure Draft argues that a liquidity premium must be considered because of the illiquidity of insurance contracts. In para. 31, it states that: 'as a result of the principle in paragraph 30, if the cash flows of an insurance contract do not depend on the performance of specific assets, the discount rate shall reflect the yield curve in the appropriate currency for instruments that expose the holder to no or negligible credit risk, with an adjustment for illiquidity ...'. On 3 March 2010, CEIOPS published the Task Force Report on Liquidity Premium 'containing technical considerations regarding the application of a liquidity premium for the valuation of insurance liabilities, principles for extrapolation and considerations on the choice of the reference risk-free rate'.[25]

For solvency purposes, CEIOPS argues that:

'The illiquidity of an insurance liability measures the extent up to which its cash flows are certain in amount and in timing, due consideration being given to the resilience to forced sales. Most life insurance liabilities can be considered to be at least partially illiquid. A prerequisite for the application of a liquidity premium to illiquid liabilities is the existence of objective and reliable methods allowing to measure the degree of illiquidity'.[26]

However, some people affirm that a liquidity premium is not coherent with a current fulfillment value because insurance contracts are evaluated on a contractual obligation basis without considering their marketability. On the contrary, a liquidity premium is perfectly consistent with a current exit value that represents the transfer value of the contract.

Even if a liquidity adjustment to the discount rate is admitted, another important problem remains: how to determine the liquidity adjustment value. CEIOPS defines one model that companies may adopt but IASB does not specify anything.

5.4.2 Acquisition costs of insurance contracts

Acquisition costs – for example, the fees paid to distribution networks (traditional agents, brokers or banks) to compensate their activities in selling insurance contracts – clearly represent an expense for companies from an economic point of view. At present, there is no specific indication in international accounting principles about the elements that are included in these expenses and how they must be considered in financial statements.[27]

The 91/674/EEC Directive affirms that: 'acquisition costs shall comprise the costs arising from the conclusion of insurance contracts. They shall cover both direct costs, such as acquisition commissions or the cost of drawing up the insurance document or including the insurance contract in the portfolio, and indirect costs, such as advertising costs or the administrative expenses[28] connected with the processing of proposals and the issuing of policies' (art. 40). Referring to the definition, it should be noted that the Insurance Directive includes in the acquisition costs both direct and indirect costs (such as, for example, the administrative expenses joined with the issuing of policies).

Referring to the reporting, the Directive permits acquisition costs to be considered either as current expenses or as capitalized costs. However, the solution adopted has an important effect on the economic results: in the first hypothesis, all of the acquisition costs paid in the year are considered as expenses in the income statement; in the second, there is a limited effect on the income statement for the acquisition costs of the period because only a part of these are considered.

The IASB Exposure Draft states that incremental acquisition[29] costs must be included in the present value of the fulfillment cash flows and other acquisition costs *'must be identified as an expense when incurred'*.[30] There are two aspects to note: the limitation of acquisition costs to only incremental ones and the evaluation of these expenses directly in the cash flow.

The first aspect is innovative, referring to what is defined by the Directive and is very sensitive because it can lead to a different accounting treatment of these charges depending on the type of distribution channel chosen by companies. It produces a significant disadvantage for direct sales networks, because in the case of direct sales it is impossible to demonstrate the incremental nature of the cost.

The evaluation of acquisition costs directly in cash flows is innovative too but it refers to a common actuarial practice that consists in the calculation of Zillmer's reserve.[31]

5.4.3   The proposal for a 'new' income statement for insurance companies

Another important issue to reflect on is the definition of the statement for comprehensive income. The models examined are numerous and it is possible to find advantages as well as critical issues for most of them. The assumption made by the IASB is to identify a statement to analyze economic performance that is consistent with the criteria defined to measure insurance liabilities (measurement drives presentation). To achieve this consistency, there must be at least the following information in the income statement:

- the effects of the risk margin and the residual margin in the period covered by the measurement model of technical liabilities (the separation between the effects of the two margins can be exposed directly in the income statement or may be shown in the notes to financial statements);
- the difference between expected and actual cash flows;
- the economic effects due to change in the estimates;
- interest existing on the insurance liabilities.

Before examining the approach favoured by the IASB, it may be useful to present briefly all the possible models of income reporting and their positive and negative points.

The first model, which the staff of the IASB have tried several times to eliminate, is based on 'pure flow' or 'volume': it considers the premiums received and the claims paid, adjusted for economic competence, and is very similar to models used in traditional life business (written premium approach). This model shows the volumes that characterize the activities of companies but has two important limitations: it is not compatible with the definition of income given in the IASB project Revenue Recognition and it cannot be identified with the results obtained in terms of the performance management insurance contract. In this case, the information about the profitability of contracts should be provided in the notes. However, it must be underlined that this approach allows the preservation of the existing ratio series for premiums and claims and is very useful in the construction of major indices for the sector such as, for example, the loss ratio, given by the relationship between premiums and claims.

The second model proposed by the IASB (earning premium approach) is still based on premiums and claims incurred but in this instance only one part of the premium is considered (allocating the premium throughout the term of the contract). This approach is similar to the models traditionally used for non-life. In this case, changes in expectations in terms of claims and expenses, as well as the difference between estimated losses and claims incurred, have an effect on the statement of income. It is not easy to reconcile those amounts with changes in value that occurred in the technical provisions. This model is however compatible with the definition of income of the Revenue Recognition project.

The third model examined by the IASB – and that preferred – (summarized margin approach) is based on presentation in the income statement of the 'clean margins'. This model has the advantage of helping the reader to immediately detect the changes in the value of insurance liabilities and the different drivers of performance. But it is not possible to obtain details on premiums and claims in line with those of today (you need to ask about a specific disclosure in the notes) and also the presentation of this line is not fully congruent with the definition of income in the project on Revenue Recognition.

The fourth model combines elements of the traditional income statement with innovative features (expanded margin approach). It should be able to combine the advantages of both models. However, its presentation may be complex and expensive and also it determines an unclear definition of 'income'. The IASB, however, states that *'it creates a new issue'*.

As mentioned, the IASB prefers the approach based on margins and, in particular, the summarized margin approach with the exception of the hypothesis of accounting treatment of short-term contracts, for which they request an indication of premiums and claims in the income statement.

The preferred approach for margin chosen by the IASB is the most different from existing accounting practice in Europe where the volume approach is at present the most widely applied and where the analysis of some ratios (such as loss and combined ratio) is fundamental for the actuary in the process of pricing the product, for the analyst who wishes to assess the strategic positioning of the company, for third parties who seek to understand the firm's position in relation to the actual loss referring to that expected in the agreement phase.[32]

5.5 Conclusions

From the few elements examined two important considerations emerge. The first concerns the 'complexity' of the rules defined to build financial insurance statements (and, in particular, the measurement model of technical provisions and the valuation assumptions adopted).

It is worth noticing that in the recent past, the IASB adopted an 'expanded' approach in defining accounting principles. Sometimes the IASB instead of principles often issues technical rules. The latest approach is a little dangerous from two points of view:

- technical rules must be changed every time you discover different practices in the economic reality. This means continuously changing rules which does not help comparability and transparency of financial statements and increases the costs;
- new accounting principles defined by IASB sometimes mix accounting rules with mathematical tools and statistics. This determines the 'complexity' of principles and also the possibility that the company boards delegate some important decisions to technical offices.

The second concerns the fact that the Exposure Draft, although several steps ahead of the Discussion Paper, is not fully representative of the insurance business in its financial statements. In this case the replies that users, preparers and academics give to the first ED question, referring to the capacity of the new measurement model to produce relevant information, will be very important. It is possible that, even if in most cases ED produces an increase in the amount of useful information, for some relevant aspects further reflection will be necessary. These are the hypothesis of the insurance liabilities measurement model of long life contracts, the relationship between IFRS 9, IAS 40 and other IASs that define rules to evaluate assets that cover technical liabilities, the new income statement based on a full margin approach.

EFRAG, in its comment letter issued on 14 December 2010,[33] affirms that:

'EFRAG considers that the measurement model proposed in the ED will be a step forward in accounting for insurance contracts. EFRAG considers that the proposed measurement model increases the relevance of information for users since there will be more consistency and comparability in the financial statements and eliminate the existing diversity of accounting principles used for the measurement of liability. However, EFRAG believes that the IASB should explore in more details the issues around what constitutes the performance of an insurer and how this should be presented in the financial statements.

We also have the concern about some of the other proposals where we do not believe that they will improve the usefulness of information provided ...'.

It is worth noting that the IASB has launched an Advisory Panel to consider the definition and utility of the business model for the accounting rules. This is due to increasingly frequent requests by companies to have accounting principles that reflect the business reality so that financial statements represent the business and, at the same time, a true and fair view.

Finally, it is important to note that while this book was being printed discussion of the main aspects of IFRS 4 Exposure Draft has continued and the deadline to issue the new IFRS 4 has been modified (first semester of 2012 instead of the end of 2011).

The model to evaluate technical reserves, especially for short-term contracts, is being studied again to define a modified approach[34] but it is not yet perfectly clear if it represents a simplification or an approximation of the basic approach.

The accounting mismatches have been analyzed in detail to verify the possibility of a solution using OCI instead of changing some general principles fixed in ED (for example, instead of the 'lock-in' of interest rates in the quantification of technical reserves when assets evaluated exist in front of these reserves are evaluated at amortized cost).

Some other models to represent income results[35] have been analyzed in order to increase the level of disclosure of financial statements referring to the technical solutions adopted and margins obtained by the companies.

From the above comments it is easy to see that, at this stage, some important decisions about insurance contract representation are not definitive. IASB may express only "tentative decisions" and therefore the future of the financial statements of insurance companies still has to be decided.

Notes

1. Regulation (EC) No. 1606/2002 of the European Parliament and of the Council of 19 July 2002 on the application of international accounting standards, is available on: www.eur-lex.europa.eu.
2. 'An entity shall apply this IFRS to: (a) insurance contracts (including reinsurance contracts) that it issues and reinsurance contracts that it holds; (b) financial instruments that it issues with a discretionary participation feature (see paragraph 35). IFRS 7 Financial Instruments: Disclosures requires disclosure about financial instruments, including financial instruments that contain such features', IFRS 4, par. 2. 'This [draft] IFRS does not address other aspects of accounting by insurers, such as accounting for their financial assets and financial liabilities, other than those mentioned in paragraph 2(b) (see IFRS 9 Financial Instruments, IFRS 7 Financial Instruments: Disclosures,

IAS 32 Financial Instruments: Presentation and IAS 39 Financial Instruments: Recognition and Measurement), except in the transition requirements in paragraph 102' (IFRS, para. 3).

3. 'An entity shall not apply this IFRS to:

(a) product warranties issued directly by a manufacturer, dealer or retailer (see IAS 18 Revenue and IAS 37 Provisions, Contingent Liabilities and Contingent Assets).

(b) employers' assets and liabilities under employee benefit plans (see IAS 19 Employee Benefits and IFRS 2 Share-based Payment) and retirement benefit obligations reported by defined benefit retirement plans (see IAS 26 Accounting and Reporting by Retirement Benefit Plans).

(c) contractual rights or contractual obligations that are contingent on the future use of, or right to use, a non-financial item (for example, some license fees, royalties, contingent lease payments and similar items), as well as a lessee's residual value guarantee embedded in a finance lease (see IAS 17 Leases, IAS 18 Revenue and IAS 38 Intangible Assets).

(d) financial guarantee contracts unless the issuer has previously asserted explicitly that it regards such contracts as insurance contracts and has used accounting applicable to insurance contracts, in which case the issuer may elect to apply either IAS 39, IAS 32 and IFRS 7 or this Standard to such financial guarantee contracts. The issuer may make that election contract by contract, but the election for each contract is irrevocable.

(e) contingent consideration payable or receivable in a business combination (see IFRS 3 Business Combinations).

(f) direct insurance contracts that the entity holds (i.e., direct insurance contracts in which the entity is the policyholder). However, a cedant shall apply this IFRS to reinsurance contracts that it holds' (IFRS4, para. 4).

4. For some details of LAT, see: IASB, *Liability Adequacy Test*, Agenda Paper 10G, February 2006, available on www.iasb.org; International Actuarial association, IASP 6, *Liability Adequacy Testing, Testing for Recoverability of Deferred Transaction Costs, and Testing for Onerous Service Contracts under International Financial Reporting Standards*, June 2005, available on: www.actuaries.org.

5. For further information see the IASB site (www.ifrs.org) the part of standard development dedicated to insurance contracts.

6. For further information see http://www.ifrs.org/Current+Projects/IASB+Projects/Insurance+Contracts/Project+history.htm.

7. See Dickinson (2003, pp. 151–75). On the methods to measure technical liabilities, it is possible to read: Christiansen (2008, pp. 787–96); Gerber (1997); Kassberger et al. (2009, pp. 419–33); Ohlsson and Lauzeningks (2009, pp. 203–8).

8. IASB, Discussion Paper, June 2007, para. IN21, available on: www.ifrs.org.

9. IASB, Discussion Paper, para. 31.

10. 'In the Board's view, a measurement using the three building blocks will provide several benefits to users of an insurer's financial statements:

(a) relevant information about the amount, timing and uncertainty of future cash flows arising from existing insurance contracts.

(b) explicit and more robust estimates of cash flows and margins.

(c) a consistent approach to changes in estimates.

(d) an appropriate and consistent approach for all types of insurance (and reinsurance) contracts. This will:

(i) provide a coherent framework to deal with more complex contracts (such as multi-year, multi-line or stop loss contracts) and to resolve emerging issues without resorting to unprincipled distinctions and arbitrary new rules.

(ii) limit the need for arbitrary rules on such matters as embedded derivatives, financial reinsurance, and amendments to existing contracts'. in IASB, Discussion Paper, para. IN20.

11. IASB, Discussion Paper, para. 35.
12. IASB, Discussion Paper, para. 56.
13. IASB, Discussion Paper, pars 68–69.
14. IASB, Discussion Paper, para. 76.
15. IASB, Discussion Paper, pars 87–88.
16. Exposure Draft, para. 17. For methods of valuation, see: American Academy of Actuaries (2002); International Association of Insurance Supervisors (2003); Institute of Actuaries of Australia (2002); Laganá et al. (2006); Dickinson (2003, pp. 151–75 (25); Girard (2002).
17. Exposure Draft, para. 22.
18. Exposure Draft, para. 30.
19. Exposure Draft, para. 35.
20. A lot of papers exist that examine the techniques adoptable to determine risk adjustment: see Briys and Varenne (1995).
21. Exposure Draft, B76.
22. Exposure Draft, 17.
23. 'EFRAG supports a measurement approach for insurance liabilities that is based on the expected present value of the fulfillment cash flows (future cash outflows less future cash inflows). We agree that the portfolio is the appropriate level of measurement for the probability weighted cash flows of insurance contracts. We have concerns about the different levels of measurement required by the proposals as we believe that a consistent unit-of-account should apply throughout the standard for all building blocks', in EFRAG, Comment letter on IASB Exposure Draft Insurance Contracts, issued on 14 December 2010, available on: www.efrag.org.
24. 1. "The value of technical provisions shall be equal to the sum of a best estimate and a risk margin as set out in paragraphs 2 and 3.

    2. The best estimate shall correspond to the probability-weighted average of future cash-flows, taking account of the time value of money (expected present value of future cash-flows), using the relevant risk-free interest rate term structure.

    The calculation of the best estimate shall be based upon up-to-date and credible information and realistic assumptions and be performed using adequate, applicable and relevant actuarial and statistical methods.

    The cash-flow projection used in the calculation of the best estimate shall take account of all the cash in- and out-flows required to settle the insurance and reinsurance obligations over the lifetime thereof.

    The best estimate shall be calculated gross, without deduction of the amounts recoverable from reinsurance contracts and special purpose vehicles. Those amounts shall be calculated separately, in accordance with Article 81.

    3. The risk margin shall be such as to ensure that the value of the technical provisions is equivalent to the amount that insurance and reinsurance

undertakings would be expected to require in order to take over and meet the insurance and reinsurance obligations.

4. Insurance and reinsurance undertakings shall value the best estimate and the risk margin separately", Directive 2009/138/EC, art. 77, available on: www.eur-lex.europa.eu.

25. CEIOPS, *Task Force on Illiquidity Premium*, 2010, available on: www.gcactu aries.org.

26. CEIOPS, *Task Force on Illiquidity Premium*, 2010, available on: www.gcactu aries.org., p. 8.

27. See also: IASB Staff Paper 5C, *Acquisition Costs*, Meeting of April 2009, available on: www.iasb.org.

28. 'Administrative expenses shall include the costs arising from premium collection, portfolio administration, handling of bonuses and rebates, and inward and outward reinsurance. They shall in particular include staff costs and depreciation provisions in respect of office furniture and equipment in so far as these need not be shown under acquisition costs, claims incurred or investment charges', Directive 91/674/EEC art. 41.

29. The cash flow must include: 'the incremental costs of selling, underwriting and initiating an insurance contract for those contracts that have been issued and that the insurer has incurred because it has issued that particular contract ... Thus, these costs are identified at the level of an individual insurance contract rather than at the level of a portfolio of insurance contracts', Exposure Draft on Insurance Contracts, para. B61f.

30. Exposure Draft on Insurance Contracts, para. 39.

31. Gerber (1997). *Controversies Surrounding* The University of Western Ontario, London, Ontario, ust 23–25.

32. In its Letter to IASB, EFRAG comments: 'We do not believe that the IASB has sufficiently explored issues around what constitutes the performance of an insurer and how this should be presented in the financial statements. We believe that the proposals as currently drafted do not offer a complete approach to performance reporting by an insurer. We would recommend that the IASB explore these issues in more detail to improve the decision-usefulness of the information for users of an insurer's financial statements', in EFRAG, *Comment letter on IASB Exposure Draft Insurance Contracts*, issued on 14 December 2010, available on: www.efrag.org.

33. EFRAG, *Comment letter on IASB Exposure Draft Insurance Contracts*, issued on the 14 of December 2010, available on www.efrag.org.

34. IASB, Premium allocation approach: A two model solution, 14 July 2011, available on: www.ifrs.org.

35. IASB, Statement of comprehensive income, 13 June 2011, available on: www.ifrs.org.

References

American Academy of Actuaries (2002) *Fair value of insurance liabilities: principles and methods*, September 2002, available on: www.actuary.org.

Briys, E. and F. Varenne (1995) 'On the Risk of Life Insurance Liabilities: Debunking Some Common Pitfalls', Wharton, November 1995, no. 96–29, available on: www.fic.wharton.upenn.edu.

CEIOPS, *Task Force on Illiquidity Premium*, 2010, available on: www.gcactu aries.org.

Christiansen, M. C. (2008) 'A sensitivity analysis of typical life insurance contracts with respect to the technical basis', *Insurance: Mathematics and Economics*, XLII, 2, pp. 787–96.

Dickinson, G. (2003), 'The Search for an International Accounting Standard for Insurance: Report to the Accountancy Task Force of the Geneva Association', *The Geneva Papers*, XXVIII, 2, pp. 151–75.

Directive 2009/138/EC, art.77, available on: www.eur-lex.europa.eu.

EFRAG, *Comment letter on IASB Exposure Draft Insurance Contracts*, issued on the 14 of December 2010, available on: www.efrag.org.

Gerber, H. U. (1997) *Life Insurance Mathematics*, 3rd edn. Swiss Association of Actuaries (Berlin: Springer).

Girard, L. N. (2002) 'An Approach To Fair Valuation of Insurance Liabilities Using the Firm's Cost of Capital', *North American Actuarial Journal*, VI, available on: www.soa.org.

IASB, *Liability Adequacy Test*, Agenda Paper 10G, February 2006, available on: www.iasb.org.

IASB, *Discussion Paper on insurance Contracts*, June 2007, available on: www. ifrs.org.

IASB, Staff Paper 5C, *Acquisition Costs*, Meeting of April 2009, available on: www. iasb.org.

IASB, *Exposure Draft on Insurance Contracts*, issued on July 2010, available on: www.ifrs.org.

International Actuarial Association, IASP 6, *Liability Adequacy Testing, Testing for Recoverability of Deferred Transaction Costs, and Testing for Onerous Service Contracts under International Financial Reporting Standards*, June 2005, available on: www.actuaries.org.

International Association of Insurance Supervisors, *Quantifying and assessing insurance liabilities*, Discussion Paper, December 2003, available on: www. iais.org.

Institute of Actuaries of Australia, *Guidance Note. 353, Evaluation of General Insurance Technical Liabilities*, December 2002, available on: www.actuaries. asn.au.

Kassberger, S., R. Kiesel and T. Liebmann (2008) 'Fair valuation of insurance contracts under Levy process specification', *Insurance: Mathematics and Economics*, XLII, 1, pp. 419–33.

Laganá, M., M. Perina, I. Von Köppen-Mertes and A. D. Persaud (2006), 'Implications for Liquidity from Innovation and Transparency in the European Corporate Bond Market', *ECB Occasional Paper* 50.

Ohlsson, E. and J. Lauzeningks (2009), 'The One-year Non-life Insurance Risk', *Insurance: Mathematics and Economics*, XLV, 2, pp. 203–8.

Regulation (EC) No. 1606/2002 of the European Parliament and of the Council of 19 July 2002 on the application of international accounting standards, available on: www.eur-lex.europa.eu.

6
Studying the Bancassurance Phenomenon: A Literature Review

Ornella Ricci

6.1 Introduction

The academic literature dealing with the combination of the banking and the insurance industries is not very extensive, reflecting the fact that bancassurance is a relatively recent phenomenon, especially in the US, where it has been allowed only since 1999 with the passage of the Gramm–Leach–Bliley Act (GLBA). A much wider empirical research stream deals with bank diversification in activities beyond the traditional deposits and lending business, but engagement in the insurance activity is often treated as an aside. As outlined in Chen et al. (2009), most studies focusing on bancassurance have only been descriptive in nature, providing a broad insight into the economic rationales, advantages and drawbacks for all of the involved institutions. Only a few authors have provided quantitative findings on the viability of bancassurance combinations as a new business model for financial firms. Empirical analyses focusing on bancassurance are hindered not only by the recent development of the phenomenon, but also by the availability of limited public information: for example, looking at a bank profit and loss account, it is quite difficult to distinguish the weight of the insurance business from other sources of non-interest income. And it is not easy to collect information on different forms of cooperation between the banking and the insurance industries, especially in respect of 'soft integration', such as non-equity strategic alliances or cross-selling agreements. As a consequence, there are only few empirical analyses devoted to bancassurance and studies comparing the performance registered by alternative organizational models (for example, captive, joint venture, and so on) are even more rare, based on surveys of managers and then limited to their relevant, but personal, experience.

The objective of this chapter is to provide a review of the empirical literature dealing with the bancassurance phenomenon. This review does not aim to be totally exhaustive, rather, it attempts to highlight the main methodologies applied by researchers and the most relevant findings. Special attention is paid to recent contributions, in which the analysis of the phenomenon has benefited from the opportunity to observe real bancassurance experiences.[1] The remainder of the chapter is organized as follows:

- section 6.2 discusses papers dealing with the *diversification hypothesis*, supposing that the shift towards fee-income business offers the opportunity of improving the risk/return profile of a bank portfolio of activities. This is a quite general research stream, considering many types of bank diversification and not specifically devoted to bancassurance. However, it often provides relevant empirical findings also referred to combinations between the banking and the insurance activities. Comparisons of the risk/return effects of a diversification or a specialization strategy are generally conducted with a long-run perspective and can be based on data at the firm or at the industry level. In some cases the empirical analysis is not founded on actual experience, but on hypothetical situations. Starting from information at the industry level it is possible to conduct portfolio simulations and measure the effect of several possible combinations of traditional and non-traditional activities. Another common methodology is based on the construction of synthetic combined entities resulting from potential M&As between real existing firms;
- section 6.3 also examines studies providing a performance comparison of diversified versus specialized institutions, adopting the different point of view of the *scope economies hypothesis*, positing that diversification can enhance efficiency through the exploitation of cost and revenue synergies among several financial activities. As the direct estimation of scope economies is a quite problematic issue, most recent studies have moved to the wider concept of X-efficiency, that is the general management ability in combining production factors;
- section 6.4 analyzes contributions adopting a different standpoint and turning to stock prices reaction to the announcement of relevant events concerning bancassurance. Several event studies have been devoted to measuring investors' reaction to regulatory changes removing existing barriers among different sectors of the financial services industry;

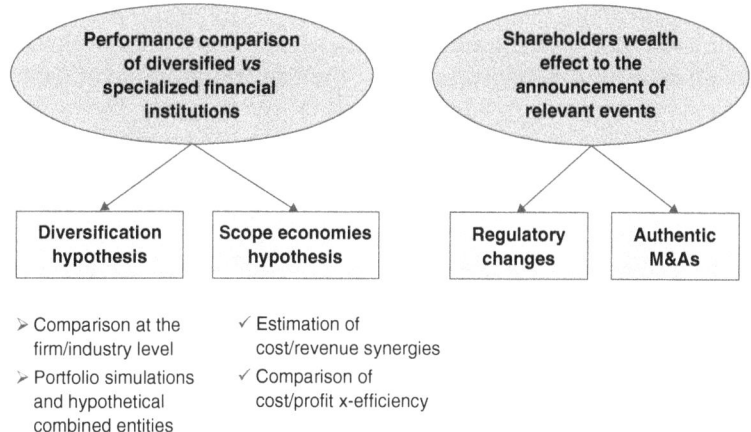

Figure 6.1 Studies on bank diversification
Source: Author's elaboration.

- section 6.5 continues with papers based on event studies, summarizing the main findings of empirical analyses assessing the wealth effect of authentic M&As involving banks and insurance companies;
- section 6.6 completes the overview of the bancassurance empirical literature discussing recent studies that specifically focus on the combination between the banking and the insurance activities but cannot be classified in one of the previous groups;
- section 6.7 reports some conclusions also mentioning the main evidence provided in studies based on surveys and aimed at selecting the best organizational bancassurance models. The objective of this final section is to highlight the current state of the art and identify some directions for future bancassurance research.

In every section, a higher level of detail is provided for empirical contributions specifically dealing with the bancassurance phenomenon. The logical structure of the literature review is illustrated in Figure 6.1.

6.2   Testing the diversification hypothesis: how the shift towards non-traditional lending activities affects the risk/return profile of banks

The financial services industry has experienced a general trend towards greater integration and consolidation in all developed countries. Banks have become increasingly active in businesses different from the traditional deposits and lending activity. Many researchers have tried to test the so-called diversification hypothesis in order to assess if diversification results in an improvement of the risk/return profile of banks. This kind of study adopts a long-run perspective and generally consider the point of view of several stakeholders. From the standpoint of the regulators and supervisors, aiming at the preservation of the financial sector's stability, possible changes in the risk profile of financial firms is probably the main concern. Managers, shareholders and investors can also be willing to undertake more risk if the increase in the expected return is sufficiently relevant.

There is a large number of studies comparing the long-term risk/return profile of specialized versus diversified banks. Generally, the degree of functional diversification in the non-lending business is measured with reference to both an asset and an income standpoint. A widely adopted indicator is the ratio between non-interest income and total operating income that effectively captures all revenues deriving from non-traditional banking activities, such as trading and fiduciary services, underwriting securities, underwriting and/or distributing insurance policies. In a complementary way, it is possible to calculate the ratio of loans to total assets, measuring lending specialization and adding information to the income-based indicator because, as outlined in Baele et al. (2007, page 2010), 'One should be careful not to interpret the loan-to-asset ratio as an alternative indicator of the reliance of a bank on interest income, since other types of assets such as securities also generate interest revenues'.

Laeven and Levine (2007) introduce similar measures, named asset and income diversity. They are calculated as:

$$1 - |2x - 1| \qquad (6.1)$$

where x is the proportion of net loans in total earning assets or the weight of non-interest income in total operating income. Asset and income diversity take values between zero and one with higher values indicating greater diversification. Rumble and Stiroh (2006) define another indicator of diversification, using a logic similar to a Herfindahl–Hirschman Index of concentration, calculated as:

$$DIV = 1 - (SH_{NET}^2 + SH_{NON}^2) \qquad (6.2)$$

where SH_{NET} and SH_{NON} are, respectively, the share of total operating revenue coming from net interest income and non-interest sources.

The index takes a value between 0 (all revenues coming from a single source) and 0.5 (an even split between net and non-interest income).

Less frequently, the level of diversification is measured with reference to standard industrial classifications used for statistical purposes, such as the SIC/NAIC codes at different levels of detail: so a financial firm operating in only one segment is specialized, while one having two or more segments can be considered diversified.

The diversification measures outlined above are examined as one of the main determinants of the risk/return profile of banks. Performance and risk can be evaluated with reference to market or accounting data. Every approach presents some advantages and drawbacks. Market data are forward-looking, able to reflect valuations and expectations of investors, but their use is restricted to publicly traded firms. This is a strong limitation in studies dealing with the financial services industry, especially when involving non-banking firms (for example, insurance companies, security firms) that are rarely listed on stock markets. Accounting data are available also for small and unlisted institutions, but are backward looking and can be distorted by management policies for smoothing earning over time. In addition to this, accounting standards can vary among countries or through time (for example, the introduction of IAS/IFRS in the European Union) leading to possible bias in international and panel data analyses.

6.2.1 Studies using market data to assess the risk/return effects of diversification

First of all, studies using market data are considered. Before mentioning their main results, it is important to clarify the indicators they use to measure banks' performance and risk. The most common indicators are stock market returns and the relative variability over a defined time interval. Some studies dealing with diversification effect (for example, Stiroh, 2006) propose a portfolio view of banking with interest and non-interest activities. For a financial firm engaged in two different businesses, A and B, standard portfolio theory suggests that expected return and its variance are the following:

$$E(R) = wE(R_A) + (1-w)E(R_B) \tag{6.3}$$

and

$$\sigma^2 = w^2\sigma_A^2 + (1-w)^2\sigma_B^2 + 2w(1-w)\sigma_{A,B} \tag{6.4}$$

where w is the amount invested in the A activity. So the effect of diversification on bank returns depends on the relative profitability of non-interest income activities with respect to traditional lending. The impact on risk derives from the volatility of the two components and also their degree of correlation.

Other studies consider the total volatility of equity returns to assess the effect of diversification on its systematic and idiosyncratic components. For example, with reference to a single index model, excess returns for the i-th bank are calculated as (for example, Baele et al., 2007):

$$R_{i,t} = \beta_{i,t} R_{m,t} + e_{i,t} \tag{6.5}$$

where R_m is the excess return of the market index.

The total variance of equity returns for the i-th bank is:

$$\sigma_{i,t}^2 = \beta_{i,t}^2 \sigma_{m,t}^2 + \sigma_{e,t}^2 \tag{6.6}$$

where the first and second terms represent, respectively, the systematic and the idiosyncratic components of risk.

Finally, some contributions try to assess if diversified institutions are evaluated at a premium or a discount, using the market to book value ratio or Tobin's q (for example, Laeven and Levine, 2007) calculated as:

$$Q_j = \frac{\begin{array}{c} market\_value\_common\_equity + book\_value \\ \_preferred\_shares + book\_value\_debt \end{array}}{book\_value\_assets} \tag{6.7}$$

In order to shed more light on the effect of functional diversification a good metric is the Excess Value, obtained as the difference between the effective Tobin's q of the j-th bank and the Tobin's q it would have if it was disentangled into several specialized institutions (adjusted Tobin's q):

$$AdjQ_j = \sum_{i=1}^{n} a_{ji} Q^i \tag{6.8}$$

where Q^i is the average Tobin's q for institutions specialized in the i-th activity and a_{ji} is the weight of the i-th activity in the j-th bank, in terms of asset or income (for example, Laeven and Levine, 2007; Elsas et al. 2010). The Excess Value can be also measured with respect to the firm market to book value ratio (and not the Tobin's q) and can be considered a direct measure of the market discount or premium due to bank diversification.

The remainder of this section summarizes the main findings of studies adopting the cited metrics to assess advantages and drawbacks of banks' engagement in non-traditional activities. This research stream, which initially dealt principally with US financial firms, has gradually extended to consider European and cross-country samples.

Investigating US publicly traded bank holding companies (hereafter, BHCs) over the period 1980–93 (with a sample ranging from 81 observations in 1993 to 134 in 1986), Demsetz and Strahan (1997) find a positive relationship between size and diversification. Large and diversified BHCs experienced a reduction in firm-specific risk, but in terms of total risk this advantage is offset by a lower capital ratio and the engagement in riskier activities, such as commercial and industrial loans (instead of real estate and consumer loans), trading, derivatives and foreign deposits. According to their results, diversification seems to produce not a risk reduction benefit, but a potential positive effect on profitability (given that riskier activities are generally more remunerative). These findings are consistent with Stiroh (2006), which examines equity market returns for a sample of 635 US BHCs over the period 1997–2004 (3,198 total year observations). Results provide evidence of similar returns for banking institutions significantly engaged in non-interest activities with respect to their more specialized competitors, but with a higher volatility. The author concludes that the shift towards non-interest income is probably due to internal agency problems or managerial incentives to expand into new businesses and that stakeholders should be concerned about the engagement in activities that do not appear more profitable, but are clearly more volatile. Extending the analysis not only to banks, but also to security firms and insurance companies, Schmid and Walter (2009) confirm the evidence in favour of the hypothesis that diversification destroys economic value in financial firms. The relationship between Excess Value and diversification is explored for a sample of 664 US financial firms over the period 1985–2004 (with about 4,000 total year observations). The evidence of a diversification discount is tested with the inclusion of several control variables and the use of an instrumental variables regression excludes that results are driven by a self-selection bias (that is, that the decision to diversify is taken by bad performers trying to improve their situation). Further analyses reveal two notable exceptions: combinations of commercial banks and insurance companies or investment banking activities, both exhibiting a significant valuation premium.

Laeven and Levine (2007) analyzing a sample of 836 large banks from 43 different countries over the period 1998–2002 (with a total of 3,415 year observations) find that financial conglomerates that engage in different activities have a lower market value than if they were broken into specialized institutions. The negative relationship between market value and diversification results from the regression of Tobin's q or Excess Value on asset and income diversity, controlling for year and country effects. The robustness of results is tested by including in the regression model some firm-specific variables (for example, market share), banking industry features (for example, CR3 ratio) and country factors (for example, GDP growth). Other robustness checks are carried out against endogeneity, to ensure that the discount is driven by diversification and not by other firm characteristics that make more likely the decision to diversify. The authors conclude that it is difficult to identify a single factor explaining the diversification discount, but their findings are consistent with theories that indicate how scope economies are not sufficiently large to compensate intensified agency problems in financial conglomerates.

Examining a sample of 143 European banks from 17 different countries (EU-15 area, Norway and Switzerland, for a total of 1,200 year observations) Baele et al. (2007) find quite different results with respect to Laeven and Levine (2007), in favour of a positive relationship between Tobin's q and the degree of functional diversification. It might be an indication that the stock market considers potential cost and revenue synergies able to exceed the disadvantage of increased complexity and the associated agency costs. However, the authors raise some cautions: on the risk side, findings provide evidence of a positive relationship between functional diversification and systematic risk, so that financial conglomerates, in the regulators' perspective, are entities needing to be carefully monitored. The relationship with idiosyncratic risk is non-linear: diversification seems to reduce firm-specific risk to a certain extent, but too much reliance on non-interest income can make the bank less safe. The existence of a positive relationship between Tobin's q and functional diversification is confirmed by De Jonghe and Vander Vennet (2008) in a study focused mainly on investigating the impact of efficiency and competition on banking firms' market value.

It is evident that studies assessing whether diversification creates or destroys value find quite mixed and contrasting evidence. Results appear also to be driven by the geography of the investigated samples: analyses dealing with US financial firms are in favour of a diversification discount (and also the cross-country analysis of Laeven and Levine

2007), while studies dealing with Europe show the opposite evidence of a diversification premium. In the opinion of Baele et al. (2007, page 2020) this geographic difference could be due to the fact that 'European banks have been able to operate broader franchises and establish longer track records'. A more recent study by Elsas et al. (2010) contributes to this debate, providing evidence on a cross-country sample of 380 large banks over the period 1996–2008, for a total of 3,348 year observations. The authors find robust evidence against a conglomerate discount, analyzing market to book value and a measure of profitability with respect to a very detailed measure of diversification, constructed in the logic of equation 2 and also distinguishing different sources of non-interest income (commission, trading and other). While the regression analysis does not provide evidence of a significant relationship between the market to book value and the functional diversification, diversification results to positively affect profitability without affecting the cost of equity in a systematic way. The evidence of this indirect value effect via bank profitability also appears to remain confirmed during the subprime crisis. It seems that the most recent contributions attempt a deep exploration of the financial conglomeration phenomenon, and also consider less evident relationships and the possible role of latent variables. In this direction, it is important to cite the study by Klein and Saidenberg (2010) finding that investors prefer simple organizational structures and penalize BHCs with many subsidiaries with respect to more compact and centralized institutions. Even though this analysis is not related to the expansion of bank focus, it is interesting in the debate, suggesting that the conglomeration discount often found in the literature may be due to the complexity of organizational structures and not to activity diversification.

This section ends with the discussion of van Lelyveld and Knot (2009), a paper that focuses specifically on bancassurance combinations, in contrast to previous studies which had treated the issue solely as an aside. The investigated sample includes the 45 financial conglomerates identified in the EU list published in 2006.[2] In the perspective of the EU regulator (see Directive 2002/87/EC), financial conglomerates are entities engaged in both banking/securities and insurance activities, so can be considered bancassurance combinations. These institutions are compared with specialized peers: the 45 largest EU banks (on the basis of total assets) and the 45 largest insurance companies (on the basis of gross premiums written). Accounting information is drawn from Bankscope and ISIS and stock prices from Datastream, with reference to the period 1990–2005. Given that most financial conglomerates do not decompose their accounting data by sector in their consolidated reporting, the authors separately consider individual data for the banking and the insurance components, even if they do not precisely sum up to the consolidated balance sheet. Excess Value is calculated with respect to the market to book value ratio, considering the weights of the banking and the insurance activities in terms of both total assets and total profits before taxes. This metric does not provide evidence of a structural conglomeration discount. Its average is not significantly far from zero, and there is a lot of volatility: about half of the sample shows a premium, while the other half does not. Three possible drivers of different market valuation are investigated:

- Size. The dimension of the financial conglomerate can be considered as a proxy for its degree of complexity. The regression analysis provides evidence that small conglomerates tend to experience a premium and the large ones a discount;
- Degree of mixedness. A fully mixed conglomerate, not having a main business, can be viewed as particularly opaque, a firm that is difficult to manage and to analyze. Empirical results, however, do not provide strong support to this hypothesis;
- Riskiness. As the risk decreases for diversification effect there is a value shift from shareholders to debt holders. Data confirm that this shift is priced, finding a positive relationship between risk (measured as the volatility of stock prices or as the firm leverage) and Excess Value.

Finally, the time trend is found to be positively related to Excess Value, signalling that over time investors may have become more familiar with the financial conglomerate business model. The authors comment that their results, in contrast with previous literature using similar methodologies, can be explained by sample composition, including recent data on bancassurance conglomerates. It is then probable that the combinations between banking and insurance are expected to produce more synergies than other types of financial conglomeration and that investors in the stock market have recently learned to appreciate diversified entities.

6.2.2   Studies using accounting data to assess the risk/return effects of diversification

A large number of studies conduct empirical analyses with the use of accounting data. These contributions generally adopt the ROE and

ROA standard measures of global performance while other profitability indicators, such as the gross margin or interest spreads, are considered less frequently. Risk is often defined as the volatility of the preferred performance measures (σ_{ROE} and σ_{ROA}), or as the coefficient of variation, that is the ratio between standard deviation of profitability and its mean. A compact evaluation based on risk-adjusted measures of performance is also quite common (that is, ROE/σ_{ROE} and ROA/σ_{ROA}). Finally, the probability of failure of a given institution can be proxied by the Z-score, calculated as:

$$Z\text{-}score = \frac{\overline{ROA + E/A}}{\sigma_{ROA}} \qquad (6.9)$$

where E/A is the ratio of equity to total assets. The Z-score indicates the number of standard deviations that profits must fall to lead the bank to insolvency. The higher the value the lower the probability of default.

A first set of contributions examine accounting data aggregated for a large sample of banks or at the entire industry level in order to assess the different risk profile of interest and non-interest activities. Recalling portfolio theory (see equation 6.4), the impact on risk depends on the relative volatility of the two revenue streams and their degree of correlation. As outlined in De Young and Roland (2001, page 56),

> The conventional wisdom among many bankers, bank regulators, and bank analysts is that fee-based earnings are more stable than loan-based earnings (because they believe that fee-based activities are less sensitive to movements in interest rates and to economic downturns), and that increasing the share of fee-based activities in a traditional portfolio of banking products reduces overall earnings volatility...

The authors raise some doubts about this view, for several reasons now briefly recalled. First of all, lending activities are based on the relationship banking model: switching and information costs make it difficult to change partner for both borrowers and lenders so that interest revenue tends to be relatively stable over time. On the other hand, in the fee-income-based business the level of competition is higher, the demand is more volatile and customers are not influenced by relevant information costs. In addition to this, once the relationship is established, an increase in the amount of loans leads to an increase only in interest expenses (variable costs) while the growth in fee-based income may require a shift in fixed costs (that is, additional personnel). Finally, the lack of regulatory capital requirements for fee-based business with respect to traditional lending can give incentive to operate with a higher financial leverage and thus higher earnings volatility.

Smith et al. (2003) examine a large set of 2,655 European banks, with accounting data available for the entire observed period, finding that the increase of non-interest income share in total operating income has been accompanied by an increase in variability. However, given that interest and non-interest income seem to have a negative correlation in several countries, non-interest income can still play a role in stabilizing banks' total operating revenues. Different results are found in Stiroh (2004) analyzing aggregate US banking industry data provided by the Federal Deposit Insurance Corporation (FDIC), on a quarterly frequency over the period 1984–2001. As in Smith et al. (2003), there is evidence of an increase in the share of non-interest income and in its volatility. In addition, US aggregate data also show a strong increase in the degree of correlation between the two revenue streams, probably due to the development of cross-selling policies. If different products are sold to the same customer base, interest and non-interest income may be exposed to the same shocks (that is, a worsening of financial conditions for certain firms or industries). Finally, observing the response to changes in GDP, the authors find only limited support for the idea that a shift towards non-interest income can reduce the cyclical nature of bank revenue.

An analysis of both return and risk effects of diversification is conducted by Verweire (1999) comparing financial conglomerates, defined as bancassurance combinations, against their more specialized competitors, both banks or insurance companies. The sample includes 125 total year observations for financial conglomerates, 473 for banks and 393 for insurance companies over the period 1992–96, located in Belgium and the Netherlands. The findings reveal that financial conglomerates are more profitable and stable than their specialized competitors, even if operating at a higher leverage. This result is substantially confirmed by additional analyses dealing with the banking and the insurance industries considered separately. To our knowledge, this is the only study based on a long-run comparison of accounting data and focusing on bancassurance. A large number of contributions is devoted to investigating the more general issue of bank diversification in non-traditional activities.

With regard to market data, studies relating diversification to accounting measures of performance and risk are not conclusively in favour or against the shift towards non-interest income. De Young and Rice (2004) analyze a large set of 4,712 US banks from 1989 to 2001 (with a total of 37,135 year observations) with a twofold objective: determine which bank characteristics drive diversification and what is the impact of diversification on performance and risk. The empirical analysis reveals that size is positively related to diversification, but well-managed banks rely more on traditional lending activities. Some financial and technological innovations (that is, cashless transactions and mutual funds) lead to an increase in fee-based income, while others (that is, mortgage securitization) have a negative impact on diversification from the lending business. The increase in non-interest income is found to be associated with both higher profitability and volatility. The net result is a worsening in the level of the attained risk-adjusted performance. Stiroh (2004) explores a huge sample of US banks over 1978 to 2000 (the number of observations ranges from 14,117 in 1979 to 8,110 in 2000), concluding that the share of non-interest income is negatively related to risk-adjusted performance and positively affects the probability of failure. Rumble and Stiroh (2006) analyze quarterly data over 1997–2002 for 1,816 US financial holding companies (hereafter, FHCs) confirming the 'dark side of diversification': diversification benefits are not large enough to compensate the effect of increased exposure to non-interest activities, which are more volatile but not more profitable than lending activities. So the shift towards fee-based business results in a decline in risk-adjusted profits. The absence of risk/return benefits for US diversified banks is also confirmed by Yaeger et al. (2007).

Different findings are outlined in Chiorazzo et al. (2008), analyzing a balanced panel data of 85 Italian banks over the period 1993–2003. The empirical investigation shows a positive relationship between the share of non-interest income and the risk-adjusted performance, also highlighting some differences between small and large banks: the former seem to gain diversification advantages only if they start with a low level of fee-based activities. Finally, the attained performance appears to be more influenced by the absolute value of non-interest income rather than by its composition. The authors make hypotheses to explain contrasting results for US and Italian banks. A possible reason is that larger institutions might be able to invest more resources in ICT and to better exploit scope economies: so the difference could be due to the relatively small size of US banks. Other possible explanations can be derived by some features of the EU banking industry: fee-based relationships appear quite stable and durable, even in the absence of relevant informational and switching costs; the low degree of cross-selling reduces the correlation between interest and non-interest income. Finally, it could also be that the shift towards fee-based business has been accompanied by a modernization process improving the performance of Italian banks, typically ICT-deficient with respect to the US.

Lepetit et al. (2008) investigate the risk implications of banking diversification using both market and accounting data in a sample of 734 European banks from 1996 to 2002. They find that banks with a higher share of non-interest income are riskier than their more specialized competitors. However, the negative effect of diversification is not universal, but depends on bank size and income composition. The analysis, in fact, also reveals that greater reliance on fee and commission income is associated with higher risk, but this is not always the case for trading income. For smaller banks, the engagement in trading activities can also imply a decrease in risk.

6.2.3   Studies testing the diversification hypothesis on synthetic M&As

The literature reviewed in the last two sections considers banking diversification as the shift from the lending business to activities generating non-interest income. Another way to test if diversification can improve the risk/return profile of banks is to analyze combinations with other financial firms, mainly security and insurance companies. In the past, especially in the US – where regulatory barriers to conglomeration fell in 1999 – the lack of available data on effective M&As has been a major drawback for empirical studies on conglomeration, leading researchers to examine synthetic combinations.

Contributions dealing with simulated M&As are reviewed very briefly, it being possible to find several more recent studies considering actual deals. The effect of simulated combinations can be estimated on the basis of market or accounting data. Among studies using market data, Allen and Jagtiani (2000) consider the effect of combining banking, securities and insurance activities on both total and systematic risk. Equity returns for the synthetic entity are constructed as a value-weighted average of equity returns for each component, on the basis of total assets. Total volatility is decomposed into its systematic and idiosyncratic components adopting a two-factor model accounting for both market and interest rate risk. Total risk appears to decline with the combination of banks with securities and insurance companies. However, both the components of systematic risk (market and interest rate factors) increase with the engagement in securities underwriting, while insurance does not impact significantly on market risk and reduces the exposure to interest rate risk. Using a different methodology based on an option pricing model, Estrella (2001) reaches similar conclusions, finding that mergers between banking institutions and life or P&C insurance companies are likely to experience diversification gains, while the high volatility of securities returns offset the effect of less than perfect correlation with banks.

Other studies looks at synthetic combinations of different financial firms using accounting data. Boyd et al. (1993)[3] examine the impact of diversification on risk (measured as the volatility of ROA) and probability of failure (using a Z-score measure). Findings provide evidence in favour of the engagement in life or P&C insurance activities, but not in securities underwriting, real estate and insurance brokerage. Their results are confirmed by Laderman (2000), using a very similar methodology. The author also carries on some portfolio simulations in order to derive optimal weights for the investment in several non-banking activities, showing that the weights minimizing the bankruptcy probability tend to be higher than those minimizing the variance of returns. In addition to this, weights calculated with the two different objectives lead to a different ranking of various businesses in which the bank can expand. Lown et al. (2000), investigating potential combinations between banks, insurers, real estate and security firms, obtain slightly different evidence for the US market: as in the studies previously cited, they conclude in favour of the combination between banking and life insurance industries, but they find P&C increasing the probability of failure, as in the case of securities.

It is possible to notice that studies examining simulated M&As between different financial firms achieve quite consistent results: they generally conclude in favour of banks' engagement in the insurance industry but not in securities underwriting. All of the cited authors agree in findings that evidence of risk diversification benefits for the combination of banking and life insurance activities, while contrasting results are highlighted for the P&C business.

As far as we are aware, there are only a few studies using the simulated M&As' methodology and dealing specifically with bancassurance combinations. With reference to the UK market, Genetay and Molyneux (1998) explore possible combinations between commercial banks, building societies and life insurers, both mutual or stock companies. Their sample includes 16 commercial banks, 66 building societies, 14 mutual life insurers and 27 proprietary life insurers over the period 1988–92.

Hypothetical combined entities are evaluated on the basis of risk and return accounting measures. In terms of risk reduction, the most attractive combinations are found to be those between building societies and mutual life insurers, leading to a significant risk reduction, accompanied by a less than proportional decrease in profits. The least attractive are mergers between building societies and proprietary life insurers, reducing returns and increasing their coefficient of variation, although not in a significant way. The combination of commercial banks with both types of insurance companies appears to lead to a return and risk reduction, but not statistically significant. A more recent contribution is the study of Nurullah and Staikouras (2008) dealing with a European sample considering 45 banks, 40 life insurers, 12 non-life insurers and 11 insurance brokers over the period 1990–99. Their analysis of the risk/return effects of bancassurance combinations is conducted on the basis of accounting data (return on asset, volatility of returns and Zeta score) distinguishing life, non-life underwriting and insurance broking. The pre-merger comparison among different industries reveals that non-life underwriting and insurance broking are both more profitable and riskier (in terms of ROA volatility) than the banking business, while life underwriting is not significantly different from banking. Regarding the probability of failure, all of the insurance activities result in greater exposure to bankruptcy than banking. In order to assess the effect of hypothetical M&As it is important to also account for correlation among the activities investigated, positive for insurance underwriting and negative for insurance broking, with different magnitude and level of statistical significance. The authors conclude that combinations of banking and insurance broking is a viable strategy, improving profitability without affecting risk. More caution has to be taken with banking engagement in life insurance underwriting that boosts both profitability and risk. The worst candidate for bancassurance combination is non-life insurance underwriting that increases risk without advantages in terms of profitability.

Finally, it is important to notice that, as outlined in Genetay and Molyneux (1998), the methodology based on simulated M&As does not account for either management ability to identify the best partners for bancassurance combinations or for the exploitation of cost and revenue synergies that may improve the risk/return profile of the combined entity, that is simply obtained as a sum of the two partners. Considering that the best partners could ask a merger premium that reduces overall benefits, this approach can be considered simple, but realistic, at least in providing a lower bound to diversification benefits.

6.3 Testing the scope economies hypothesis: potential efficiency gains of bank diversification in non-lending activities

While a large number of studies are devoted to assessing the risk reduction advantage of banking diversification into other financial activities, there are only a few studies trying to estimate the effect in terms of efficiency. This is quite surprising since cost and revenue synergies are commonly recognized as one of the main economic rationales for corporate diversification. As noted by Klein and Saidenberg (2000, p. 5),

Risk reduction is not a satisfactory efficiency rationale for diversification. At least in the case of publicly traded banks, shareholders can always reduce their risk by holding a diversified portfolio of non diversified banks, gaining the risk-reduction advantages of diversification without incurring the costs of managing a large organization. For this reason, diversification would be beneficial only if it provides some kind of economies of scope'.

For Allen and Jagtiani (2000, p. 496),

'It is important to point out, however, that risk diversification is only one of the reasons generally offered to justify integrating non-bank financial activities with banking. Our results suggest that this reason alone is insufficient to justify the creation of universal banks. Indeed, if there are net gains to universal banking, gains from synergies and demand effects must be powerful enough to overcome the disadvantages of increased systematic risk exposure documented in this paper'.

The estimation of (cost and revenue) scope economies, however, has always appeared as a quite problematic issue in the banking empirical literature. Scope economies occur when it is more economical to produce two (or more) products jointly in a single firm than in separated specialized units (Berger et al., 1987). The earlier definition of scope economies is referred to the cost side: synergies can arise from spreading fixed cost on a wider range of products or from cost complementaries. Cost complementaries between Y_1 and Y_2 occur when the marginal cost of Y_1 (or Y_2) decreases by increasing the production of Y_2 (or Y_1); cost complementaries between all product combinations are a sufficient, but not necessary, condition for the existence of scope economies.

From a theoretical point of view, it is very simple to understand how similar synergies can be realised in bancassurance combinations or in other diversified financial firms. From the cost side, we can think of the opportunity of (see for example Berger, 2001):

- sharing physical inputs (like offices or computers), staff costs and distribution net;
- employing common information systems, investment departments, account service centres;
- reusing managerial expertise or information;
- obtaining capital with larger issue size.

Berger et al. (1994) point out that scope economies can also arise from the revenue side. The idea is that a consumer could be willing to pay higher prices for one-stop banking, because of reductions in user transaction and search cost associated with consuming different financial services offered by the same provider, often at the same location. However, their empirical analysis does not find evidence of revenue scope economies between deposits and loans, over the period 1978–90, for both small and large banks. In their opinion 'this result for the provision of current banking services, where benefits are most likely to occur if they occur at all, is suggestive of similarly small synergies from an expansion of banking powers into new service areas' (Berger et al. 1994, p. 22).

The difficulty in detecting scope economies is not a peculiarity of bancassurance, but a problem concerning all financial industries: various studies find evidence of scope economies (Murray and White, 1984; Kim, 1986; Humphrey and Pulley, 1993), while others are not able to detect significant synergies (Berger et al. 1987; Hunter et al. 1990; Berger et al. 2000). Verweire (1999) observes that these results could depend on study fragmentation: most findings are taken from analyses dealing with scope economies within a single product category (for example, Berger, 2001), as deposits and loans for banks. In this case a major problem is to find real firms fully specialized, that have zero output for the other product(s), for example, banks that produce only deposits or loans in a mutually exclusive way. Studies dealing with scope economies in different product categories, as in bancassurance combinations, do not meet this problem; there are several econometric difficulties to solve. Parametric methods for the measurement of efficiency often use a translog specification for the cost function: being multiplicative in outputs, it has the unfortunate property of having a predicted cost of zero for each of the specialised firms, for example, $C(Y_1,0) = C(0,Y_2) = 0$ (Berger and Humphrey, 1994). So economies of scope cannot be easily calculated. As observed in Hughes and Mester (1993), replacing a null output with a small quantity arbitrarily chosen involves potentially excessive extrapolation outside the sample. A frequently applied solution is the definition of within the sample scope economies, in which the zero level of output is substituted with the minimum observed in the sample. In this way, it is possible to measure the increase (or decrease) in cost of dividing up the outputs into relatively specialized banks, 'but none more specialised than the most specialised bank in the sample' (Mester, 1996, p. 1032). Nevertheless, any finding of scope economies can be eliminated by setting the observed minimum sufficiently close to zero, that it mirrors exactly what happens in the case of a real specialised firm (Berger and Humphrey, 1994). Furthermore, the data available in bank financial statements do not always allow the isolation of the output produced thanks to the engagement in the insurance business. Generally, it is only possible to disentangle interest-based business from fee-based business where the latter includes insurance among various activities (for example, investment banking). As a consequence, the scope economies estimation using the available data would not enable researchers to establish whether bancassurance is a viable strategy for realizing cost and revenue synergies.

In addition, various empirical studies (Berger and Humphrey, 1994, 1997) show that both scale and scope economies are less important than management ability in combining production factors, the so-called X-efficiency. As suggested by Cummins et al. (2003), X-efficiency can also provide indirect evidence for the existence of scope economies, if diversified firms significantly outperform specialized ones.

With reference to the bancassurance phenomenon, existing studies using frontier methodologies to estimate X-efficiency have adopted the banking or the insurance points of view in a mutually exclusive way.

From the banking side we find only a handful of studies dealing specifically with efficiency gains from diversification. Allen and Rai (1996) adopt a stochastic frontier approach to examine cost efficiency of banks during the period 1988–92, for a sample of 15 different countries. They analyze two groups of countries: universal banking countries that allow the integration between traditional and investment banking and separated banking countries that do not. The authors also account for size effects, finding that large banks in separated banking countries have the largest measure of input inefficiency. Vander Vennet (2002) uses a parametric methodology in order to measure cost and profit efficiency in European banks in 1995–96: his results show that financial conglomerates are more revenue efficient than specialised banks and that universal banks are more efficient on both the cost and revenue sides. Casu and Girardone (2004) use both statistical and mathematical approaches to measure the efficiency of Italian financial conglomerates between 1996 and 1999 and find evidence of an increase in profit efficiency.

It is important to underline that all these studies adopt a definition of banking diversification that is different from the concept of bancassurance: Allen and Rai (1996) study universal banking intended as a combination of traditional and investment banking; Vander Vennet (2002) analyses financial conglomerates defined as combinations between traditional and investment banking or insurance; Casu and Girardone (2004) consider as financial conglomerates all Italian banking groups, following the idea that they generally experienced a trend towards conglomeration during the observed period.

From the insurance side, despite the existence of a quite extensive efficiency literature, we can find only a few studies using frontier methodologies and dealing with the bancassurance phenomenon (Hwang and Gao, 2005; Barros et al. 2006).

Hwang and Gao (2005) analyze life insurance companies operating in the Irish market, measuring cost efficiency during the period 1991–2000 with a stochastic frontier approach. The efficiency scores obtained are then regressed on a set of covariates in order to detect the main drivers of performance. The authors conclude that size, market share and a dummy indicating bancassurance companies are all positively related to cost efficiency in a statistically significant way. The adopted operational definition of bancassurance is 'the distribution of insurance products by banks': consequently, bancassurance firms are those 'centred on selling insurance through the established distribution channels of their associated banks'. The criterion used appears only related to the distribution system, while banks' presence in the ownership structure of insurance companies is not explicitly considered.

Barros et al. (2006) use a stochastic frontier approach in order to measure cost efficiency in the Portuguese life insurance industry, during the period 1995–2003. Instead of following a two-stage approach, two dummies are included directly in the deterministic kernel of the frontier: in this way the authors distinguish between foreign- and Portuguese-owned companies and between those companies belonging to banking groups and those not bank-owned. Results show that the bancassurance dummy is positively related to cost efficiency, even if not statistically significant. In this case the bancassurance phenomenon is considered only from an ownership perspective; there is a failure to recognize that equity links with banking institutions are not the only way to access their branches to distribute insurance.

It is possible to find other recent studies dealing with the relationship between life insurance efficiency and the use of different distribution systems, but bancassurance is completely ignored (for example, Klumpes, 2004) or considered as a possible, marginal alternative for insurance companies using different channels (for example, Trigo-Gamarra, 2007). This is probably due to the fact that these studies deal with the UK and Germany, countries in which bancassurance is not as common as in France or Italy (see Chapter 3).

6.4 The market reaction to the announcement of regulatory changes removing barriers among different sectors of the financial services industry

In the US, the passage in 1999 of the Gramm–Leach–Bliley Act (hereafter, GLBA) was a fundamental event for the financial services industry, removing existing barriers between banking, security underwriting and insurance. Many authors have tried to estimate the market reaction to the new opportunities and challenges deriving from this crucial legislative innovation. Under the *synergies hypothesis*, financial firms are expected to have a positive reaction to the admission into previously forbidden activities because investors value the possibility of realizing cost and revenue economies and exploiting cross-selling opportunities. On the other hand, the *increased competition hypothesis* predicts a negative reaction, because all industries face the threat of new entrants in their market. In addition, the *takeover hypothesis* expects the most likely targets to experience positive stock returns. All of the following contributions use an event study methodology to estimate the market reaction to the relevant announcement; generally, the abnormal returns obtained are then regressed on a set of covariates in order to detect which are the main drivers of value creation or destruction.

The effect of the GLBA was partially anticipated by the bancassurance megamerger between the bank Citicorp and the insurer Travelers Group. Johnston and Madura (2000) assess the announcement effect on several categories of financial firms – large and medium-sized banks, insurance companies and brokerage firms – finding a general positive wealth reaction, especially for large institutions. For our aims, studies examining the market reaction to this megamerger are particularly interesting when dealing specifically with the banking and the insurance industries. Carow (2001a) explores a US sample of 133 national banks, 117 state banks, 30 life, 26 health and 67 P&C insurance companies. Larger banks and life insurance companies experience positive abnormal returns, while health and P&C insurance companies do not show a significant reaction. In the opinion of the authors, the lack of negative returns for any segment is an indication that the Citicorp Travelers merger does not generate a mere wealth transfer, but real value creation. This means that investors expect the removal of regulatory barriers to produce benefits able to offset the negative effects of increased competition. Benefits are supposed to derive from implicit government guarantees for 'too-big-to-fail' organizations or from the exploitation of scope economies. In a second paper (Carow, 2001b), the author observes market reaction to the Office of the Comptroller of Currency (OCC) and Supreme Court rulings preceding the GLBA and removing some barriers between the banking and the insurance industries: all banks are allowed to distribute annuities and those based in small towns (with less than 5,000 inhabitants) can sell all types of insurance policies to customers located everywhere. An event study conducted over a sample of 89 banks and 44 insurance companies reveals that the former do not experience a significant market reaction while the latter register negative abnormal returns.[4] This result is consistent with the contestable market theory supposing that the removal of entry barriers leads to an increase in price competition that decreases the firm value of incumbents without affecting those of the potential new entrants (not expected to gain economic profits in the long run). Customers may be the only economic agents gaining a persistent advantage, but the potential price reduction due to increased competition is not estimated.

Regarding the passage of the GLBA, it is possible to find both studies investigating all types of financial firms and also contributions focusing on the reaction in a specific industry (for example, banking or insurance). Akhigbe and Whyte (2001) estimate the reaction of stock prices to the passage of the GBLA in large and medium-sized banks, brokerage firms and insurance companies, finding positive and significant abnormal returns. A regression model including the natural log of total assets and the equity to asset ratio as independent variables show different results for financial firms belonging to the three industries: with reference to banks, large and well-capitalized institutions are expected to be those able to gain more benefits from diversification opportunities. Brokerage firms experience positive returns regardless of size and appear penalized for holding excessive capital. Finally, value creation in insurance companies does not results affected by size and leverage.

Hendershott et al. (2002) obtain positive abnormal returns for all the investigated industries, relevant in investment firms and insurance companies and limited for commercial banks, that had already experienced some de facto deregulation before the passage of the GLBA. Size is found to have a positive relationship with returns, irrespective of the industry.

Carow and Heron (2002) show a positive wealth effect for large investment banks and insurance companies, while for commercial banks there are no significant abnormal returns. This result can be attributed to the fact that large banks had been enabled to engage in different financial activities by several regulatory decisions and court rulings prior to the passage of the GBLA. In addition, thrifts, finance companies and foreign banks are found to experience negative abnormal returns.

Mamun et al. (2005) focus on the effect of the GLBA passage for the banking industry and they conclude that there was a positive market reaction largely explained by a reduction in the level of systemic risk. Larger banks and banks already engaged in securities underwriting through Section 20 subsidiaries appear to have an advantage with respect to their competitors. Findings regarding the impact of banks' profitability on abnormal returns are not conclusive.

Neale and Peterson (2005) concentrate their analysis on the insurance industry, distinguishing the impact of the GLBA on life, P&C and accident and health (A&H) companies. The passage of the act is associated with positive returns, especially for life and P&C companies providing products more suitable for distribution by bank branches, while A&H insurance is structurally and legally more complicated with less standardized policies.

The analysis of Yildirim et al. (2006) examines the impact of the GLBA passage on commercial banks, investment banks and insurance companies. Commercial banks are not found to experience significant and positive abnormal returns. The authors advance two alternative hypotheses to explain this result: potential cost and revenue synergies from diversification are expected to be offset by an increase in competition, or stock prices have anticipated the effect of the GLBA, given that barriers between different sectors of the financial services industry had long been largely abolished by market practices and technology innovation. The prior engagement in securities underwriting through a Section 20 subsidiary does not result in any advantage. Positive abnormal returns are found for investment banks and insurance companies that are probably perceived as firms having a higher probability of being targets (while bank are expected to be bidders). Splitting the insurance portfolio in life, P&C and multi-line companies does not seem to significantly affect the results.

Empirical findings from event studies dealing with the announcement of the GLBA (or prior events anticipating it) seem to provide support for the synergy and takeover hypothesis, less for the increased competition theory. There are only few authors reporting negative and significant abnormal returns. Commercial banks are generally found to experience positive reactions, signalling that investors expect the realization of synergies, or no significant reaction, attributed to market practices and ruling anticipating the effect of the GLBA. Insurance companies (and security firms) generally benefit from positive wealth creation because of expected synergies or their quality of likely targets.

6.5   The market reaction to the announcement of actual bancassurance M&As

Even though it is possible to find a very extensive literature dealing with the wealth effect of banking M&As, up to ten years ago bancassurance deals were very uncommon. For example, Cybo-Ottone and Murgia (2000) in their analysis of European M&As over the period 1988–97 find only ten bancassurance deals, resulting in positive combined abnormal returns. Other studies have investigated the results of banking M&As depending on activity and/or geographic focus (for example, DeLong, 2001; Lepetit et al., 2004). Only in the last ten years researchers have had the opportunity to observe authentic bancassurance M&As both in Europe and in the USA.

Fields et al. (2007a) assess if bancassurance M&As produce positive wealth gain for the participants and whether these gains are associated with cost and revenue synergies. They explore a sample of 129 deals over the period 1997–2002, involving both European and US firms. When the deal is concluded between publicly traded firms, both the bidder and the target experience positive abnormal returns; when the target is a private company, market reaction for the bidder is found to be insignificant. A possible explanation is that most private targets are small US insurance agencies, probably not expected to be able to produce relevant synergies. Restricting the sample to deals involving only listed institutions, a univariate analysis examines the relationship with different variables: size and ROA of the bidder, ROA of the target, relative size of the target to the bidder in terms of total asset or market capitalization (as a proxy for potential scale economies) and scope economies calculated as:

$$SCOPE = \frac{(FIRM_1 + FIRM_2) - COMBINED}{COMBINED} \qquad (6.10)$$

where $FIRM_1$ and $FIRM_2$ are pre-merger values of cost and COMBINED is the after-merger value. A similar method is also applied to revenues and profits. Results show that larger and more profitable bidders are expected to create more value for their shareholders. A positive relationship with market reaction is also found for target's profitability, scale and revenue scope economies. Further investigation shows the absence of significant impact for a measure of geographic diversification, change in risk and deal characteristics (as the percentage of equity acquired and the method of payments). A multivariate regression analysis confirms this finding, also revealing a positive role for geographic diversification and a negative influence of the change in beta (systematic risk).

In a second study, Fields et al. (2007b) analyze bancassurance M&As considering the effect of some corporate governance factors:[5]

- ownership structure: managerial stockholding can be an instrument to align managers' and shareholders' interests and so to increase firm value. But at some point, the relationship can become negative, because excessive managerial entrenchment results in a low probability of takeover and, consequently, in less market discipline. Affiliated blockholding (tied to managers) can have the same effect as managerial ownership, while unaffiliated blockholding can play a positive role thanks to the ability of monitoring the behaviour of managers;
- size and composition of the board of directors: the effectiveness of strategy and decision making can be influenced by the number of directors and by their degree of independence. Directors are classified as insider if they have direct ties to the firm (for example, managers or their relatives, former employees), grey if they have some relationships that could reduce their impartiality (for example, lawyers or consultants collaborating with the firm) and outsider if they do not have relevant ties;
- executive compensation, in terms of both absolute size and relative weight of the incentive-based component.

The only corporate governance variable found to be significant in explaining bidder abnormal returns in bancassurance M&As is CEO ownership: it presents a negative coefficient, meaning that investors judge as more successful acquisitions decided by non-entrenched CEOs.

Staikouras (2009) investigates 51 multinational bancassurance deals over the period 1990–2006, also offering a comparison with a control sample of ten corporate events in which at least one participant is a bank or an insurer. Bancassurance appears to receive a positive market valuation, in contrast with the control sample, experiencing negative abnormal returns. If banking and insurance bidders are separately examined, a strong difference emerges: abnormal returns are positive and significant for bank-bidders, negative and significant for insurance-bidders. The author explains this result in terms of the stronger brand names of banks, which have a trust relationship with their customers that is as yet undeveloped in the insurance industry. It is therefore probable that banks' shareholders expect significant synergies from bancassurance while insurance shareholders are worried about banks' entrance into their business. A cross-section analysis provides evidence of a positive relationship between wealth creation and bidder profitability and relative size of the target, while the ratio of non-interest income to total operating income shows a negative impact. The evidence in favour of bancassurance is reinforced by the finding of a negative reaction to bank–insurance sell-offs, indicating that financial markets do not support bank withdrawals from hybrid entities.

The recent study of Chen and Tan (2011) sheds additional light on the wealth and risk effects of bancassurance M&As. The authors examine a sample of 72 deals over 1989–2004, in which the bidder is a European bank and the target is an insurance company (located in Europe in 61 cases, in other countries for the remaining 11). First of all, the post-merger risk profile of acquirers is examined with reference to a world market index, a home market index and a banking home index, finding no significant changes. Possible bancassurance M&A effects are also analyzed with reference to the systematic risk component. With respect to the world market index there are no significant shifts. For the entire sample there is an increase in the beta relative to the home market index, not confirmed when results are taken separately for domestic and cross-country deals. Only domestic deals are found to produce a reduction in the home banking index beta. When part of the income comes from the insurance business, a reduction in the covariance with the home banking index is expected; on a theoretical basis, if the insurer operates in another country this reduction should be even larger, but this is not supported by empirical findings. On the wealth side, bancassurance M&As show positive abnormal returns for bank bidders engaged in domestic deals, and no significant stock price reaction for those involved in cross-country operations. A regression analysis reveals that deal size and previous bidder experience in M&As operations have a positive relationship with shareholders value creation.

6.6 Other studies dealing with the bancassurance phenomenon

This section discusses some recent studies that have focused specifically on bancassurance, adopting a methodology and/or a perspective different from those analyzed in previous sections.

Okeahalam (2008) examines cost and income information at the individual customer level, obtaining data from leading banking and insurance companies in South Africa over the period 1999–2004. A regression analysis models the price of financial products – present in the database – as a function of different variables, including the number of products packaged in the bundle, a bancassurance dummy and some proxies for the intensity of demand and competition. Findings show that bancassurance reduces the price of financial services included in the bundle. One of the tested hypotheses is that if the point-of-sale and the delivery firm have cross-holdings, and so already cooperate, the price reduction effect of bancassurance is less significant. Empirical findings seem to support this idea: in the case of independent firms, bancassurance reduces service fees by about 6 per cent, while in the case of existing cross-holdings the reduction is only about 2 per cent. At the same time, if there is already a bancassurance arrangement in place, potential synergies deriving from a cross-holding may be less relevant. Results show that cross-holdings without previous bancassurance arrangements reduce prices by about 4.5 per cent, while in case of bancassurance already in place the impact is less than 1 per cent. The author observes that (page 157) 'The results could also imply that to some extent, bancassurance and cross-holdings are substitutes. Firms with cross-holdings will likely pursue bancassurance, although bancassurance may not necessarily lead to cross-holdings. Cross-holdings would be an expensive method of achieving bancassurance'.

Chen et al. (2009) investigate the main determinants of bancassurance in a sample of 71 banks engaged in insurance activities, operating in 28 different countries over the period 1999–2003. The dependent variable of their regression analysis is the percentage of banks' total income deriving from insurance premiums. Regressors can be grouped in three different categories:

- a set of bank-specific factors, relative to size, risk (measured as the standard deviation of daily share prices on an annual basis), efficiency (measured as the annual percentage change in the cost–income ratio), profitability (measured as the annual percentage change of revenues to total assets);
- dimension and competitiveness of the industry;
- macroeconomic conditions of the country (per capita GNI and inflation rate).

Results show that size, efficiency and profitability positively affect bancassurance, while there is an inverse relationship with company risk. Competitiveness also has a positive relationship with banks' engagement in the insurance industry while economic development does not seem to have a significant effect. Finally, inflation has a positive net impact (so it seems that the negative effect on customer demand for saving products is more than offset by the benefit for firms in terms of lower value of their liabilities).

The study of Lorent (2010) aims at identifying the main determinants of life insurance consumption in 90 different countries, with reference to the year 2005. The author includes a large list of explanatory variables, found to be significant in previous analyses, such as social factors (for example, social security expenditure as a percentage of GDP), economic factors (for example, per capita GDP, inflation rate, real investment rate, financial development), demographic factors (religion, old and young dependency ratios, life expectancy, education), institutional and legal indicators. The innovative contribution to the existing literature is given by the inclusion of other variables, accounting for the relationship between the banking and the insurance industries. Results provide evidence that two of these factors play a significant role in determining the level of life insurance consumption. The first is *bancassurance*, indicating whether the financial regulation applied in the country allows banks to engage in the insurance business. From a theoretical point of view, the author has no specific expectation regarding the sign of this coefficient: it could be that bancassurance companies are able to exploit scale and scope economies, resulting in more efficient provision of life policies, or that specialized insurers have a better knowledge of the market and customer needs. In addition to this, mixed companies could have the disadvantage of being large, complex and opaque institutions.

Empirical findings are in favour of the second hypothesis, showing that life insurance consumption is lower in countries allowing for the combinations of the banking and the insurance industries. Consistently, the bank zeta score also appears to be negatively related to life insurance demand. A higher ratio of the score means a low probability of default, and so higher customers' confidence in the banking system. Another way to look at this ratio is to consider that it increases with profitability. This may lead to greater competition in the financial services industry and to the substitution of life insurance policies with banking savings products.

6.7   Conclusions

The aim of this final section is to highlight the state of the art and future perspectives for empirical research into bancassurance. Before proceeding to this, it is important to mention some other studies that deal with the selection of the best organizational structure for the combination of banking and insurance activities. These contributions are based on multiple criteria decision-making problems (MCDM), solved with the Analytic Hierarchy Process (AHP) introduced by Saaty (1980). The AHP is a method for modelling the choice among different alternatives (for example, bancassurance organizational structures) on the basis of several criteria. A panel of interviews is conducted in order to assess the mutual importance of the criteria and evaluate each alternative in terms of these criteria. Finally, the AHP is applied to synthesize all responses in only one scale to obtain a global ranking of possible alternatives.

Korhonen and Voutilainen (2006) compare alternative structures of financial alliance between the banking and insurance industries:[6] simple cross-selling agreements, alliances of independent partners (that are cross-selling agreements reinforced by cross-ownership or joint ownership of third parties) and control by ownership (when a bank controls an insurance company, or vice versa, and when the same holding company controls both banks and insurance companies). The study adopts the standpoint of Finnish top managers, asked to evaluate each alternative on the basis of the following nine different criteria: maximize the efficiency of product development; implement the one-door principle; compromise possibly conflicting earnings logics as well as possible; maximize the efficiency of customer relationship management; optimize cost and revenue synergies; minimize channel conflicts; optimize required solvency capital; maximize investor power and, finally, maximize the efficiency of sales management. Results show that, from a managerial point of view, one of the most important criteria is the exploitation of cost and revenue synergies and that control by ownership is the favourite model. However, the authors also outline that this model is not always feasible for smaller institutions, such as local banks and mutual insurers. In addition to this, risk-averse managers seem to prefer cross-selling agreements or alliances between independent partners. Similar results are obtained by Lin et al. (2009) with reference to the Taiwan market.

In a second paper, Korhonen et al. (2006a) investigate the same bancassurance alliances, interviewing a panel of experts from the Finnish supervisory authorities. The different standpoint, with respect to top managers in banking and insurance, is quite evident looking at the criteria that emerged for the comparison: the equality of the member companies of the alliance; system risk management;the capability of the authorities to supervise the alliance as well as possible; the flexibility of the alliance with respect to changes in its environment; the optimal functioning of insurance and finance markets; synergies brought about by the alliance; the sufficiency of capital and dependency of the alliance on the competence of the executive management. It is clear that supervisors pay more attention than top managers to risk and capital adequacy issues. Consistent with their view, supervisors seem to prefer cross-selling agreements and alliances between independent partners, considering control by ownership models to be too complex and opaque. Nevertheless, financial conglomerates may be a compromise solution if risk management and transparency are improved as a consequence of new legislation and stronger collaboration among authorities charged with supervision in different sectors of the financial services industry.

In a third paper, Korhonen et al. (2006b) explore the client perspective, interviewing a panel of experts from Finnish customers and labour market organizations. As expected, comparison criteria are different from those chosen by top managers and regulators, resulting in the following: equal treatment of customers, sustainability and reliability of the operations, transparency and comparability of the products, understandable division of risks between a customer and the financial corporation, system risk management, economies of scale and availability of services. The point of view of customers, preferring softer forms of integration, is more similar to that of supervisors than to that of top managers. Once again, financial conglomerates seem able to represent a compromise solution if transparency and comparability of products are improved.

These contributions are based on interviews and reflect opinions from different categories of stakeholders, not supported by an analysis of actual risk and return performance in different bancassurance organizational models. In addition to this, they deal with the specific case of the Finnish (or Taiwanese) financial services industry, so that it is difficult to extend their conclusions to other countries.

In order to identify some directions for future research, the results of all studies specifically focusing on bancassurance and cited in previous sections are summarized in Table 6.1. Apart from some exceptions, findings seem to be conclusive as in favour of the combination of banking and insurance activities, especially with respect to life business or to insurance broking. Results are less positive about the engagement in the P&C or A&H businesses that undoubtedly have less complementaries and similarities with commercial banking. Studies based on hypothetical M&As generally provide evidence of an improvement in the risk/return profile of the synthetic combined entity compared to the involved parties prior to the merger. Capital markets usually show a positive reaction to the announcement of bancassurance M&As or to the passage of new legislation removing existing barriers between different sectors of the financial services industry. In addition to this, bancassurance combinations are not subject to the conglomeration discount hypothesized by a large part of corporate diversification theory. This evidence is even more positive if we consider that it contrasts with the more general literature dealing with banking diversification, often finding that the shift towards non-traditional lending activities has more drawbacks than advantages for banks. However, it is important to highlight some limitations of these studies. In contributions that are based on simulated M&As the risk/return profile of the resulting combined entities is obtained applying the portfolio theory that considers the relative profitability and volatility of the banking and the insurance industries stand alone and their correlation. What is left aside are all the potential positive and negative effects deriving from actually mixing two businesses in a new larger institution: are the cost and revenue scope economies significant enough to offset the increased organizational complexity, the possible conflicts of interest and the agency costs? The fact that there is no direct observation of a real combined entity prevents giving an answer. Other empirical analyses dealing with bancassurance adopt the event study methodology. Event studies are able to measure, under some assumptions, shareholders' value creation due to stock price reactions. This means that a short-run perspective is adopted and no indications are provided relative to the

Table 6.1 Empirical studies providing quantitative findings on the bancassurance phenomenon

YEAR	AUTHORS	METHODOLOGY	SAMPLE	MAIN RESULTS
1998	Genetay and Molyneux	Accounting data. Hypothetical bancassurance combinations are evaluated on the basis of return (ROA) and risk measures (standard deviation and coefficient of variation of ROA, Z-score)	UK sample. 16 commercial banks, 66 building societies, 14 mutual and 27 proprietary life insurers over 1988–1992	From a risk/return perspective, combinations between building societies and mutual life insurers are preferable to those with proprietary life insurers. The mergers of commercial banks with both types of insurance companies appear to lead to a risk reduction, but not statistically significant
1999	Verweire	Accounting data. Performance comparison among financial conglomerates and their specialized competitors, both banks and insurance companies	Belgian and Dutch sample. Unbalanced panel of 125 year obs for FCs, 473 for banks and 393 for insurers over 1992–1996	Financial conglomerates are more profitable and stable than their specialized competitors, even if operating at a higher leverage
2001a	Carow	Market data. An event study is conducted to estimate stock price reaction to the Citicorp-Travelers merger in both the banking and the insurance industry	US sample. 133 national banks, 117 state banks, 30 life, 26 health and 67 P&C insurance companies. Different event windows	Larger banks and life insurance companies experience positive abnormal returns, while A&H and P&C insurance companies do not show a significant reaction
2001b	Carow	Market data. An event study is conducted to estimate stock price reaction to OCC and Supreme Court rulings removing some barriers between the banking and the insurance industry	US sample. 89 banks and 44 insurance companies. Different event windows	Insurance companies experience negative abnormal returns, while banks do not register a significant market reaction

(continued)

2005	Hwang and Gao	Accounting data. Stochastic Frontier Analysis is applied to estimate cost efficiency of life insurance companies. Bancassurance is defined as the distribution of policies through bank branches	Irish sample. 10 life insurance companies over 1991–2000	The dummy indicating the distribution of insurance policies by bank branches is positively related to cost efficiency and the coefficient is statistically significant
2006	Barros et al.	Accounting data. Stochastic Frontier Analysis is applied to estimate cost efficiency of life insurance companies. Bancassurance is defined as equity links between banks and insurance companies	Portuguese sample. 14 life insurance companies over 1995–2003	The dummy indicating the ownership by a bank institution is positively related to cost efficiency, but the coefficient is not statistically significant
2007a	Fields et al.	Market data. An event study is conducted in order to estimate stock price reaction to bancassurance M&As	International sample. 129 bancassurance deals over 1997–2002	When the deal involves listed institutions, both the bidder and the target experience positive abnormal returns. Value creation is positively related to size, profitability and potential scale and scope economies
2007b	Fields et al.	Market data. An event study is conducted in order to estimate stock price reaction to bancassurance M&As. The role of several corporate governance factors is estimated	International sample. 129 bancassurance deals over 1997–2002. Only US bidders for corporate governance data	The only corporate governance variable found to be significant in explaining bidder abnormal returns is CEO ownership, with a negative coefficient, meaning that investors prefer acquisitions decided by non-entrenched CEOs

Table 6.1 Continued

YEAR	AUTHORS	METHODOLOGY	SAMPLE	MAIN RESULTS
2008	Nurullah and Staikouras	Accounting data. Hypothetical bancassurance combinations are evaluated on the basis of return (ROA) and risk measures (standard deviation of ROA, Z-score)	European sample. 45 banks, 40 life insurers, 12 non-life insurers and 11 insurance brokers over 1990–1999	Combinations of banking and insurance broking improve profitability without affecting risk. Banks' engagement in life insurance underwriting boosts both profitability and risk. Combinations of banking and non life insurance underwriting increase risk without advantages on profitability
2008	Okeahalam	Price information. Assessment of the effect of bancassurance on the price of financial products	South African sample. More than 11,000 customers records over 1999–2004	Bancassurance reduces the price of bundled financial products. The positive effect on customers is more relevant when there are no previous cross-holdings
2009	van Lelyveld and Knot	Market data. Comparison of the market to book value ratio and excess value between specialized competitors and financial conglomerates	EU sample. 45 FCS, 45 large banks and 45 large insurance companies over 1990–2005	No evidence of universal diversification discount. The eventual discount is driven by size, risk and more or less familiarity with the financial conglomerate business model

2009	Staikouras	Market data. An event study is conducted in order to estimate stock price reaction to bancassurance M&As. The role of several corporate governance factors is estimated	International sample. 51 bancassurance deals over 1990–2006	Bancassurance deals experience a positive value creation while the market show a negative reaction to bank-insurance sell-offs. If banking and insurance bidders are separately examined, a strong difference emerges: abnormal returns are positive and significant for bank-bidders, negative and significant for insurance-bidders
2009	Chen et al.	Accounting data. The percentage of banks' total income deriving from insurance is measured as a function of different firm specific factors, banking industry and macroeconomic variables	International sample. 71 banks engaged in insurance over 1999–2003	Results show that bank size, efficiency, competition and profitability are directly related to bancassurance, also accompanied by a reduction in risk
2010	Lorent	Macroeconomic and financial industry data. Assessment of the bancassurance impact on the consumption of life insurance	International sample. 90 different countries in 2005	Life insurance consumption is lower in countries where bancassurance is allowed and where banks are more profitable and less risky
2011	Chen and Tan	Market data. Event study of bancassurance M&As. Risk profile of entities resulting from bancassurance M&A is evaluated with reference to a world market index, a home market index and a banking home index	European sample. 72 bancassurance deals in which the bidder is a European bank over 1989–2004	Positive abnormal returns for bidder banks engaged in domestic deals, and no significant reaction for cross country operations. No significant risk change with respect to the world market index. Reduction in the home banking index beta only for domestic deals

effective performance attained by bancassurance combinations in the long run. If a bancassurance deal registers positive cumulative abnormal returns it is possible to affirm that investors expect the combined entity to have a better risk/return profile of the involved parties before the merger or to exploit relevant cost and revenue synergies boosting efficiency and productivity, but this does not guarantee that this will be the case.

The only way to assess if bancassurance is a viable business model for financial firms is to consider its performance in the long run, compared to more specialized competitors. Studies adopting a long-run perspective are also needed to shed more light on the key issue of cost and revenue synergies. The efficiency issue, in fact, is particularly poorly investigated, probably due to difficulties in detecting and measuring revenue and cost scope economies. A possible solution may be represented by the investigation of X-efficiency, as outlined in section 6.3. If bancassurance combinations are found to systematically overperform their specialized banking and insurance competitors, from the point of view of either costs or profits, then it is possible to deduce that there are positive synergies offsetting eventual diseconomies due to large size and complexity. Further research on bancassurance performance in the long run is also necessary to assess performance differences among several organizational models. It is likely that there is no best bancassurance model, but that the success of different forms of cooperation depends strongly on the features of the subjects involved, the characteristics of the national financial services industry and also on the institutional and economic framework of the country under investigation.

Notes

1. For a detailed and comprehensive review of previous bancassurance literature, see Genetay and Molyneux (1998).
2. Filters for data availability reduces the number of observed financial conglomerates to 29.
3. Boyd et al. (1993) use also market data with substantially similar results.
4. Brokerage insurance firms experience positive abnormal returns. This can be explained by the fact that banks are only allowed to sell insurance policies and brokerage firms are the most likely bank partner for underwriting.
5. Corporate governance information is available only for US bidders.
6. A more detailed description of possible models for the alliance between the banking and the insurance industries can be found in Voutilainen (2005).

References

Akhigbe, A. and A.M. Whyte (2001) 'The Market's Assessment of the Financial Services Modernization Act of 1999', *The Financial Review*, XXXVI, 4, 119–38.

Allen, L. and J. Jagtiani (2000) 'The Risk Effects of Combining Banking, Securities, and Insurance Activities', *Journal of Economics and Business*, LII, 6, 485–97.

Allen, L. and A. Rai (1996) 'Operational Efficiency in Banking: an International Comparison', *Journal of Banking & Finance*, XX, 4, 655–72.

Baele, L., O. De Jonghe and R. Vander Vennet (2007) 'Does the Stock Market Value Bank Diversification?', *Journal of Banking & Finance*, XXXI, 7, 1999–2023.

Barros, C.B., N. Barroso and M.R. Borges (2006) 'Measuring Efficiency in the Life Insurance Industry with a Stochastic Frontier Model', paper presented at the 28th International Congress of Actuaries, May 28–June 2, in Paris, France.

Berger, A. (2001) 'The Integration of the Financial Services Industry: Where are the Efficiencies?', *North American Actuarial Journal*, IV, 3, 25–52.

Berger, A., D. Cummins., M. Weiss and H. Zi (2000), 'Conglomeration versus Strategic Focus: Evidence from the Insurance Industry', *Journal of Financial Intermediation*, IX, 4, 323–62.

Berger, A., G. Hanweck and D. Humphrey (1987), 'Competitive Viability in Banking: Scale, Scope, and Product Mix Economies', Research Papers in Banking and Financial Economics from Board of Governors of the Federal Reserve System (U.S.), no. 82.

Berger, A. and D. Humphrey (1997) 'Efficiency of Financial Institutions: International Survey and Direction for Future Research', Board of Governors of the Federal Reserve System, Finance and Economics Discussion Series, no. 97-11.

Berger, A. and D. Humphrey (1994) 'Bank Scale Economies, Mergers, Concentration, and Efficiency: the US Experience', Wharton School Centre for Financial Institutions, University of Pennsylvania, working paper no. 94-25.

Berger, A., D. Humphrey and L. Pulley (1994) 'Do Consumers Pay for One Stop Banking? Evidence from a Non Standard Revenue Function' Board of Governors of the Federal Reserve System, Finance and Economics Discussion Series, no. 93-30.

Boyd, J.H., S.L. Graham and R.S. Hewitt (1993) 'Bank Holding Company Mergers with Nonbank Financial Firms: Effects on the Risk of Failure', *Journal of Banking & Finance*, XVII, 1, 43–63.

Casu, B. and C. Girardone (2004) 'Financial Conglomeration: Efficiency, Productivity and Strategic Drive', *Applied Financial Economics*, XIV, 10, 687–96.

Carow, K. (2001a) 'The Citicorp–Travelers Merger: Challenging Barriers between Banking and Insurance', *Journal of Banking & Finance*, XXV, 8, 1553–71.

Carow, K. (2001b) 'The Wealth Effects of Allowing Bank Entry into the Insurance Industry', *Journal of Risk and Insurance*, LXVIII, 1, 129–50.

Carow, K.A. and R.A. Heron (2002) 'Capital Market Reactions to the Passage of the Financial Services Modernization Act of 1999', *The Quarterly Review of Economics and Finance*, 42, 3, 465–85.

Chen, Z., D. Li., L. Liao., F. Moshirian and C. Szablocs (2009) 'Expansion and Consolidation of Bancassurance in the 21st Century', *Journal of International Financial Markets, Institutions & Money*, XIX, 4, 633–44.

Chen, Z. and J. Tan (2011) 'Does Bancassurance Add Value for Banks? Evidence from Mergers and Acquisitions between European Banks and Insurance Companies', *Research in International Business and Finance*, XXV, 1, 104–12.

Chiorazzo, V., C. Milani and F. Salvini (2008), 'Income Diversification and Bank Performance: Evidence from Italian Banks', *Journal of Financial Services Research*, XXXIII, 3, 181–203.

Cummins, D., M. Weiss and H. Zi (2003) 'Economies of Scope in Financial Services: a DEA Bootstrapping Analysis of the US Insurance Industry', Unpublished working paper, The Wharton School of the University of Pennsylvania.

Cybo-Ottone, A. and M. Murgia (2000) 'Mergers and Shareholder Wealth in European Banking', *Journal of Banking & Finance*, XXIV, 6, 831–59.

Demsetz, R.S. and P.E. Strahan (1997) 'Diversification, Size, and Risk at Bank Holding Companies', *Journal of Money, Credit and Banking*, XXIX, 3, 300–13.

De Jonghe, O. and R. Vander Vennet (2008) 'Competition Versus Efficiency: What Drives Franchise Values in European Banking?', *Journal of Banking & Finance*, XXXII, 9, 1820–35.

DeLong, G.L. (2001) 'Stockholder Gains from Focusing versus Diversifying Bank Mergers', *Journal of Financial Economics*, LIX, 2, 221–52.

DeYoung, R. and T. Rice (2004) 'Noninterest Income and Financial Performance at U.S. Commercial Banks', *Financial Review*, XXXIX, 1, 101–27.

DeYoung, R. and K.P. Roland (2001) 'Product Mix and Earnings Volatility at Commercial Banks: Evidence from a Degree of Total Leverage Model', *Journal of Financial Intermediation*, X, 1, 54–4.

Elsas, R., A. Hackethal and M. Holzhäuser (2010) 'The Anatomy of Bank Diversification', *Journal of Banking & Finance*, XXXIV, 6, 1274–87.

Estrella, A. (2001), 'Mixing and Matching: Prospective Financial Sector Mergers and Market Valuation', *Journal of Banking & Finance*, XXV, 12, 2367–92.

Fields, L., D. Fraser and J. Kolari (2007a) 'Bidder Returns in Bancassurance Mergers: Is There Evidence of Synergy?', *Journal of Banking & Finance*, XXXI, 12, 3646–62.

Fields, L., D. Fraser and J. Kolari (2007b) 'Is Bancassurance a Viable Model For Financial Firms?', *Journal of Risk and Insurance*, LXXIV, 4, 777–94.

Genetay, N. and P. Molyneux (1998) *Bancassurance* (London: Palgrave Macmillan).

Hendershott, R.J., D.E. Lee and J.G. Tompkins (2002) 'Winners and Losers as Financial Service Providers Converge: Evidence from the Financial Modernization Act of 1999', *The Financial Review*, XXXVII, 1, 53–72.

Hughes, J.P. and L.J. Mester (1993) 'A Quality and Risk-Adjusted Cost Function for Banks: Evidence on the "Too-Big-To-Fail" Doctrine', *Journal of Productivity Analysis*, IV, 3, 293–315.

Humphrey, D. and L. Pulley (1993) 'The Role of Fixed Costs and Cost Complementarities in Determining Scope Economies and the Cost of Narrow Banking Proposals', *Journal of Business*, LIVI, 3, 437–62.

Hunter, W., S. Timme and W. Yang (1990) 'An Examination of Cost Subadditivity and Multiproduct Production in Large US Banks', *Journal of Money, Credit and Banking*, XXII, 4, 504–25.

Hwang, T. and S. Gao (2005) 'An Empirical Study of Cost Efficiency in the Irish Life Insurance Industry', *International Journal of Accounting, Auditing and Performance Evaluation*, II, 3, 264–80.

Johnston, J. and J. Madura (2000) 'Valuing the Potential Transformation of Banks into Financial Service Conglomerates: Evidence from the Citigroup Merger', *The Financial Review*, XXXV, 2, 17–36.

Kim, H.Y. (1986) 'Economies of Scale and Economies of Scope in Multiproduct Financial Institutions: Further Evidence from Credit Unions', *Journal of Money, Credit and Banking*, XVIII, 2, 220–6.

Klein, P.G. and M.R. Saidenberg (2000) 'Diversification, Organization and Efficiency: Evidence from Bank Holding Companies', in P.T. Harker and S.A. Zenios (eds), *Performance of Financial Institutions* (Cambridge: Cambridge University Press).

Klein, P.G. and M.R. Saidenberg (2010) 'Organizational Structure and the Diversification Discount: Evidence from Commercial Banking', *The Journal Of Industrial Economics*, LVIII, 1, 127–55.

Klumpes, P.J.M. (2004) 'Consolidation and Efficiency in the Major European Insurance Markets', *Journal of Business*, LXXVII, 2, 257–73.

Korhonen, P., L. Koskinen and Raimo Voutilainen (2006a) 'A Financial Alliance Compromise between Executives and Supervisory Authorities', *European Journal of Operational Research*, CLXXV, 2, 1300–10.

Korhonen, P., L. Koskinen and Raimo Voutilainen (2006b) 'A Customer View on the Most Preferred Alliance Structure between Banks and Insurance Companies', *ZfB*, LIIVI, 2, 139–64.

Korhonen, P. and R. Voutilainen (2006) 'Finding the Most Preferred Alliance Structure between Banks and Insurance Companies', *European Journal of Operational Research*, CLXXV, 2, 1285–99.

Laderman, E.S. (2000) 'The Potential Diversification and Failure Reduction Benefits of Bank Expansion into Non Banking Activities', Federal Reserve Bank of San Francisco Working Papers in Applied Economic Theory, no. 2000-01.

Laeven, L. and R. Levine (2007) 'Is There a Diversification Discount in Financial Conglomerates?', *Journal of Financial Economics*, LXXXV, 2, 331–67.

Lepetit, L., E. Nysa, P. Rous and A. Tarazi (2008) 'Bank Income Structure and Risk: An Empirical Analysis of European Banks', *Journal of Banking & Finance*, XXXII, 8, 1452–67.

Lepetit, L., S. Patry and P. Rous (2004) 'Diversification versus Specialization: an Event Study of M&As in the European Banking Industry', *Applied Financial Economics*, XIV, 9, 663–9.

Lin, C.T., Y.F. Lin and C.R. Wu (2009) 'Selecting the Preferable Bancassurance Alliance Strategic by Using Expert Group Decision Technique', *Expert Systems with Applications* XXXVI, 2, 3623–9.

Lorent, B. (2010) 'The Link between Insurance and Banking Sectors: An International Cross-Section Analysis of Life Insurance Demand', Université Libre de Bruxelles, Working Papers CEB no. 10-040.

Lown, C.S., C.L. Osler, P.E. Strahan and A. Sufi (2000) 'The Changing Landscape of the Financial Services Industry: What Lies Ahead?', *FRBNY Economic Policy Review*, October.

Mamun, A., M.K. Hassan and N. Maroney (2005) 'The Wealth and Risk Effects of the Gramm–Leach–Bliley Act (GLBA) on the US Banking Industry', *Journal of Business Finance & Accounting*, XXXII, 1/2, 351–88.

Mester, L. (1993) 'Efficiency of Banks in the Third Federal Reserve District', Wharton School Centre for Financial Institutions, University of Pennsylvania, working paper no. 94-13.

Mester L. (1996) 'A Study of Bank Efficiency Taking into Account Risk-Preferences', *Journal of Banking & Finance*, XX, 6, 1025–45.

Murray, J. and R. White (1984) 'Economies of Scale and Economies of Scope in Multiproduct Financial Institutions: a Study of British Columbia Credit Unions', *The Journal of Finance*, XXXVIII, 3, 887–902.

Neale, F.R. and P.P. Peterson (2005) 'The Effect of the Gramm–Leach–Bliley Act on the Insurance Industry', *Journal of Economics and Business*, LVII, 4, 317–38.

Nurullah, M. and S.K. Staikouras (2008) 'The Separation of Banking from Insurance: Evidence from Europe', *Multinational Finance Journal*, XII, 3/4, 157–84.

Okeahalam, C. (2008) 'Does Bancassurance Reduce the Price of Financial Service Products?', *Journal of Financial Services Research*, XXXIII, 3, 147–62.

Rumble, A. and K. J. Stiroh (2006) 'The Dark Side of Diversification: The Case of US Financial Holding Companies', *Journal of Banking & Finance*, XXX, 8, 2131–61.

Saaty, T. (1980) *The Analytic Hierarchy Process—Planning, Priority Setting, Resource Allocation* (New York: McGraw-Hill).

Schmid, M.M. and I. Walter (2009) 'Do Financial Conglomerates Create or Destroy Economic Value?', *Journal of Financial Intermediation*, XVIII, 2, 193–216.

Smith, R., C. Staikouras and G. Wood (2003) 'Non-interest Income and Total Income Stability', Bank of England Working Paper, no. 198.

Staikouras, S.K. (2009) 'An Event Study Analysis of International Ventures between Banks and Insurance Firms', *Journal of International Financial Markets, Institutions & Money*, XIX, 4, 675–91.

Stiroh, K.J. (2004) 'Diversification in Banking: Is Noninterest Income the Answer?', *Journal of Money, Credit and Banking*, XXXVI, 5, 853–82.

Stiroh, K.J. (2006) 'A Portfolio View of Banking with Interest and Noninterest Activities', *Journal of Money, Credit, and Banking*, XXXVIII, 5, 1351–61.

Trigo-Gamarra, L. (2007) 'Single- versus Multi-Channel Distribution Strategies in the German Life Insurance Market: A Cost and Profit Efficiency Analysis', University of Rostock, Institute of Economics, Thuenen-Series of Applied Economic Theory, working paper no. 81.

van Lelyveld, I. and K. Knot (2009) 'Do Financial Conglomerates Create or Destroy Value? Evidence for the EU', *Journal of Banking & Finance*, XXXIII, 12, 2312–21.

Verweire, K. (1999) 'Performance Consequences of Financial Conglomeration with an Empirical Analysis in Belgium and the Netherlands', PhD thesis, University of Ghent.

Vander Vennet, R. (2002), 'Cost and Profit Efficiency of Financial Conglomerates and Universal Banks in Europe', *Journal of Money, Credit and Banking*, XXXIV, 1, 254–82.

Voutilainen, R. (2005) 'Comparing Alternative Structures of Financial Alliances', *The Geneva Papers*, XXX, 327–42.

Yeager, T.C., F.C. Yeager and E. Harshman (2007), 'The Financial Services Modernization Act: Evolution or Revolution?', *Journal of Economics and Business*, LIX, 4, 313–39.

Yildirim, H.S., S.A. Kwag and M.C. Collins (2006) 'An Examination of the Equity Market Response to The Gramm–Leach–Bliley Act Across Commercial Banking, Investment Banking, and Insurance Firms', *Journal of Business Finance & Accounting*, XXXIII, 9/10, 1629–49.

7
Studying the Bancassurance Phenomenon: An Empirical Exploratory Analysis on a European Sample[1]

Franco Fiordelisi and Ornella Ricci

7.1 Introduction

As outlined in Chapter 6, cost and revenue synergies are commonly recognized as one of the main economic rationales for bank diversification into the insurance industry. Nevertheless, there are only a very few studies dealing with efficiency issues and specifically focussing on bancassurance. This chapter aims to present the empirical analysis conducted on a European sample in order to answer the following research question: are banks engaged in the insurance business more cost and profit efficient than their competitors specialised in traditional and investment banking?

The remainder of the chapter is structured as follows: section 7.2 describes the methodology used to measure cost and profit efficiency; section 7.3 deals with sample selection criteria and variables included in the cost and profit efficiency models; section 7.4 presents the main results, while section 7.5 concludes.

7.2 Methodology

Efficiency is estimated using the Stochastic Frontier Analysis (SFA) contemporaneously introduced by Aigner et al. (1977) and Meeusen and Van Den Broeck (1977). For the deterministic kernel of the frontier a translog specification is adopted:[2]

$$\ln TC = a_0 + \sum_k a_k \ln y_k + \sum_j b_j \ln p_j$$

$$+ \frac{1}{2}\left(\sum_k \sum_j c_{kj} \ln y_k \ln y_j + \sum_k \sum_j d_{kj} \ln p_k \ln p_j \right)$$

$$+ \sum_k \sum_j g_{kj} \ln y_k \ln p_j + \varepsilon \qquad (7.1)$$

where TC is total cost for the i-th firm; y_k are quantities of outputs or netputs (quasi-fixed inputs that cannot be adjusted in the short run); p_j are input prices. As usual, symmetry and linear homogeneity restrictions are imposed standardising total cost TC and input prices p_j by the last input price. The peculiarity of the SFA is to disentangle the error term in two main components $\varepsilon_i = v_i + u_i$. The first represents the standard statistical noise, accounting for measurement errors, bad luck and other factors unspecified in the cost function. The v_is are generally assumed to be i.i.d. normal random variables with mean zero and constant variance equal to σ_v^2. The second component is a non-negative inefficiency term, added to the cost frontier representing minimum cost. The u_is are generally assumed to be i.i.d. random variables with a half normal or a truncated normal distribution and constant variance equal to σ_u^2. They provide a Farrell (1957) type measure of relative inefficiency, intended as the distance from the best practice. In panel data model, the inefficiency component can be expressed as:

$$u_{it} = \{\exp[\eta(T - t)]\}u_i \qquad (7.2)$$

where the u_is are defined as above; η is a parameter to be estimated, T is the last period of observation and t the current one. If η is supposed equal to zero, a non-time-varying efficiency model is defined. When the time parameter is not imposed to be null, efficiency can be increasing or decreasing, (respectively, $\eta > 0$ or $\eta < 0$).

Alternative profit efficiency is also estimated in order to account for possible synergies on the revenue side. The profit efficiency concept is more meaningful than the cost efficiency one. As noted by Berger and Mester (1997, p. 9): 'it's based on the more accepted goal of profit maximization, which requires that the same amount of attention is paid to raising a marginal dollar of revenues as to reducing a marginal dollar of costs'. The alternative profit efficiency specifies profits given the level of outputs, rather than the output prices. As outlined in Berger and Mester (1997), this last method can provide useful information when one or more of the following conditions hold: output markets are not perfectly competitive; the quality of products and services is not homogeneous between different firms; firms cannot achieve every output scale or product mix; output prices cannot be accurately measured. The frontier definition is the same as in the cost case, except for the dependent variable. Total cost is replaced with total profit and the inefficiency term (u_{it}) is subtracted as in the production case, given that the frontier represents maximum profit.

Defining the inefficiency component as identically distributed in the sample implies the assumption that all the firms investigated share the same production technology and comparable environmental conditions. Recent studies on performance of financial business (for example, Bos et al., 2005) underline that in the case of sample heterogeneity efficiency estimates can be strongly biased, reflecting two factors that are difficult to distinguish: the actual managerial skills in combining production factors and the impact of exogenous factors out of management control. In order to build an accurately shared frontier (that is, a realistic benchmark of reference for all the companies in the sample) it is, then, essential to deal with the problem of heterogeneity.

In order to account for potential data heterogeneity, Coelli et al. (1999) suggest two different approaches based on the inclusion of environmental conditions and/or firm-specific factors in the frontier model. The first approach (labelled as 'Case 1') assumes that environmental conditions/ firm-specific factors directly influence the production structure, so that each firm faces a different cost or profit frontier. As such, the z_m exogenous factors terms are added to the deterministic kernel of the frontier that is the same as in equation 7.1 plus $(\Sigma_{m=1}^{M} \theta_m \ln z_{m,it})$. The efficiency estimates obtained in Case 1 are measures of efficiency net of exogenous influences. In the second approach (labelled as 'Case 2' and well known as the 'Technical Inefficiency Effects model', proposed by Battese and Coelli, 1995), all firms in the sample share the same production technology, but some firm-specific factors (that is, out of management control, at least in the short term) influence the distance from best practice. As such, the deterministic kernel of the frontier is the same as in equation (7.1) and the inefficiency components u_{it}s are now assumed to be distributed independently, but not identically. For each observation, the inefficiency effect is obtained as the truncation at zero of a normal distribution, with the mean μ_{it}, that is a function of M firm-specific conditions:

$$\mu_{it} = \delta_0 + \sum_{m=1}^{M} \delta_m z_{m,it} \qquad (7.3)$$

Efficiency estimates in Case 2 incorporate the effect of firm-specific factors and these can be viewed as gross measures of efficiency. To obtain net efficiency scores, it is sufficient to replace firm-specific conditions with the most favourable in the sample (see Coelli et al., 1999). Using these models it is possible to overcome the limitations of a *two-step* approach in which the predicted inefficiency effects are regressed upon a vector of variables supposed to influence firm performance. As outlined in Battese and Coelli (1993) and Battese et al. (1998), this approach suffers from a strong inconsistency: unless the second step regression coefficients are all equal to zero, the covariates influence the inefficiency level. This is in contrast with the assumption of inefficiency terms identically distributed across the sample (traditionally used in the first stage frontier analysis). Kumbhakar and Lovell (2000) note that it is difficult to choose if an exogenous variable is a characteristic of the production frontier or a determinant of productive (in)efficiency (that is, choosing between the Case 1 and Case 2 models). This can be done on the basis of theoretical reasons or through statistical hypothesis testing. From the former point of view the Case 2 model is more convenient because, as outlined in Bos et al. (2005), it allows the analysis to account for heterogeneity across firms and still benchmark all of them against an identical frontier.

From the statistical point of view, a possible solution is to construct an artificial nested model (see for example Coelli et al., 1999; Glass and McKillop, 2006) that includes environmental variables both in the translog function and as determinants of inefficiency. Then this nested model is compared with Case 1 and Case 2 models on the basis of a likelihood ratio test to determine which approach supplies the best fit to sample data.

7.3 Data and variables

This section describes the investigated sample and variables used in the research design. Specifically, section 7.3.1 presents sample selection criteria, section 7.3.2 discusses the choice of input and output variables and section 7.3.3 deals with firm-specific factors included in the frontier model to account for heterogeneity.

7.3.1 Sample selection criteria

First of all, bancassurance has to be defined from an operational point of view. As such, a bank is classified as a 'Bancassurance Combination' (BC) when the two following conditions are met:

- the bank is engaged in the life insurance activity through a captive company or a joint venture;
- the ratio of non-interest income to total revenues exceeds 20 per cent.

Banks not meeting both conditions are defined as a residual cluster and named 'Not Bancassurance-oriented Institutions' (NBIs): so NBIs can either be specialised commercial banks, either combinations between commercial and investment banking, while banks specialised in investment banking or in another particular business, such as consumer finance or leasing, are excluded. This approach is also consistent with recent developments in EU regulation, recognising bancassurance as a relevant kind of diversification. Under the European regulatory framework, insurance activity has to be conducted through separated entities: so it was necessary to check for the condition that the bank consolidates at least one insurance subsidiary.[3] Annual statements and ownership information for the year 2005 are derived from the Fitch/IBCA database Bankscope.[4] Consistent with the aim of assessing the effects of controlling insurance subsidiaries, it is more informative to collect consolidated financial statements rather than individual ones.

Dropping observations with missing (or extreme) values and eliminating foreign subsidiaries, the final sample consists of 278 banks in the EU-15 area (see Table 7.1), with different institutional types: commercial, savings and cooperative.

Table 7.1 Overview of the selected sample in the EU-15 banking industry

Country	NBIs	BCs	Tot
Austria	14	1	15
Belgium	4	1	5
Denmark	19	3	22
Finland	2	2	4
France	48	11	59
Germany	23	1	24
Greece	13	0	13
Ireland	3	2	5
Italy	18	22	40
Luxembourg	0	0	0
Netherlands	5	3	8
Portugal	4	0	4
Spain	51	9	60
Sweden	1	3	4
UK	9	6	15
Total	**214**	**64**	**278**

Notes: BCs: Bancassurance combinations, NBIs: Not bancassurance-oriented institutions.
Source: Author's own elaboration on Bankscope data.

7.3.2 Input and output definition

In the existing literature, it is possible to identify two main approaches used for output definition in the banking industry (Berger and Humphrey, 1997):

- the *production approach*: banks are considered as institutions providing some services to their customers; these services can be measured in terms of physical quantities, for example, the number of accounts or transactions over a given time period;
- the *asset or intermediation approach*: banks are viewed as mediators between the demand and the supply of funds. This approach has been widely used in banking studies dealing with efficiency (Vander Vennet, 2002; Casu and Molyneux, 2003; Casu and Girardone, 2004; Becalli et al., 2006; Fiorentino et al., 2006) and there is a large consensus on which variables should be selected: labour, fixed assets and deposits as inputs; loans, securities and other earning assets as outputs.

The production approach is preferable for evaluating the efficiency of single branches, while the intermediation approach may be more appropriate for evaluating entire financial institutions.

There is also a third option, the *value added approach* (see for example Resti, 1997; Fiordelisi and Molyneux, 2006; Battaglia et al., 2010), that identifies inputs and outputs depending on the contribution of bank items (from both sides of the balance sheet) to create value added. Under this view, customer deposits are considered as an output, together with loans and securities, given that commissions and services fees are generally higher than interest paid on customers' accounts. Total net loans (Y_1), total other earning assets (Y_2)[5] and total customer deposits (Y_3) are defined as outputs while labour, fixed assets and total funding are considered inputs. The price of labour (p_1) is obtained dividing personnel expenses by the number of employees.[6] The price of fixed assets (p_2) is calculated as total expenses for depreciation and amortisation relative to fixed assets, while the cost of funding (p_3) is defined as the ratio of total interest expenses to the sum of total deposits and other funding.

As dependent variables, Total cost (TC) is defined as the sum of interest and other operating expenses and Total Profit (TP) as pre-tax profit. Using a translog specification, it is necessary to solve the problem of sample firms with negative values of profits, for which it is not possible to take the logarithm. A common adjustment (e.g. Vander Vennet, 2002; Casu and Girardone, 2004; Fiordelisi and Molyneux, 2006) is to add the constant term $\theta = |\pi^{min}| + 1$ to every firm profit in the sample. In this case, θ should also be subtracted from both the numerator and the denominator of the firm PE expression (see, for example, Berger and DeYoung, 2002). If the number of firms exhibiting a loss is small relative to the sample size, a solution can also be dropping relative observations as in Humphrey and Pulley (1997) or in Huang (2000). Finally, profit efficiency can be redefined as follows (see for example De Young and Hasan, 1998; Akighbe and McNulty, 2003):

$$PE_i = \begin{cases} \dfrac{\pi_i}{\pi_{max}} & if \; \pi_i > 0 \\ 0 & if \; \pi_i \leq 0 \end{cases} \tag{7.4}$$

In the sample there are only nine banks exhibiting a loss: so it is better to drop these observations rather than running the adjustment described[7] above. As a consequence, the profit efficiency estimation is based on a sample of 269 firms. Rogers (1998) observes that non-traditional banking activities should be considered when measuring output in efficiency studies. His output definition also has been used in Vander Vennet (2002) in order to better account for output diversification beyond traditional banking. In the attempt to represent modern banking production, in a second specification traditional outputs are replaced by revenue flows: total interest income (Y_1'), representing traditional banking intermediation, and total non-interest income (Y_2') accounting for fee based activities (as insurance). Summary statistics for the input and output variables are presented in Table 7.2 for both the full sample and the two subgroups of BCs and NBIs.

7.3.3 Firm-specific factors and environmental conditions included to account for heterogeneity

To face possible estimation bias it is important to account for potential heterogeneity between the two subsamples, using the Case 1 or the Case 2 models explained in section 7.2. In order to consider differences across the banks analysed, the model includes a set of firm-specific factors supposed to be out of management control, at least in the short run, but able to influence the performance attained. Firm-specific factors to be included in the model have been chosen on the basis of two simple criteria:

• variables should have an influence on the production structure or the inefficiency distribution, on the basis of theoretical literature and evidence from empirical studies;

Table 7.2   Descriptive statistics of input and output variables for the EU-15 banking sample over 2005

	Variable	Mean	Std. Dev.	Min	Max
Full sample (278 observations)					
TC	Total cost	2,944,217	8,097,469	5,160	69,500,000
y1	Total loans	35,500,000	82,800,000	34,500	613,000,000
y2	Total other earning asset	36,000,000	118,000,000	6,163	864,000,000
y3	Total customer deposits	29,800,000	75,600,000	49,020	500,000,000
p1	Price of labour	63.2679	21.1780	26.3398	235.4430
p2	Price of fixed asset	0.1435	0.1238	0.0240	1.1111
p3	Price of funding	0.0220	0.0080	0.0080	0.0569
y1'	Net interest income	2,542,131	6,477,178	3,700	41,700,000
y2'	Non-interest income	830,005	2,506,219	430	17,900,000
TP	Total profits	583,752	1,493,540	−881,800	10,600,000
E	Equity	3,279,360	7,486,409	6,200	50,500,000
Bancassurance combinations (64 observations)					
TC	Total cost	9,122,497	14,100,000	17,600	69,500,000
y1	Total loans	102,000,000	134,000,000	34,500	613,000,000
y2	Total other earning asset	117,000,000	213,000,000	185,120	864,000,000
y3	Total customer deposits	87,800,000	126,000,000	399,728	500,000,000
p1	Price of labour	67.9321	24.2939	29.1385	173.3174
p2	Price of fixed asset	0.1381	0.1378	0.0278	1.1111
p3	Price of funding	0.0221	0.0083	0.0080	0.0458
y1'	Net interest income	7,677,966	10,900,000	16,100	41,700,000
y2'	Non-interest income	2,778,478	4,499,214	15,500	17,900,000
TP	Total profits	1,834,991	2,555,768	−881,800	10,600,000
E	Equity	9,717,090	12,800,000	24,900	50,500,000
Not Bancassurance-oriented institutions (214 observations)					
TC	Total cost	1,096,508	3,458,772	5,160	35,600,000
y1	Total loans	15,500,000	43,200,000	36,800	385,000,000
y2	Total other earning asset	11,700,000	44,800,000	6,163	441,000,000
y3	Total customer deposits	12,500,000	38,100,000	49,020	317,000,000
p1	Price of labour	61.8729	20.0054	26.3398	235.4430

(*continued*)

Table 7.2 Continued

	Variable	Mean	Std. Dev.	Min	Max
p2	Price of fixed asset	0.1451	0.1196	0.0240	0.7143
p3	Price of funding	0.0220	0.0079	0.0101	0.0569
y1'	Net interest income	1,006,180	3,060,827	3,700	30,600,000
y2'	Non-interest income	247,284	836,167	430	8,248,000
TP	Total profits	209,549	598,183	−171,400	5,684,000
E	Equity	1,354,057	2,845,038	6,200	23,000,000

Note: All values are in € thousands, except for relative prices of fixed assets and funding.
Source: Author's own elaboration on Bankscope data.

Table 7.3 Measuring cost and profit efficiency in the EU-15 banking industry over 2005 (bank-specific factors introduced in the model to account for sample heterogeneity)

	LN_TA	E/TA	NII/TR	LN_INTG	COMM	LISTED
NBIs_mean	15.6523	0.0892	0.2124	7.4097	0.4019	0.2991
BCs_mean	17.9717	0.0604	0.2606	12.0418	0.5938	0.6719
diff NBIs-BCs	−2.3194	0.0288	−0.0482	−4.6321	−0.1919	−0.3728
t-stat[a]	−8.8364	6.5044	−3.5347	−9.0847	−2.7253	−5.5677
p-value	0.0000	0.0000	0.0006	0.0000	0.0076	0.0000

Notes: BCs: Bancassurance combinations, NBIs: Not bancassurance-oriented institutions.
[a] Two sample t-test of differences in mean between BCs and NBIs, under the assumption of unequal variance.
H_0: mean(NBIs)−mean(BCs) = 0, H_1: mean(NBIs)−mean(BCs) ≠ 0.
Source: Author's own elaboration on Bankscope data.

- variables show a significant difference in means between the two subgroups, so that they are suitable to consider the peculiarity of banks diversifying into the insurance business and banks engaged only in traditional and investment banking.

The list of variables selected is reported in Table 7.3 together with the results from testing difference in means between the two subgroups (under the assumption of unequal variance). In detail, the following variables are considered:

- *Size (LN_TA)*. The relationship between size and efficiency has always received great attention in efficiency studies, representing an important policy issue, especially during M&A waves. Even though there are no clear conclusions and results change depending on methodologies applied (as outlined in Weill, 2004) accounting for size difference is certainly significant. The mean values of the natural log of total assets (*LN_TA*) shows that BCs are, on average, larger than NBIs;

- *Risk (E/TA)*. Many efficiency studies outline the importance of accounting for bank risk preferences (see for example Mester, 1996; Laeven, 1999; Altunbas et al., 2000). The ratio between equity and total asset (*E/TA*) is considered as an indicator of management risk preferences. It is possible to note that BCs are more risky than NBIs, showing a lower mean level of capitalisation;

- *Diversification (NII/TR)*. Consistently with the research topic, the degree of diversification is supposed to have a relevant impact on bank operational performance. Given that the ratio of non-interest income to total revenues (*NII/TR*) has been used as a criterion to identify BCs it is obvious that their degree of diversification is larger than in NBIs. However it is important to notice that diversification is also quite high in NBIs;

- *Intangible Assets (LN_INTG)*. There is a growing attention on soft investment, such as advertisement, R&D expenditures or investments enhancing human capital and the future ability of firms to create value. To our knowledge only a few studies have related this issue to efficiency (see for example Casolaro and Gobbi, 2006 and Beccalli, 2007 relative to investments in ICT). Intangible assets may have an influence on operational efficiency. BCs show a greater value of investment in intangibles (as for total assets the natural log is considered, *LN_INTG*): this is probably due to the fact that they are more often large financial groups;

- *Institutional type (COMM)*. The sample investigated includes banks of different institutional types: commercial, savings and cooperative. The institutional model adopted by the bank can influence the production structure and the conditions faced in competition with other institutions, as outlined in many studies (between the others Altunbas et al., 2001; Bos et al., 2005). A dummy variable, named *COMM*, distinguishes commercial banks from savings and cooperatives; its mean shows that BCs are more often commercial banks;

- *Listing (LISTED)*. The sample comprises both listed and unlisted banks. Corporate governance mechanisms can influence firm performance, more or less subject to shareholder control or to take over threats: Beccalli et al. (2006) show the existence of a positive relationship between efficiency and stock performance. So listed banks, more exposed to competitive pressures, may pay particular attention to efficiency. A dummy, named *LISTED*, distinguishes between listed and unlisted banks: as expected, BCs are more often listed companies with respect to NBIs.

Many studies dealing with cross-country comparison of financial firms performance (Dietsch and Lozano-Vivas, 2000; Maudos et al., 2002; Casu and Molyneux, 2003; Beccalli, 2004; Fiordelisi and Molyneux, 2006) show that nationality has an important influence on the efficiency level. Despite the harmonisation process followed by EU members, there are still significant differences across several economic and institutional contexts. Following this literature a set of country dummies (CD_k) is included to synthetically control for different national conditions.[8]

7.4   Results

First, empirical findings from the base model are presented, analysing the resulting frontiers and outlining its limitations (section 7.4.1). Second, the applied solution for the sample heterogeneity problem and the inclusion of firm specific factors is discussed. Finally, results from the preferred model are examined, commenting on differences in the mean level of cost and profit efficiency between the two subsamples of BCs and NBIs and the impact of the included exogenous factors (section 7.4.2).

7.4.1   Base model

Table 7.4 reports results for cost and profit efficiency, with both input and output specifications, under the Base Model, in which BCs and NBIs are supposed to share the same technology and the same environmental conditions. In this case the frontier model is specified as in equation (7.1), without the inclusion of exogenous factors.

Cost efficiency seems to have a very similar level between the two subgroups. With the value added approach NBIs are more efficient while under the specification with traditional and non-traditional banking output BCs have a small advantage and less variability than NBIs. Moving to the profit side, BCs show a marginal advantage (not statistically significant) in both input and output specifications. These results are consistent with Vander Vennet (2002) showing that: 'specialised banks are more efficient in traditional intermediation activities ... while conglomerates appear to be slightly better managed when non traditional activities are included ... In terms of profit efficiency,

Table 7.4 Measuring cost and profit efficiency in the EU-15 banking industry over 2005. Base Model – Pooled frontier

Group	Mean	Std dev	Min	Max
Panel A – COST EFFICIENCY				
VALUE ADDED APPROACH				
NBIs (n = 214)	0.8208	0.0985	0.4356	0.9589
BCs (n = 64)	0.7949	0.0998	0.5066	0.9473
Test of difference in mean[a]	t stat = 1.8286		p-value 0.0704	
TRADITIONAL AND NON TRADITIONAL BANKING OUTPUT				
NBIs (n = 214)	0.8141	0.0840	0.3273	0.9567
BCs (n = 64)	0.8255	0.0710	0.6115	0.9490
Test of difference in mean[a]	t stat = −1.0755		p-value 0.2843	
Panel B – ALTERNATIVE PROFIT EFFICIENCY				
VALUE ADDED APPROACH				
NBIs (n = 206)	0.6413	0.1680	0.0646	0.9224
BCs (n = 63)	0.6737	0.1476	0.3147	0.9064
Test of difference in mean[a]	t stat = −1.4759		p-value 0.1427	
TRADITIONAL AND NON TRADITIONAL BANKING OUTPUT				
NBIs (n = 206)	0.6831	0.1374	0.107133	0.9274
BCs (n = 63)	0.6936	0.1225	0.3558	0.9025
Test of difference in mean[a]	t stat = −0.5752		p-value 0.5663	

BCs: Bancassurance combinations, NBIs: Not bancassurance-oriented institutions.
[a] Two sample t-test of differences in mean between BCs and NBIs, under the assumption of unequal variance.
H_0: mean(NBIs)−mean(BCs) = 0, H_1: mean(NBIs)−mean(BCs) ≠ 0.
Source: Author's own elaboration on Bankscope data.

financial conglomerates achieve a slightly higher efficiency level than their specialised peers, but the difference is only marginally significant' (Vander Vennet, 2002, p. 266–7).

As outlined in section 7.2, comparisons based on a common frontier can be conducted only if all the firms in the sample share the same production technology and comparable environmental conditions: this assumption is quite strong for BCs and NBIs, engaged in a different mix of activities. So in order to avoid estimation bias, it is necessary to control for poolability between the two subgroups. To this aim a generalised log-likelihood ratio test is run; the LR statistic is defined by:

$$\lambda = -2\{\ln[L(H_0)] - \ln[L(H_1)]\} \tag{7.5}$$

where $\ln[L(H_0)]$ is the value of the log-likelihood function for the stochastic frontier estimated by pooling the data and $\ln[L(H_1)]$ is the sum of the values of the log-likelihood functions for the two separated frontiers for BCs and NBIs (Battese et al. 2004). The degrees of freedom for the Chi-square distribution are the difference between the number of parameters estimated under H_1 and H_0. Results for the poolability test are reported in Table 7.5.

The null hypothesis of poolability between the two subgroups is always rejected, concluding that a common frontier is not applicable to the sample investigated.

Allen and Rai (1996) find that it is not possible to compare banks from universal and separated banking countries on the basis of a common frontier, while Vander Vennet (2002) concludes that poolability between banks with different degrees of conglomeration can be accepted, except for the cost model with specification of traditional and non-traditional banking output. This difference, beyond the selection of a different sample, is probably also due to the definition of different subgroups and to the consideration of consolidated statements.

Rejecting poolability, it is possible to consider cost and profit frontiers obtained for each subgroup; results from these separated frontiers are reported in Table 7.6, even though they are not helpful to the purpose of comparing BCs and NBIs against a common benchmark.

Table 7.5 Measuring cost and profit efficiency in the EU-15 banking industry over 2005 (Log-likelihood ratio test for poolability of BCs and NBIs under the base model frontier)

TEST PERFORMED	TEST STAT[a]	CRITICAL VALUE	DECISION
Cost frontier with the value added approach	$\chi^2 = 50.90$	$\chi^2_{(0.05)} = 41.34$	Reject H_0
Cost frontier with traditional/non-traditional output	$\chi^2 = 53.81$	$\chi^2_{(0.05)} = 32.67$	Reject H_0
Profit frontier with the value added approach	$\chi^2 = 78.41$	$\chi^2_{(0.05)} = 41.34$	Reject H_0
Profit frontier with traditional/non-traditional output	$\chi^2 = 41.93$	$\chi^2_{(0.05)} = 32.67$	Reject H_0

[a] The LR statistic is $\lambda = -2\{\ln[L(H_0)] - \ln[L(H_1)]\}$ where $\ln[L(H_0)]$ is the value of the log-likelihood function for the stochastic frontier estimated by pooling the data and $\ln[L(H_1)]$ is the sum of the values of the log-likelihood functions for the two separated frontiers for BCs and NBIs.

Source: Author's own elaboration on Bankscope data.

Table 7.6   Measuring cost and profit efficiency in the EU-15 banking industry over 2005 (Base Model – Separated Frontiers)

Group	Mean	Std dev	Min	Max
Panel A – COST EFFICIENCY				
VALUE ADDED APPROACH				
NBIs (n = 214)	0.8148	0.1039	0.4204	0.9636
BCs (n = 64)	0.9737	0.0027	0.9656	0.9813
TRADITIONAL AND NON TRADITIONAL BANKING OUTPUT				
NBIs (n = 214)	0.8034	0.0923	0.2969	0.9525
BCs (n = 64)	0.8983	0.0410	0.7595	0.9667
Panel B – ALTERNATIVE PROFIT EFFICIENCY				
VALUE ADDED APPROACH				
NBIs (n = 206)	0.6214	0.1874	0.0551	0.9304
BCs (n = 63)	0.7550	0.1959	0.2903	0.9980
TRADITIONAL AND NON TRADITIONAL BANKING OUTPUT				
NBIs (n = 206)	0.6972	0.1219	0.1295	0.9223
BCs (n = 63)	0.9471	0.0053	0.9320	0.9612

Notes: BCs: Bancassurance combinations, NBIs: Not bancassurance-oriented institutions.
Source: Author's own elaboration on Bankscope data.

Analysing results from separated cost frontiers, using the value added approach, BCs all look similar, with a very high mean efficiency and a low standard deviation: on the other hand, NBIs show a lower level of mean efficiency and a larger variability. In addition to this, the value of the log-likelihood function for BCs is less than that obtained using ordinary least squares. This means that this specification is unable to detect a significant inefficiency component in the subgroup of BCs. The specification using traditional and non-traditional banking output shows a greater variability in the efficiency estimation for both BCs and NBIs: in any case BCs seem more efficient than NBIs. Mean profit efficiency is higher for BCs with both input and output specifications: standard deviation, in this case, is lower for BCs under the specification with traditional and non-traditional banking output.

In order to construct a shared frontier, the heterogeneity problem has to be solved including firm specific factors and environmental variables considering mean differences between the two subgroups.

7.4.2   Accounting for heterogeneity

From the point of view of this research comparisons based on separated frontiers are not very significant. So it is necessary to construct a model accounting for heterogeneity between the two subgroups in which the LR test allows for poolability between BCs and NBIs. In order to do this, it is possible to use both the Case 1 and the Case 2 models explained in section 7.2, including environmental/firm-specific variables directly in the production function or as determinants of the inefficiency component. Even though Case 2 is more convenient for our purpose, the statistical method to select the model providing the best fit to sample data is also tried.

As suggested by the literature dealing with efficiency measurement (see, for example, Coelli et al., 1999; Glass and McKillop, 2006) a log-likelihood ratio test is used to contrast the two null hypotheses associated with the Case 1 and the Case 2 models against the alternative hypothesis represented by the artificial nested model. The relative test statistic is calculated as in equation (7.5), where $\ln[L(H_0)]$ is the value of the log-likelihood function for the null hypotheses corresponding to the Case 1 or the Case 2 model, and $\ln[L(H_1)]$ is the value of the log-likelihood function for the alternative artificial nested model. The degrees of freedom for the Chi-square distribution involved are the number of parameters settled at zero under the null. Results from these tests are reported in Table 7.7.

In both cases the null hypothesis is rejected in favour of the nested model, so the statistical approach is unable to discriminate which model, between Case 1 and Case 2, provides the best fit to the data. In this case the preferred specification can be selected on the basis of theoretical motivations. The model in which variables are directly included in the deterministic portion of the frontier determines different benchmarks for sample units with different exogenous factors. As a consequence, the Case 2 model appears preferable because it allows the consideration of heterogeneity among firms and still benchmark all of them against an identical frontier. Before taking any comparison on the basis of the resulting common frontiers it is important to control that this specification solves the heterogeneity problem, allowing for poolability between BCs and NBIs. As in the case of the base model a log-likelihood ratio test is run. Results from this test are reported in Table 7.8.

The variables included allow construction of a common frontier in three out of four cases (except for profit efficiency under the value added approach). So it is reasonable to compare BCs and NBIs against

Table 7.7   Measuring cost and profit efficiency in the EU-15 banking industry over 2005. Testing Case 1[a] and Case 2[b] models against the artificial Nested model[c]

TEST PERFORMED	TEST STAT[d]	CRITICAL VALUE	DECISION
Cost Efficiency – Value Added approach			
Case 1 (H_0) against Nested (H_1)	$\chi^2 = 60.91$	$\chi^2_{(0.05)} = 30.14$	Reject H_0
Case 2 (H_0) against Nested (H_1)	$\chi^2 = 120.25$	$\chi^2_{(0.05)} = 30.14$	Reject H_0
Cost Efficiency – Traditional And Non Traditional Banking Output			
Case 1 (H_0) against Nested (H1)	$\chi^2 = 62.41$	$\chi^2_{(0.05)} = 30.14$	Reject H_0
Case 2 (H_0) against Nested (H1)	$\chi^2 = 73.37$	$\chi^2_{(0.05)} = 30.14$	Reject H_0
Alternative Profit Efficiency – Value Added approach			
Case 1 (H_0) against Nested (H_1)	$\chi^2 = 105.45$	$\chi^2_{(0.05)} = 30.14$	Reject H_0
Case 2 (H_0) against Nested (H_1)	$\chi^2 = 99.58$	$\chi^2_{(0.05)} = 30.14$	Reject H_0
Alternative Profit Efficiency – Traditional And Non Traditional Banking Output			
Case 1 (H_0) against Nested (H_1)	$\chi^2 = 76.81$	$\chi^2_{(0.05)} = 30.14$	Reject H_0
Case 2 (H_0) against Nested (H_1)	$\chi^2 = 71.01$	$\chi^2_{(0.05)} = 30.14$	Reject H_0

Notes:
[a] Case 1 model: environmental/firm-specific factors are supposed to influence the production structure and are directly included in the deterministic kernel of the frontier.
[b] Case 2 model: environmental/firm-specific factors are supposed to influence the distance from the best practice and determine the inefficiency distribution.
[c] Nested model: environmental/firm-specific factors are included both in the deterministic kernel of the frontier and as determinants of inefficiency.
[d] The LR statistic is $\lambda = -2\{\ln[L(H_0)] - \ln[L(H_1)]\}$ where $\ln[L(H_0)]$ is the value of the log-likelihood functions under the null hypotheses corresponding to Case 1 and Case 2 models and $\ln[L(H_1)]$ is the value of the log-likelihood function for the alternative artificial nested model.
Source: Author's own elaboration on Bankscope data.

a common frontier, as shown in Table 7.9. Under the value added approach there is a slight cost advantage in favour of NBIs, but it is not statistically significant. Results from alternative profit efficiency are not reported because of the rejection of the poolability test.

Moving to the specification with traditional and non-traditional banking output, results provide evidence of a strong and statistically significant advantage for BCs on both the cost and the profit sides. So under the value added approach there are no significant gaps between BCs and NBIs, while NBIs result more performing when non-traditional banking output is considered.

Including exogenous factors as determinants of the inefficiency component permits the analysis of their effect on attained performance,

Table 7.8 Measuring cost and profit efficiency in the EU-15 banking industry over 2005 (Log-likelihood ratio test for poolability between BCs and NBIs under the Case 2 model[a])

TEST PERFORMED	TEST STAT[b]	CRITICAL VALUE	DECISION
Cost frontier – value added approach	$\chi^2 = 48.82$	$\chi^2_{(0.05)} = 62.83$	Accept H_0
Cost frontier – traditional/ non-traditional output	$\chi^2 = 47.78$	$\chi^2_{(0.05)} = 53.38$	Accept H_0
Profit frontier – value added approach	$\chi^2 = 129.13$	$\chi^2_{(0.05)} = 62.83$	Reject H_0
Profit frontier – traditional/ non-traditional output	$\chi^2 = 29.6$	$\chi^2_{(0.05)} = 53.38$	Accept H_0

[a] Case 2 model: environmental/firm specific factors influence the distance from the best practice and are the determinants of the inefficiency distribution.
[b] The LR statistic is $\lambda = -2\{\ln[L(H_0)] - \ln[L(H_1)]\}$ where $\ln[L(H_0)]$ is the value of the log-likelihood function for the stochastic frontier estimated by pooling the data and $\ln[L(H_1)]$ is the sum of the values of the log-likelihood functions for the two separated frontiers for BCs and NBIs.
Source: Author's own elaboration on Bankscope data.

Table 7.9 Measuring cost and profit efficiency in the EU-15 banking industry over 2005 (Pooled Frontier including firm specific factors as determinants of (in) efficiency)

INPUT/OUPUT SPECIFICATION	NBIs MEAN	BCs MEAN	T-STAT[a]	P-value
COST EFFICIENCY				
Value added approach	0.8549	0.8446	0.5613	0.57
Traditional and non-traditional banking output	0.7793	0.8844	−5.9992	0.00
ALTERNATIVE PROFIT EFFICIENCY				
Traditional and non-traditional banking output	0.6672	0.7135	−1.6509	0.10

BCs: Bancassurance Combinations, NBIs: 'Not bancassurance-oriented' Institutions.
[a] Two sample t-test of differences in mean between BCs and NBIs.
H_0: mean(NBIs)−mean(BCs) = 0, H_1: mean(NBIs)−mean(BCs) ≠ 0.
Source: Author's own elaboration on Bankscope data.

studying the signs and the significance of the resulting coefficients. These are reported in Table 7.10 for both firm-specific factors and country dummies included to account for national differences.

Firm size *(LN_TA)* appears always positively related to efficiency (the coefficient is negative and statistically significant in two out of three cases). In the efficiency literature dealing with financial firms there are

Table 7.10   Measuring cost and profit efficiency in the EU-15 banking industry over 2005 (Firm-specific factors determining the inefficiency distribution)

| | COST EFFICIENCY | | PROFIT EFFICIENCY |
| | (value added approach) | (traditional and non-traditional output) | (traditional and non-traditional output) |
VARIABLE	COEFFICIENT	COEFFICIENT	COEFFICIENT
LN_TA	−0.0806***	−0.0198	−0.2455***
E/TA	0.0712	−0.3337***	−1.0651***
NII/TR	0.2599***	−0.3638***	0.0148
LN_INTG	0.0048	−0.0154*	−0.0024
COMM	0.0695	−0.0591	−0.0466
LISTED	0.0752	−0.0183	−0.1683
Austria_dummy	−0.2141	0.0709	0.1588
Belgium_dummy	0.2981	0.3114	−3.558***
Denmark_dummy	0.2403	−0.3584	−1.3564
Finland_dummy	−0.3568	0.4814***	−2.955***
France_dummy	0.2222	−0.1820	0.4581
Germany_Dummy	0.4369	0.2659**	0.1593
Greece_dummy	0.7099**	0.7446***	−0.2876
Ireland_dummy	−0.8232	−0.0705	0.3014
Italy_dummy	0.5925*	0.2210	−0.0353
Netherlands_dummy	−0.4284	0.1213	−0.0448
Portugal_dummy	0.3443	0.3083	−0.4469
Spain_dummy	−0.0937	0.3672***	−1.0664**
Sweden_dummy	0.3483	−0.7485	−0.1521

Note:
A coefficient >0 means a positive effect on the inefficiency component u_i and then a negative relationship with efficiency; the opposite for a coefficient <0. *p-value<0.1; **p-value<0.05; ***p-value<0.01.
Source: Author's own elaboration on Bankscope data.

mixed results on the relationship between efficiency and size. While there is a large number of studies dealing with scale economies, only a few analyses have investigated bank size as a determinant of X-efficiency. Worthington (1998) finds that larger organisations have an advantage in managing institutional operations observing that '... larger building societies direct more managerial inputs into identifying and resolving inefficiency; ex ante one would expect a negative coefficient when cost inefficiency is regressed against total asset' (Worthington, 1998, p. 463). Vander Vennet (2002) finds that cost efficiency is largely unrelated to size, while the smallest banks appear less profit-efficient. Weill (2004) tries different frontier techniques to study the relationship between size and efficiency, finding that Data Envelopment Analysis (DEA) efficiency scores increase monotonically with size, while there is no a clear trend for SFA and DFA scores. In any case, restricting the analysis to the comparison between only extreme classes, all approaches agree in assigning a better performance to the largest banks, except in Switzerland. In their SFA analysis, Cavallo and Rossi (2002) include both the natural logarithm of total assets and three dummies to distinguish among small, medium and large banks, with different results across countries.

The relationship with the level of capitalisation *(E/TA)* is ambiguous: when the coefficients are significant they signal a positive relationship between capitalisation and efficiency. This agrees with Mester (1993) underlying that this does not mean that banks can enhance their efficiency by a higher capital asset ratio, but 'it may be an indication that higher capital ratios may prevent moral hazard' (Mester, 1993, p. 23). If a bank's capital level decreases, managers have an increasing incentive to take on excessive risk, engaging in activities that do not create value for shareholders. This sign of the relationship is confirmed by Worthington (1998) but contrasts with the results in Cavallo and Rossi (2002) and Casolaro and Gobbi (2006) which show a negative relationship between capitalization and efficiency for both cost and profit models. The authors recognised that the casualty is ambiguous because 'Large capital ratios may follow from excess capacity or may be due to agency problems as long as more efficient banks can signal their quality through a high leverage ...' (Casolaro and Gobbi, 2006, p. 25). Mixed results are presented in Casu and Girardone (2004).

The level of diversification *(NII/TR)* shows different coefficients depending on the definition of inputs and outputs. Under the value added approach it has a positive sign, showing a negative relationship between diversification and cost efficiency. This is consistent with the finding of a small advantage in favour of NBIs when non-traditional output is not considered. On the other hand, using the specification with traditional and non-traditional banking output, the coefficient is negative and statistically significant, meaning that there exists a direct relationship between cost efficiency and diversification. In addition, this result is consistent with the finding of an advantage for BCs using this approach. Moving to the profit case the coefficient is not statistically significant: so there is no evidence in favour of the one-stop banking theory.

The amount of investment in intangibles *(LN_INTG)* shows coefficients of different signs and levels of significance. This is probably due to the fact that these assets enhance firm ability to realise profit or to reduce costs only in the long run, while the analysis refers to the balance sheet of a specific financial year.

The dummy linked to institutional type (*COMM*) is never significant, meaning that commercial banks do not have a structural advantage on cooperative and savings banks as confirmed in other studies (for example, Altunbas et al., 2001; Weill, 2004; Girardone et al., 2004).

Studying the dummy linked to listing (*LISTED*), listed companies seem to be more efficient than unlisted companies from both the cost and the profit sides when using the specification with traditional and non-traditional banking output. A reverse relationship is revealed under the value added approach. The coefficients, however, are not significant.

Country dummies are quite different from one model to another:[9] Greece and Italy seem to have a cost disadvantage under the value added approach; when non-traditional activities are included the disadvantage for Italy disappears while it remains for Greece, together with Germany, Finland and Spain. On the profit side Belgium, Finland and Spain show an advantage. It is then possible to affirm that even a different geographical distribution of BCs and NBIs across Europe can influence the mean level of efficiency in the two subgroups.

In order to assess the impact of firm-specific factors on the attained performance, net efficiency scores are also measured (supposing that all the firms in the sample share the same conditions, that is, the most favourable).

Net efficiency scores for both the cost and the profit cases are reported in Table 7.11 for every model (except for alternative profit efficiency

Table 7.11 Measuring cost and profit efficiency in the EU-15 banking industry over 2005 (Case 2 Model: net cost efficiency scores)

INPUT/OUTPUT SPECIFICATION	NBIs MEAN	BCs MEAN	T-STAT[a]	P-VALUE
NET COST EFFICIENCY				
Value added approach	0.9661	0.9683	−0.6947	0.49
Traditional and non-traditional banking output	0.9789	0.9824	−3.4030	0.00
NET PROFIT EFFICIENCY				
Traditional and non-traditional banking output	0.9128	0.9326	−2.7499	0.01

BCs: Bancassurance combinations, NBIs: Not bancassurance-oriented institutions.
[a] Two sample t-test of differences in mean between BCs and NBIs.
H_0: mean(NBI)−mean(BC) = 0, H_1: mean(NBI)−mean(BC) ≠ 0.
Source: Author's own elaboration on Bankscope data.

under the value added approach, for which the hypothesis of poolability between the two subgroups is rejected).

On the cost side, with respect to gross efficiency scores, the substantial parity between BCs and NBIs under the value added approach is confirmed. The advantage for BCs resulting from the use of traditional and non-traditional banking output is still significant but strongly reduced. Moving to the profit side the advantage for BCs is still evident but not so relevant as in terms of gross efficiency scores. This probably means that the considered firm-specific factors play a very important role in determining the performance of banking institutions.

7.5 Conclusions

This chapter has compared banks diversifying into the insurance business (Bancassurance Combinations, BCs) with banks operating only in traditional and investment banking ('Not bancassurance-oriented institutions', NBIs). Following Vander Vennet (2002), BCs are defined as banks consolidating an insurance company and presenting a ratio of non-interest income to total revenues greater than 20 per cent.

BCs and NBIs are quite heterogeneous with respect to some firm-specific factors, such as size, level of capitalisation, amount of investment in intangibles, institutional type, listing and, for definition, level of diversification. In order to avoid estimation bias in efficiency scores due to sample heterogeneity, the model incorporates the cited firm-specific factors as determinants of (in) efficiency, together with a set of country dummies to synthetically account for differences across nations. The inclusion of these exogenous factors allows a shared benchmark between the two subgroups to be obtained and analyses their impact on the attained performance, avoiding the problems of a two-step procedure.

Results from the investigated European sample show that BCs and NBIs have a very similar performance under the value added approach, while BCs present a strong advantage under the definition of traditional and non-traditional banking output, on both the cost and the profit sides. Analysing the coefficients assumed by firm-specific factors it is possible to conclude that differences between the two subgroups are also influenced by size and level of capitalisation. For diversification, results depend on the approach used in input and output definition. The coefficient assumed under the value added approach indicates a negative relationship with efficiency, while the coefficient under the specification with traditional and non-traditional banking output shows a positive relationship (statistically significant only on the cost side). Calculating net efficiency scores (that is, assuming that all sample firms share the same conditions) the advantage of BCs is strongly reduced so that the firm-specific factors included can explain a large proportion of differences across the two subgroups.

It is possible to conclude that in order to compare BCs and NBIs it is crucial to account for sample heterogeneity and that there is only weak evidence in favour of the soundness of bancassurance strategy: for the European sample investigated, the advantage of BCs is highly sensitive to the definition of input and output variables and is substantially reduced when net efficiency scores are considered.

In order to give a complete evaluation of the bancassurance phenomenon the insurance side should also be investigated, assessing whether life insurance companies controlled by banks are more efficient than their independent competitors.

Notes

1. This chapter is mostly based on Ornella Ricci's PhD thesis, made under the supervision of Franco Fiordelisi.
2. For simplicity, subscripts referring to time and single firms are omitted.
3. Banking institutions identified as financial conglomerates (under Article 3 of Directive 2002/87/EC) in the list edited by the Mixed Technical Group on April 2006 are included in the sample as BCs.
4. Ownership information was also checked analysing company annual statements and websites.
5. Two different definitions are given for Y_2: Total Securities and Total Other Earning Assets. As expected, results are very similar given that Total Securities is the main component of Total Other Earning Assets.
6. The number of employees is not always available in the IBCA database: so many studies use the ratio between personnel expenses and total assets (for example, Vander Vennet 2002; Casu and Girardone 2004; Fiordelisi and Molyneux, 2006). Given the relatively small size of our sample it was possible to fill in the gap with a search of institutional bank/group websites.
7. Rather than making a data transformation (that is, adding the constant θ to every observation in the sample), it is preferable to estimate alternative profit efficiency using the original data set since the loss of information is very small (less than 3.5 per cent of the sample).
8. Selected banks operate in the EU-15 area. In the final sample there are no observations for Luxembourg. As usual, one dummy (UK_dummy) is dropped from the model to avoid multicollinearity.
9. The sign and the magnitude of country dummies coefficients should be interpreted in comparison with the omitted variable that is UK_dummy.

References

Aigner, D., C. Lovell and P. Schmidt (1977) 'Formulation and Estimation of Stochastic Frontier Production Function Models', *Journal of Econometrics*, VI, 1, 21–37.

Akighbe, A. and J. McNulty (2003) 'The Profit Efficiency of Small US Commercial Banks', *Journal of Banking and Finance*, XXVII, 2, 307–25.

Allen, L. and A. Rai (1996) 'Operational Efficiency in Banking: An International Comparison', *Journal of Banking & Finance*, XX, 4, 655–72.

Altunbas, Y., L. Evans and P. Molyneux (2001) 'Bank Ownership and Efficiency', *Journal of Money, Credit and Banking*, XXXIII, 4, 926–54.

Altunbas, Y., H. Ming, P. Molyneux and R. Seth (2000) 'Efficiency and Risk in Japanese Banking', *Journal of Banking and Finance*, XXIV, 10, 1605–28.

Battaglia, F., V. Farina, F. Fiordelisi and O. Ricci (2010) 'The Efficiency of Cooperative Banks: The Impact of Environmental Economic Conditions', *Applied Financial Economics*, XX, 17, 1363–76.

Battese, G. and T. Coelli (1993) 'A Stochastic Frontier Production Function Incorporating a Model for Technical Inefficiency Effects', Department of Econometrics, University of New England, working paper in Econometrics and Applied Statistics.

Battese, G. and T. Coelli (1995) 'A Model for Technical Inefficiency Effects in a Stochastic Frontier Production Function for Panel Data', *Empirical Economics*, XX, 2, 325–32.

Battese, G., T. Coelli and C.D.S. Prasada Rao (1998) *An Introduction to Efficiency and Productivity Analysis* (Boston: Kluwer Academic Publishers).

Battese, G., T. Coelli, D. Prasada Rao and C. O'Donnel (2004), 'A Metafrontier Production Function for Estimation of Technical Efficiencies and Technology Gaps for Firms Operating Under Different Technologies', *Journal of Productivity Analysis*, XXI, 1, 91–103.

Beccalli, E. (2004) 'Cross-country Comparison of Efficiency: Evidence from the UK and Italian Investment Firms', *Journal of Banking and Finance*, XXVIII, 6, 1363–83.

Beccalli, E. (2007) 'Does IT Investments Improve Bank Performance? Evidence from Europe', *Journal of Banking and Finance*, XXXI, 7, 2205–30.

Beccalli, E., B. Casu and C. Girardone (2006) 'Efficiency and Stock Performance in European Banking', *The Journal of Business, Finance and Accounting*, XXXIII, 1–2, 245–62.

Berger, A. and R. De Young (2002) 'Technological Progress and the Geographic Expansion of the Banking Industry', Federal Reserve Bank of Chicago, working paper 2002–07.

Berger, A. and D. Humphrey (1997) 'Efficiency of Financial Institutions: International Survey and Direction for Future Research', Board of Governors of the Federal Reserve System (US), Finance and Economics Discussion Series no. 97-11.

Berger, A. and L. Mester (1997) 'Inside the Black Box: What Explains Differences in the Efficiencies of Financial Institutions?', Wharton School Centre for Financial Institutions, University of Pennsylvania, working paper 97-04.

Bos, J., F. Heid, M. Koetter, J. Kolari and C. Kool (2005) 'Inefficient or Just Different? Effects of Heterogeneity on Bank Efficiency Score', Deutsche Bundesbank Banking Supervision Discussion Papers no. 15/2005.

Casolaro, L. and G. Gobbi (2006) 'Information Technology and Productivity Changes in the Banking Industry', Temi di discussione Banca d'Italia.

Casu, B. and C. Girardone (2004) 'Financial Conglomeration: Efficiency, Productivity and Strategic Drive', *Applied Financial Economics*, XIV, 10, 687–96.

Casu, B. and P. Molyneux (2003) 'A Comparative Study of Efficiency in European Banking', *Applied Economics*, XXXV, 17, 1865–76.

Cavallo, L. and S. Rossi (2002), 'Do Environmental Variables Affect the Performance and Technical Efficiency of the European Banking Systems? A Parametric Analysis Using the Stochastic Frontier Approach', *The European Journal of Finance*, VIII, 1, 123–46.

Coelli, T., S. Perelman and E. Romano (1999) 'Accounting for Environmental Influences in Stochastic Frontier Models: With Application to International Airlines', *Journal of Productivity Analysis*, XI, 3, 251–73.

DeYoung, R. and I. Hasan (1998) 'The Performance of De Novo Commercial Banks: A Profit Efficiency Approach', *Journal of Banking and Finance*, XXII, 5, 565–87.

Dietsch, M. and A. Lozano-Vivas (2000) 'How the Environment Determines Banking Efficiency: A Comparison between French and Spanish Industries', *Journal of Banking and Finance*, XXIV, 6, 985–1004.

Farrell, M.J. (1957) 'The Measurement of Productive Efficiency', *Journal of the Royal Statistical Society*, Series A (General) CXX, 3, 253–90.

Fiordelisi, F. and P. Molyneux (2006) *Shareholder Value in Banking* (London: Palgrave Macmillan).

Fiorentino, E., A. Karmann and M. Koetter (2006) 'The Cost Efficiency of German Banks: a Comparison of SFA and DEA', Deutsche Bundesbank, discussion paper no. 10/2006.

Girardone, C., P. Molyneux and E. Gardener (2004) 'Analysing the Determinants of Bank Efficiency: The Case of Italian Banks', *Applied Economics*, XXXVI, 3, 215–27.

Glass, J.C. and D.G. McKillop (2006) 'The Impact of Differing Operating Environments on US Credit Union Performance, 1993–2001', *Applied Financial Economics*, XVI, 17, 1285–300.

Huang, T. (2000) 'Estimating X-Efficiency in Taiwanese Banking Using a Translog Shadow Profit Function', *Journal of Productivity Analysis*, XIV, 3, 225–45.

Humphrey, D. and L. Pulley (1997) 'Banks' Responses to Deregulation: Profits, Technology, and Efficiency', *Journal of Money, Credit and Banking*, XXIX, 1, 73–93.

Kumbhakar, S.C. and C.A.K. Lovell (2000) *Stochastic Frontier Analysis* (Cambridge: Cambridge University Press).

Laeven, L. (1999) 'Risk and Efficiency in East Asian Banks', The World Bank Policy Research Working Paper Series no. 2255.

Maudos, J., J. Pastor, F. Pérez and J. Quesada (2002) 'Cost and Profit Efficiency in European Banks', *Journal of International Financial Markets, Institutions and Money*, XII, 1, 33–58.

Meeusen, W. and J. Van Den Broeck (1977) 'Efficiency Estimation from Cobb-Douglas Production Functions with Composed Error', *International Economic Review*, XVIII, 2, 435–44.

Mester, L. (1993) 'Efficiency of Banks in the Third Federal Reserve District', Wharton School Center for Financial Institutions, University of Pennsylvania, Working Paper no. 94-13.

Mester, L. (1996) 'A Study of Bank Efficiency Taking into Account Risk-Preferences', *Journal of Banking and Finance*, XX, 6, 1025–45.

Resti, A. (1997) 'Evaluating the Cost-Efficiency of the Italian Banking System: What Can Be Learned from the Joint Application of Parametric and Non-Parametric Techniques', *Journal of Banking and Finance*, XXI, 2, 221–50.

Rogers, K.E. (1998) 'Nontraditional Activities and the Efficiency of US Commercial Banks', *Journal of Banking & Finance*, XXII, 4, 467–82.

Vander Vennet, R. (2002) 'Cost and Profit Efficiency of Financial Conglomerates and Universal Banks in Europe', *Journal of Money, Credit and Banking*, XXXIV, 1, 254–82.

Weill, L. (2004) 'Measuring Cost Efficiency in European Banking: A Comparison of Frontier Techniques', *Journal of Productivity Analysis*, XXI, 2, 133–52.

Worthington, A. (1998) 'Efficiency in Australian Building Societies: An Econometric Cost Function Approach', *Applied Financial Economics*, VIII, 5, 459–67.

8
Studying the Bancassurance Phenomenon: A Two-Sided Analysis on the Relevant Case of Italy[1]

Franco Fiordelisi and Ornella Ricci

8.1 Introduction

Most studies dealing with bancassurance provide readers with descriptive analysis by discussing economic rationales, advantages and drawbacks for all the institutions involved. In contrast, there are few studies providing an empirical assessment of the bancassurance business. More specifically, as outlined at the end of the previous chapter, there are no empirical analyses measuring bancassurance cost and profit efficiency gains from both the banking and the insurance perspectives. This chapter aims to fill this gap by answering the following three research questions: (1) Are banks engaged in the insurance business more cost and profit efficient than competitors who have specialised in traditional and investment banking? (2) Are bancassurance companies more cost and profit efficient than independent companies operating in the life business? (3) Which model of bancassurance performs best?

Our analysis focuses on the Italian banking and insurance sectors over the period 2005–06.[2] The Italian case is particularly interesting since the cooperation between banks and life insurers has been well-established for a number of years: for example, the most important bancassurers were already operating in the late 1990s. Furthermore, the Italian life insurance market is the fourth largest in Europe and the sixth in the world for the volume of premiums. The contribution of this study with respect to the existing literature is manifold. First, cost and profit efficiency gains are assessed focussing on both the banking and the insurance industries: as far as we are aware, there are no other studies running a bilateral analysis of the bancassurance phenomenon. Second, it was possible to exploit a unique dataset allowing the investigation of both the ownership and the distribution perspectives of the bancassurance phenomenon. In this way, the analysis is able to consider that insurance companies can distribute their products through bank branches, even when they are not bank-participated, based on soft forms of integration (such as cross-selling agreements, non-equity strategic alliances or minority stakes). Third, quantitative findings are also provided on performance differences between various organizational models of bancassurance.

The remainder of the chapter is organized as follows. The methodology applied for the estimation of cost and profit efficiency is the same described in the previous chapter. A similar approach is also adopted in order to solve the problem of possible heterogeneity among sample firms. Section 8.2 describes the sample selection criteria and data sources; section 8.3 gives the empirical results and section 8.4 presents the study's conclusions.

8.2 Data and variables

Regarding the banking side, the operational definition of bancassurance is the same as in Chapter 7. 'Bancassurance Combinations' (BCs) are banking groups expanding their scope beyond traditional banking and entering the life business through a consolidated subsidiary while 'Not Bancassurance-oriented Institutions' (NBIs) are specialised commercial banks or institutions engaged in both commercial and investment banking not diversifying into the insurance industry. Data for consolidated annual statements and ownership information are drawn from the ABI Banking Data database and from corporate web sites. Dropping observations with missing (or extreme) values, the final banking sample consists of an unbalanced panel data of 80 annual observations: 47 for BCs (23 in 2005; 24 in 2006) and 33 for NBIs (18 in 2005; 15 in 2006).

Regarding the insurance standpoint, bancassurance companies are life insurers that: 1) are wholly owned by banks or controlled by banks with a stake greater than 50 per cent (insurance companies controlled by banks, CBs); 2) are jointly owned by a bank and an insurer, with either equal or unequal participation (joint ventures, JVs). Independent companies (ICs) are treated as a residual cluster. Data are directly obtained by the *Associazione Nazionale delle Imprese di Assicurazione* (ANIA) and INFOBILA (i.e., a database managed by ANIA). Removing observations with missing (or extreme) values, the final sample is an unbalanced panel data of 168 annual observations: 25 for CBs (13 in 2005; 12 in 2006); 43 for JVs (21 in 2005; 22 in 2006) and 100 for ICs (49 in 2005; 51 in 2006).

The definition of input and output variables is tailored to account for differences in the activities undertaken by banking and insurance companies. The banking output definition has already been discussed in Chapter 7. This analysis follows some recent studies (Rogers 1998, Vander Vennet 2002) and uses revenue flows instead of output quantities: total interest income, representing traditional banking, and total non-interest income, representing fee-based activities (such as insurance). This output specification, used in the empirical analysis presented in Chapter 7, has proven to be more suitable than the value added approach for reflecting bank diversification and comparing BCs against NBIs. Labour, fixed assets and total funding are regarded as bank inputs. Furthermore, consistently with several recent studies (for example, Altunbas et al., 2000; Girardone et al. 2004; Yildirim and Philippatos, 2007), bank equity capital is included as a netput (i.e., a quasi-fixed input that cannot be adjusted in the short run).

For the insurance side, the most recent studies (for example, Fenn et al., 2008) suggest a value-added approach in which risk pooling and bearing activities are measured by incurred benefits (i.e. the payments made to policyholders when an insured event happens), while the intermediation function is captured by the sum of funds not needed for customers claims, added to technical reserves and invested in securities. Labour, business services/materials and financial capital are considered as inputs. Costs related to labour and business services/materials are included in the insurer profit and loss account as operating expenses or investment charges. Following Fenn et al. (2008), financial capital is considered as a netput and represented by both equity and technical provisions.

Punctual definitions and summary statistics for all the variables included in the deterministic portion of the cost and profit frontiers are reported in Table 8.1, for both the banking and the insurance side.

In order to account for the heterogeneity problem, a set of firm specific factors is included in the analysis. On the banking side, the engagement in bancassurance is considered by a dummy variable (BANKASS) taking the value of 1 for Bancassurance Combinations (BCs) and 0 for Not Bancassurance-oriented Institutions (NBIs). The frontier model also incorporates other variables:

- *Size (LN_TA)* is the natural log of total assets;
- *Capital and Risk-taking (TCR%)* is the ratio between regulatory capital and total risk weighted assets;

Table 8.1 Input/output variables and firm-specific factors included in the frontier model to account for sample heterogeneity

Variable	Code	Definition
Panel A – The banking side		
Total cost*	TC	Interest expenses + operating expenses
Output 1*	y_1	Total interest income
Output 2*	y_2	Not-interest income
Input price 1	p_1	Personnel expenses/number of employees
Input price 2	p_2	Capital expenses/total fixed assets
Input price 3	p_3	Interest expenses/deposits and other funding
Total profit*	TP	Total pre-tax profit
Equity*	E	Total equity
Bancassurance	BANKASS	Engaged or not in a bancassurance strategy (dummy)
Size	LN_TA	Natural log of total assets
Capital and Risk-taking	TCR%	Total capital ratio%
Institutional type	COMM	Commercial or cooperative bank (dummy)
Listing	LISTED	Listed or unlisted institution (dummy)
Panel B – The insurance side		
Total cost*	TC	Total expenses excluding net incurred claims
Output*	y_1	Claims net of reinsurance + bonus and rebates + additions to reserves
Input price 1	p_1	(Net operating expenses + technical charges)/total assets
Input price 2	p_2	Investment charges/total assets
Total profit*	TP	Net earned premiums + investment income-total cost
Netput 1*	n_1	Total equity capital at the beginning of the period
Netput 2*	n_2	Total technical reserves at the beginning of the period
Controlled by banks	CB	Companies controlled by banks (dummy)
Joint venture	JV	Joint ventures between banks and insurers (dummy)
Distribution	%BANK	% of premiums collected by bank branches
Market power	MS	Market share in the Italian life insurance industry
Business mix	%FIN	% of products into the III or VI class of the EU directive
Specialisation	COMP	Composite company or life specialist (dummy)

* Values are in € thousands.

- *Institutional type (COMM)* is a dummy variable (1 = stock company, i.e. Società per azioni; 0 = savings or cooperative bank, that is, Banche Popolari and Banche di credito cooperativo);
- *Listing (LISTED)* is a dummy variable (1 = listed companies; 0 otherwise);
- *Time effect (YEAR)* is a year dummy (0 = 2005; 1 = 2006) to account for the time effect.

With respect to the insurance industry, the ownership features of sample life companies are considered introducing two different dummy variables: the first (CB) takes the value of 1 for life insurance companies controlled by banks and 0 otherwise; the second (JV) assumes the value of 1 for life companies partially controlled by banks (0 otherwise). The frontier model also incorporates other variables:

- *Distribution (%BANK)* is the percentage of premiums collected by bank branches (i.e., the exact weight of the banking channel for every company);
- *Market Power (MS)* is the share held by the company in the Italian life insurance market;
- *Business Mix (%FIN)* is the percentage of policies with a high financial content, falling into Class III or VI, as identified by the 96/1992 Directive (respectively, unit/index-linked and capital redemption operations);
- *Specialisation (COMP)* is a dummy variable taking the value of 1 if the firm is a composite company also offering property and casualty (P&C) insurance and 0 if it is a life specialist;
- *Time effect (YEAR)* is a dummy variable to account for the time effect (i.e. 0 = 2005; 1 = 2006).

8.3   Results

Section 8.3.1 presents the main empirical findings with respect to the banking industry while section 8.3.2 focuses on the insurance side. In section 8.3.3, main results are compared from a two-sided perspective.

8.3.1   The banking perspective

First of all, both Case 1 and Case 2 models are run in order to overcome the problem of possible sample heterogeneity. Then the two alternatives are compared on the basis of a likelihood ratio test, as explained in Chapter 7, for both the cost and the profit case. The test reveals that it is not possible to discriminate between Case 1 and Case 2 models from the cost side and that Case 2 is the preferred alternative for the frontier profit model. In addition to this, Case 2 is also preferable from a theoretical point of view, because it allows the consideration of sample firms heterogeneity and maintains a common benchmark. Focussing on Case 2 results, there is no evidence of substantial differences between BCs and NBIs (see Table 8.2, Panel A): both groups of companies display similar cost efficiency levels in terms of volatility and range between the minimum and the maximum value. Focussing on profit efficiency, mean scores are lower than for the cost case and have a larger standard deviation. BCs seem to slightly outperform NBIs on the cost side, while the latter have a higher level of profit efficiency. Since these scores are obtained from the Case 2 model estimation, these are gross measures of efficiency (i.e., these incorporate the effect of all the variables included as determinants of firm performance). Consequently, it is necessary to examine the coefficients of single firm specific factors to assess the impact of engaging (or not) in a bancassurance strategy (see Table 8.2, Panel B).

Regarding the impact of firm specific factors, firm size has no statistically significant (at the 10% confidence level or less) relationship with cost efficiency, while it displays a positive and statistically significant (at the 10% level) link with profits. This result is substantially consistent with the previous literature: e.g. Worthington (1998) points out that larger organizations direct more inputs into identifying and resolving inefficiency; Vander Vennet (2002) finds that cost efficiency is unrelated to size, while the smallest banks appear less profit efficient; Weill (2004) shows that Data Envelopment Analysis (DEA) scores increase monotonically with size, while there is no clear trend for SFA scores. Cavallo and Rossi (2002) provide evidence that results for the size-efficiency relationship strongly differ among several European countries.

The capital adequacy variable *(TCR%)* has a positive and statistically significant (at the 5% confidence level or less) link with both cost and profit efficiency. This is consistent with Mester (1993), who points out that higher capital ratios may prevent moral hazard. If a bank's capital level decreases, managers have an increasing incentive to take on excessive risk, engaging in activities that do not create value for shareholders.

The negative coefficient for the institutional type dummy *(COMM,* i.e., statistically significant at the 5% level or less) suggests that in our

Table 8.2   Measuring cost and profit efficiency in the Italian banking industry over 2005–2006 including exogenous factors as determinants of performance

	Cost efficiency				Profit efficiency			
	Mean	Std Dev	Min	Max	Mean	Std Dev	Min	Max
Panel A – Cost and profit efficiency in BCs and NBIs over 2005–2006								
BCs (47 obs)	0.9147	0.0727	0.5682	0.9786	0.6586	0.2786	0.0000	0.9726
NBIs (33 obs)	0.9087	0.1033	0.4769	0.9815	0.6973	0.2510	0.0000	0.9723
Total (80 obs)	0.9123	0.0861	0.4769	0.9815	0.6746	0.2666	0.0000	0.9726

BCs: Bancassurance combinations, NBIs: Not Bancassurance-oriented Institutions.

	Cost	Profit
Panel B – Firm-specific factors effect on cost and profit inefficiency		
LN_TA	−0.028 *(0.078)*	−0.992* *(0.527)*
TCR%	−9.103** *(4.45)*	−3.123*** *(1.06)*
COMM	−0.423** *(0.179)*	−8.859*** *(1.072)*
LIST	0.349* *(0.181)*	28.571*** *(1.075)*
BANKASS	−0.149 *(0.179)*	−0.079 *(0.984)*
YEAR	−0.344*** *(0.124)*	1.368* *(0.735)*

LN_TA is the natural log of total assets.
TCR% is the ratio between regulatory capital and total risk weighted assets.
COMM is a dummy taking the value of 1 for commercial banks and 0 otherwise.
LISTED is adummy taking the value of 1 for listed companies and 0 otherwise.
BANKASS is a dummy taking the value of 1 for bancassurance combinations and 0 otherwise.
YEAR is a dummy taking the value of 0 for the year 2005 and 1 for the year 2006.
A coefficient >0 means a positive effect on the inefficiency component and then a negative relationship with efficiency; the opposite for a coefficient <0.
***p-value<0.01 **p-value<0.05 *p-value<0.1. Values in parentheses are standard errors.

sample stock companies outperform savings and cooperatives. This is consistent with agency theory (for example, Rasmusen 1988): cooperative financial institutions are assumed to be less efficient than commercial banks since the former are characterized by the vote per person and managers are usually protected from takeover threats and not motivated by performance remuneration schemes. On both the cost and the profit side, findings show a disadvantage for listed institutions (i.e. the *LISTED* coefficient is positive and significant at the 10% confidence level or less).

This may be explained supposing that listed banks have a more complex organization and higher compliance costs than unlisted institutions. In addition to this, they may be more exposed to competitive pressure and price competition, possibly to the detriment of high profits.

Cost efficiency improved between 2005 and 2006 while profit efficiency declined (i.e., the coefficient for the YEAR variable is negative and statistically significant at the 1% confidence level for the cost case; positive and statistically significant at the 10% confidence level for profits).

For our aims, the most important variable is the dummy *BANKASS*. This variable is found not to be statistically significant at the 10% confidence level or less in either the cost or the profit models. As a robustness check, the BANKASS dummy is not significant if exogenous factors are included in the deterministic kernel of the frontier (that is, using Case 1). Overall, there are no evidence of cost and profit efficiency gains for bancassurance in itself. Consequently, performance differences between BCs and NBIs are due to factors different from company engagement in the life business: e.g., BCs may benefit from larger corporate size than NBIs or may suffer a lower level of capitalisation and higher competitive pressure.

8.3.2 The insurance standpoint

Similar to the banking case, Case 1 and Case 2 models are compared with a likelihood ratio test. Results do not allow for discrimination between the two alternatives. In the light of theoretical motivations and in order to maintain consistency with the banking analysis, the Case 2 model is selected as the preferred one. Findings reported in Table 3, Panel A,provide evidence that bancassurance companies – both fully controlled by banks (hereafter, CBs) and, especially joint ventures (hereafter, JVs) – have a higher average level of cost efficiency than independents (hereafter, ICs). Surprisingly, results for profit maximisation display the opposite situation: JVs have a substantial disadvantage with respect to both CBs and ICs.

These differences are observed with reference to gross efficiency scores incorporating the effect of firm-specific factors included in the frontier model. Consequently, it is necessary to examine the coefficients of single firm-specific factors to assess the impact of full or partial control by banking institutions (Table 8.3, Panel B). First of all, firm-specific factors related to the company's distribution model and business mix are examined: the share of premiums collected by bank branches (%BANK) and the weight of policies with a high financial content (%FIN). The former appears positively related to cost efficiency and significant at the 5% confidence level, revealing that insurance companies selling their products in collaboration with a bank benefit from relevant cost economies with respect to other distribution channels. This result is consistent with previous efficiency literature (for example, Hwang and Gao, 2005) and with studies finding a price reduction thanks to bancassurance bundling (Okeahalam, 2008). It is also confirmed by the ANIA report (2008) for the Italian life insurance market, signalling that the incidence of acquisition and administrative costs for collected premiums is reduced for bank branches with respect to agents, brokers and financial advisors. The distribution of premiums through bank branches is also positively related to profit efficiency, but the relationship is not statistically significant at the 10% level or less. Consequently, there is no strong evidence in favour of revenue synergies for insurance companies cooperating with banks. Analysis of the weight of policies with a high financial content (%*FIN*) reveals that index/unit-linked and capital redemption products are, on average, less costly to manage but also less profitable than traditional protection insurance. These types of product, especially index/unit-linked, registered strong growth rates until a few years ago, driving the success of bancassurance. Then, after the end of the most euphoric phase for capital markets, these products became less attractive for investors. Regarding the other firm specific factors, the market share (*MS*) has a positive relationship with cost efficiency. The direction of causality is not investigated in this analysis. As such, it could be that the most efficient firms are able to gain market share from their competitors or that large companies with a key role in the industry pay more attention to the pursuit of cost efficiency and, therefore, are better placed in the market for production factors. In the profit efficiency estimation, the market share coefficient is not significant, suggesting that larger firms are not able to exploit their power to charge higher prices. Finally, the dummy for composite companies (*COMP*) is positively related to both cost and profit efficiency, representing a possible indirect proof that the collaboration between life and P&C businesses realises economies of scope. This result is also consistent with Fenn et al. (2008), but its relevance is, to some extent, limited by current legislation forcing insurance companies to specialise in just one of the two areas of business. The time variable YEAR reveals an improvement in cost efficiency and a decline in profit efficiency, probably due to the increase in competitive pressures.

The CB and JV coefficients are not found to be statistically significant at the 10% level or less on both the cost and the profit side. These

Table 8.3 Measuring cost and profit efficiency in the Italian life insurance industry over 2005–2006 including exogenous factors as determinants of performance

	Cost efficiency				Profit efficiency			
	Mean	Std. Dev.	Min.	Max.	Mean	Std. Dev.	Min.	Max.
Panel A – Cost and profit efficiency for different ownership types over 2005–2006								
CBs (25 obs)	0.9429	0.0305	0.8778	0.9761	0.7734	0.1427	0.4682	0.9316
ICs (100 obs)	0.9086	0.0876	0.6138	0.9876	0.7176	0.1433	0.3789	0.9455
JVs (43 obs)	0.9559	0.0321	0.8241	0.9849	0.6780	0.1280	0.4288	0.9200
Total (168 obs)	0.9258	0.0735	0.6138	0.9876	0.7158	0.1417	0.3789	0.9455

CB controlled by banks; IC independent company; JV joint venture.

	Cost	Profit
Panel B – Firm-specific factors effect on cost and profit inefficiency		
%BANK	−0.438**	−0.055
	(0.187)	(0.088)
MS	−5.773***	1.717
	(2.093)	(2.906)
%FIN	−0.748**	0.639***
	(0.371)	(0.14)
COMP	−0.316**	−0.154**
	(0.149)	(0.07)
CB	−0.103	−0.124
	(0.097)	(0.099)
JV	−0.014	−0.1
	(0.103)	(0.087)
YEAR	−0.169**	0.304***
	(0.075)	(0.063)

Notes:
% BANK is the percentage of premiums collected by bank branches.
MS is the market share in the Italian life insurance market.
%FIN is the percentage of products falling into Class III or VI of 96/1992 EU directive.
COMP is a dummy taking the value of 1 for composite companies and 0 otherwise.
CB is a dummy taking the value of 1 for companies controlled by banks and 0 otherwise.
JV is a dummy taking the value of 1 for joint ventures and 0 otherwise.
YEAR is a dummy taking the value of 0 for the year 2005 and 1 for the year 2006.
A coefficient >0 means a positive effect on the inefficiency component and then a negative relationship with efficiency; the opposite for a coefficient <0.
***p-value <0.01 **p-value <0.05 *p-value <0.1.Values in parentheses are standard errors.

findings suggest that differences in firm performance are mainly due to the distribution system and product mix, rather than to the ownership profile. As a robustness check, it is also verified that results relative to the ownership dummies remain substantially unchanged using the Case 1 model. Consequently, bancassurance firms (both CBs and JVs) strongly rely on distribution by bank branches and these are able to realise relevant cost economies with respect to other possible channels. The cost over-performance of JVs could also be due to specialisation in financial products, which is particularly marked in companies involving both banking and insurance partners. Finally, bancassurance firms are among the largest operators in the industry and benefit from the positive link between market share and cost efficiency. These effects seem to be more relevant than scope economies derived from being a composite company, in favour of ICs.

On the other hand, in terms of profit, only two firm-specific factors play a determinant role in explaining firm performance. As a consequence, the disadvantage found for JVs can be largely explained by the concentration of the business mix on high financial content products, that is much more important than in ICs, and also with respect to CBs.

8.3.3 Banking vs insurance

Results for the banking industry do not support the hypothesis that bancassurance provides banks involved in this business with cost or profit efficiency gains. Bancassurance combinations (BCs) and Not Bancassurance-oriented Institutions (NBIs) display different mean efficiency levels, but these differences are explained by factors other than bancassurance (such as corporate size, ownership structure and capital adequacy). On the insurance side, there is evidence of substantial gains due to a bancassurance strategy. Namely, the use of bank branches reduces distribution costs for life policies. In addition, high financial content products (playing a crucial role in bancassurance companies) are found to be less costly to manage than traditional protection insurance products, but also less profitable. Overall, findings are in favour of bancassurance advantages only on the cost side, while from the more important profit perspective there are no substantial gains.

The differences between findings for banking and insurance companies are not surprising. The banks analysed display large asset size and a great variety of businesses: as such, bancassurance efficiency gains are likely to have a small impact on the bank's global cost and income structure and are consequently difficult to detect. On the insurance side, it is possible to capture straightforwardly differences due to bancassurance strategy since our data enables us to focus on the life business (i.e., the business area where banks and insurers have large synergies). Regarding the most performing bancassurance structure, JVs are found to have a greater cost performance in comparison to other types of company, but also the lowest profitability. In addition to this, performance differences appear more influenced by business variables than by ownership features.

The analysis shows that the main bancassurance gain is related to the use of a cheap distribution channel (i.e. bank branches), while the success of insurance products with a high financial content appears more volatile and strictly dependent on current market trends. As a consequence, the mix of products needs to be continuously revised according to customer needs and the evolution of the financial market. In conclusion, equity links between banks and insurance companies do not necessarily represent the best bancassurance strategy, while more flexible and reversible forms of cooperation (such as cross-selling agreements, non-equity strategic alliances and minority stakes) also seem able to enhance performance.

8.4   Conclusions

This chapter showed the result of an empirical analysis assessing cost and profit efficiency gains of bancassurance in both the banking and the insurance industries. While results provide no evidence of bancassurance gains in the banking industry, bancassurance has substantial cost efficiency gains in the insurance industry: captive companies (that is, those owned by banks) and joint ventures outperform independent companies supporting the proposition that the use of bank branches is a cheaper distribution channel than other solutions (for example, agents, brokers). Regarding profitability, the relationship between performance and the use of bank branches is still positive, but not statistically significant at 10% level or less. A key finding is that high financial content products are less costly and less profitable than traditional protection insurance, probably due also to their reduced appeal after the end of the most euphoric phase for capital markets. If the reductions in welfare state protection and social security are also considered, it seems predictable that there will be a further development of insurance products providing a 'second pillar' in addition to public social protection and guaranteeing more stable income over the life cycle.

If bancassurance success is strictly linked to distribution cost savings, while typical bancassurance policies have alternate fortune due to financial market trends, it is of crucial importance to assess the effective gains of realising ownership links that are often poorly flexible and reversible. This is a key issue especially during crisis periods, when market operators tend to refocus on the core business and regulators tend to limit the creation of huge and complex financial entities, operating in all financial sectors and increasing their systemic relevance. Analysing the case of Italy over the period 2005–06, it is possible to conclude that equity links with banking institutions do not seem to directly guarantee any advantage. As a consequence, the mix of products should be continuously revised in the light of customer needs and the evolution of the financial market, and the parties involved should also consider more flexible and reversible forms of cooperation, such as cross-selling agreements and non-equity strategic alliances. In order to have a deeper and more complete view of the phenomenon, further research should be devoted to the effects of bancassurance, using a longer time interval and a larger sample, possibly on a cross-country basis.

Notes

1. This chapter is mostly based on Ornella Ricci's PhD thesis, made under the supervision of Franco Fiordelisi.
2. For more details, see Fiordelisi and Ricci (2011).

References

Altunbas, Y., H. Ming, P. Molyneux and R. Seth (2000) 'Efficiency and Risk in Japanese Banking", *Journal of Banking and Finance*, XXIV, 10, 1605–28.
ANIA. Fact-pack Mercato Vita 2008. ANIA. www.ania.it.
Cavallo, L. and S. Rossi (2002), 'Do Environmental Variables Affect the Performance and Technical Efficiency of the European Banking Systems? A Parametric Analysis Using the Stochastic Frontier Approach', *The European Journal of Finance*, VIII, 1, 123–46.
Fiordelisi, F. and O. Ricci (2011) 'Bancassurance efficiency gains: evidence from the Italian banking and insurance industries', *European Journal of Finance*, XVII, 9–10, 789–810.
Fenn, P., D. Vencappa, S. Diacon, P. Klumpes and C. O'Brien (2008) 'Market Structure and the Efficiency of European Insurance Companies: A Stochastic Frontier Analysis', *Journal of Banking and Finance*, XXXII, 1, 86–100.
Girardone, C., E. Gardener and P. Molyneux (2004) 'Analysing the Determinants of Bank Efficiency: The Case of Italian Banks. *Applied Economics*, XXXVI, 3, 215–27.

Hwang, T. and S. Gao (2005) 'An Empirical Study of Cost Efficiency in the Irish Life Insurance Industry', *International Journal of Accounting, Auditing and Performance Evaluation*, 2, 3, 264–80.

Mester, L. (1993) 'Efficiency of Banks in the Third Federal Reserve District', Wharton School Center for Financial Institutions, University of Pennsylvania, Working Paper no. 94-13.

Okeahalam, C. (2008) 'Does Bancassurance Reduce the Price of Financial Service Products?', *Journal of Financial Services Research*, 33, 3, 147–62.

Rasmusen, E. (1988) 'Mutual Banks and Stock Banks', *Journal of Law and Economics*, XXXI, 2, 395–421.

Rogers, K.E. (1998) 'Nontraditional Activities and the Efficiency of US Commercial Banks', *Journal of Banking & Finance*, XXII, 4, 467–82.

Vander Vennet, R. (2002) 'Cost and Profit Efficiency of Financial Conglomerates and Universal Banks in Europe', *Journal of Money, Credit and Banking*, XXXIV, 1, 254–82.

Weill, L. (2004) 'Measuring Cost Efficiency in European Banking: A Comparison of Frontier Techniques', *Journal of Productivity Analysis*, XXI, 2, 133–52.

Worthington, A. (1998) 'Efficiency in Australian Building Societies: An Econometric Cost Function Approach', *Applied Financial Economics*, VIII, 5, 459–67.

Yildirim, H.S. and G.C. Philippatos (2007) 'Efficiency of Banks: Recent Evidence from the Transition Economies of Europe, 1993–2000', *The European Journal of Finance*, XIII, 2, 123–43.

Conclusions

Franco Fiordelisi and Ornella Ricci

The aim of this book has been to analyze different aspects of the bancassurance phenomenon, that is unquestionably one of the most important trend in the evolution of the European financial services industry. The first part of the book provides a description of the phenomenon, examining its historical roots and main drivers of development. Alternative bancassurance organizational models are also investigated, paying attention to the current state of cooperation between banks and insurance companies in various European countries, for different types of life and P&C products. The second part is devoted to more specific issues, relative to accounting principles and regulatory constraints, outlining their main evolution in more recent years. After a comprehensive literature review of academic studies focused on bancassurance, the last part of the book presents the empirical investigations conducted in order to measure its potential efficiency gains on both the cost and the profit sides.

As outlined in Chapter 1, tracing the origin of the phenomenon, bancassurance can be considered as a consequence of the disintermediation process and progressive relaxation of regulatory barriers to financial conglomeration. A crucial role has also been played by increasing investor demand for long term savings products, fostered by growth in income and life expectancy, accompanied by the crisis of social security systems. In this context, the cooperation between banks and insurance companies has proliferated, starting from simple cross-selling agreements and evolving into strategic alliances and ownership links.

The growth of bancassurance has been particularly impressive where the financial services industry is characterized by a strong orientation to the relationship banking model and a lower penetration of insurance products. In many European countries, for example, France, Italy, Spain and Portugal, bank branches have become the main distribution channel for life policies, while in others, for example, the UK and Germany, agents and brokers have retained the majority of the market (see Chapter 3).

Regardless of the existence of some differences across countries, it is possible to affirm that cooperation between banks and insurance companies is well developed for life policies but still at an initial stage for P&C products. This is probably due to the fact that the latter present less similarities and complementaries with the banking business and require more effort to provide branch staff with the right specific competences. It is only recently that banks have extended their offering from P&C policies bundled with banking products, i.e., payment protection and home insurance, to non-bank related products, such as car, travel, pet and health insurance (see Chapter 2). These products may present a high underwriting risk and imply some inefficiencies and difficulties in the claim management process, that is something very far from the traditional banking business. On the other hand, some P&C products have a very interesting growth potential as in the case of health insurance covering private medical expenditure, increasingly relevant as a consequence of the decrease in social welfare benefits.

It could be deduced that the main future bancassurance challenge – in terms of product range – is the expansion of the P&C business, while life activity is quite stable, mature and less challenging. Actually, this is absolutely not the case. During the 1990s bancassurance success was mainly driven by high financial content products, i.e., index- and unit-linked policies, easy to sell in a period of positive growth for capital markets, also due to the Internet boom. After the end of this euphoric phase, linked policies became much less attractive for investors who turned their attention to more traditional savings products. This relevant change in customers preferences has been stressed by the advent of the global financial crisis starting in summer 2007 provoking huge losses for investors of all over the world. In the light of these considerations, it seems predictable that there will be a further development of insurance products providing a 'second pillar' in addition to public social protection and guaranteeing a more stable income over the life cycle. As a consequence, bancassurance companies should be able not only to continuously adapt their offering to changing financial needs, but also to address new customers. It is probable, in fact, that their traditional focus will move from middle-aged, affluent customers – with considerable savings to invest – towards mass market clients in need of a supplementary pension to maintain an adequate standard of living after retirement.

The evolution of financial markets and transformations in customers demand of banking and insurance products is not the only threat for the survival and the development of bancassurance as a viable business model for financial firms. Another crucial issue is represented by the action of regulators and supervisors. As described in Chapters 4 and 5, the insurance industry is facing an unprecedented phase of regulatory changes, investing accounting rules (IAS/IFRS) and capital requirements. Solvency 2 will force insurance companies to identify the right trade-off between economic contribution and risk profile of every product offered. Even though it could also be an opportunity to redesign and innovate products, and improving their pricing, the most important and immediate consequence will be an increase in the cost of running the insurance business. In addition to this, as a response to the global financial crisis, the Basel Committee for Banking Supervision has recently issued some new rules to strengthen bank capitalization and liquidity reserves. The combined impact of Solvency 2 and Basel III provisions may exert a strong pressure on bancassurance combinations, reducing the capital benefits associated with this model. As a consequence, many banks are rethinking their strategy, sometimes deciding to refocus on their core business. At the same time, the financial crisis has also outlined the importance of insurance profit contribution, able to partially offset the slowdown in credit based products. The fundamental question is whether it is preferable to act as a simple distributor of insurance products, gaining commissions free of capital and risk implications, or it is worth being directly involved in the underwriting activity to access potentially greater synergies and returns. Obviously, there is not a unique right answer to this question, because many different exogenous and endogenous factors may contribute to the success or failure of bancassurance. Precious help can be derived from the academic literature, in order to draw useful indications from both theoretical and empirical studies devoted to financial conglomeration and bancassurance.

As shown in Chapter 6, there are only a few contributions specifically focused on bancassurance. Furthermore, most of them are based on simulated or effective M&As between banks and insurance companies, assessing risk/return effects and generally adopting a short term perspective. Surprisingly, even though cost and revenue synergies are commonly recognized as one of the main economic rationales for financial conglomeration, the efficiency issue is still poorly investigated. Chapters 7 and 8 describe the empirical analyses conducted in order to reduce this gap in the existing literature.

A first exploratory study was carried out using a European sample with the objective of comparing cost and profit efficiency between banks diversifying into the life insurance industry and their more specialized competitors. Results show that the two subgroups present quite similar levels of performance and that differences are mainly explained by firm specific factors, such as size and capitalization, that are out of management control in the short run, but able to influence the distance from best practice. Considering that findings appear very sensitive to the input and output specification applied for cost and profit functions, it is possible to conclude that the analysis does not provide any strong evidence in favour of bancassurance.

In order to obtain a deeper view of the phenomenon, a second analysis was conducted focusing on an Italian sample, for which it was also possible to explore the insurance side. Findings show that the use of bank branches provides a cost advantage with respect to other distribution channels, but there is no evidence of profit synergies, either from the banking or from the insurance standpoint. It could be due to alternate fortunes for high financial content products, generally dominating the offering of bancassurance companies. This result reinforces the conclusion that the mix of products should be continuously revised in the light of customers needs and the evolution of financial markets. Furthermore, the bancassurance cost advantage depends on distribution economies, while the bank presence in the ownership structure of the insurance company does not prove to be a relevant determinant of performance, either for captive companies or for joint ventures. As a consequence, the mix of products should be continuously revised in the light of customer needs and the evolution of the financial market, and the parties involved should also consider more flexible and reversible forms of cooperation, such as cross-selling agreements and non-equity strategic alliances.

As in all empirical studies, there are some limitations. First of all, cost and revenue scope economies are not directly measured, but are inferred from the comparison of efficiency levels in diversified and specialized competitors. This choice is supported by the most recent literature and overcomes some econometric problems linked with the estimation of scope economies. Second, at the European level it was not possible to investigate both the banking and the insurance standpoints, due to the lack of publicly available data, for example relative to the weight of bank branches as a distribution channel for sample insurance companies. So, the empirical study presented provides a two-sided analysis of the bancassurance phenomenon only for the case of Italy.

Furthermore, the cooperation between banks and insurance companies is investigated only for the life business, excluding P&C activity that is still at an initial stage. Finally, the time period under investigation is limited to 2005 and 2006. For previous years, it was not possible to have the same level of detail in information collected; for the period after 2007, the analysis would have been too influenced by the advent of the global financial crisis.

In order to have a deeper and more complete view of the phenomenon, further research should be devoted to the effects of bancassurance, using a longer time interval and a larger sample, possibly on a cross-country basis. The main reason for the scarcity of bancassurance empirical studies is the relatively short track record of the phenomenon and the lack of publicly available data. In the future, these problems will probably reduce, as an effect of improved disclosure requirements. Further research will then be essential, in order to contribute to the debate between advocates and detractors of bancassurance. This may direct managers action and policymakers interventions, making their decisions more conscious and avoiding being at the mercy of contingencies and trends.

Index

Page numbers in bold type indicate tables, figures or boxes

Lightning Source UK Ltd.
Milton Keynes UK
UKHW020903240520
363729UK00007B/497

9 781349 322596